The purpose of this book

First

For reassurance and renewed expectation to brothers and sisters in Christ who are relentlessly disappointed by sensational predictions about the Rapture, but are still here.

Second

For enlightenment of brothers and sisters in Christ who have not accepted the various teaching of futuristic theology, but do not know how to answer biblically those who do.

Table of Contents

When Bad Things Happen to Good Prophecies

✦➤☰◉☰◀✦

I am of the opinion that a writer who is able to produce a best seller has to be some sort of genius. Hal Lindsey is one of those skilled writers who engaged the whole evangelical Christian world with his book, *The Late Great Planet Earth*. That book sold millions of copies, influenced many people to convert to Jesus Christ, and introduced many more to a particular system of prophecies of Scripture.

The timing of his publication was perfect—late 1960s and early 1970s—when the Cold War was depressing and much uncertainty was hanging like a dark cloud over the world. The Berlin Wall was a monument of international tension and distrust. The Iron Curtain was formidable. Nuclear weapons were more or less mass-produced. Communism had its satanic grip on half the world. No one in his right mind gave out much hope that the world would last much longer.

In another book, Tim LaHaye saw no future after the year 2000. The human race had to face up to the possibility that the whole earth would be blasted into a late great planet. If the earth was not to be destroyed by nuclear weapons, it would certainly be poisoned by radiation, and become uninhabitable. It was a time of international tension between the free world and the enslaved world. Individuality was not the emphasis—it was an atmosphere of one half of the world against the other half, with both sides terrified to start anything.

Enter Hal Lindsey with his book about a God who is in control of the world, who has a plan that will not fail. God is sovereign over history. The great message was that Christians had nothing to fear, for before any of these horrible things would take place, God would remove His church to safety in heaven. God would continue His plan so that, after seven years of total chaos and great tribulation, Christ's thousand-year kingdom of peace would begin. This is what we all needed to hear. God is on His throne in heaven and everything is running according to His divine plan.

Then, without a shot being fired, the unbelievable happened— the Soviet Union disintegrated, no doubt in answer to the millions of faithful Russian Christians' prayers. Now, of course, we're faced with an embarrassing and frustrating dilemma. The disappearing, or "Rapture" of the church, which was ostensibly supposed to occur sometime around 1988, didn't happen. There has been a great sigh of relief, of course, but now what?

Now, more than thirty years after the publication of *The Late Great Planet Earth*, we live in a world of instant information, instant contact, instant sex, instant wealth, instant bankruptcy, instant divorce, instant insecurity, and instant boredom. The emphasis is no longer nation against nation, but on self-gratification. We think in terms of, "I deserve this. I'm worth it. I have my rights." The emphasis is on personal survival in this modern rat race.

Then once again, *right on time*, the answer is found in the best selling *Left Behind* series of books. There's no longer pressure about whether or not the world will survive, the question now becomes, "Will I survive?" The same interpretation of future events that was found in Lindsey's book is now found in Tim LaHaye's and Jerry Jenkins' many volumes—ingeniously novelized, and very exciting reading.

Will I be traveling first class in a crowded jet, and suddenly, half the passengers disappear in midair? Will the cockpit also be empty? Oh no, we're going to crash! The first time I ever heard a sermon on this subject, which included the airplane illustration, was forty-five years ago in a church in Adelaide, Australia. It scared me into a prayer of repentance and the study of God's Word.

Ever since that time, and now as a pastor, I've been questioned about the Rapture of the Church, the Great Tribulation, the second coming of Christ, the Millennium, the *Left Behind* books, and the reestablishment of Israel in the Promised Land. Isn't it disappointing that after almost six decades since Israel was established as a nation, the Rapture and the removal of the church from the planet hasn't occurred?

What's the Holdup?

Millions of evangelical, Bible-believing Christians believe the reestablishment of Israel as a nation is inseparably connected with the secret coming of Christ to gather His church (the Rapture). Back in the 1980s, more than 250,000 pastors in America received a free booklet, which emphatically declared that there were eighty-eight reasons why Christ must return in 1988. Apparently, Christ did not get a copy.

Furthermore, have you been disappointed, and made to look foolish because you told everybody you knew that you were sure Christ would return within a generation of the return of the Jews to Israel (Lindsey, *The Late Great Planet Earth*)? Or during the Gulf War (Lindsey, *The Rise of Babylon and the Persian Gulf Crisis*)? Or at the turn of the new millennium (Lindsey, *Planet Earth 2000— Will Mankind Survive*)?

In Korea, many Christians were misled into giving away all their property in anticipation of the Rapture in the fall of 1992. You may not have gone to that extreme, but perhaps you've read books and pamphlets emphasizing that the Rapture is imminent. And perhaps you urged friends and relatives to get ready and, as Lindsey recommended, "keep your eyes on the Middle East" (Lindsey, 1972, page 173).

You're not alone. According to reliable surveys, twenty million Bible-believing Christians in the United States alone believe just like you. Unfortunately for some, the Bible is now looked upon with doubt, for many have been disillusioned by failed prophetic predictions.

You may wonder about other important questions regarding the whole spectrum of end-time events: is there such a thing as the sudden, secret Rapture? The second coming? A thousand-year peaceful reign of Christ on earth? Is the "Jew the most important sign to this generation" (Lindsey)? Are the Russians coming? Are we living in the last days? Does the Bible clearly teach these things? Where does the theory of a silent, secret Rapture come from?

On two occasions, I had the opportunity to preach in Egypt. Each time, I was there for thirty days. On my second visit, I raised the following question to a number of Egyptian Presbyterian pastors: "Why do the Arab nations, or Muslims, more or less, hate American Christians so much?" The answer I got was both surprising and extremely alarming: "Western Christians think God has given up on Arabs becoming converted to Christ."

It's a very interesting fact that the person who made the greatest contribution to the New Testament (besides Jesus Himself) was Saul of Tarsus, a dangerous Jewish religious fanatic, a Pharisee who persecuted the church mercilessly. It should be comforting to the Arab nations to know that immediately after his conversion to Christ, Saul was taken to the Arabian desert for three years to be taught by Christ Himself.

Additionally, apart from Eve and Sarah, Hagar the Egyptian servant of Abraham was the only other woman in the Old Testament who was *addressed and blessed* by the Lord personally, and it happened on two occasions (Genesis 16 and Genesis 21). Of course, we know that Jesus' parents had to flee to Egypt to keep the Son of God alive, so He could fulfill Scripture: "out of Egypt have I called my son" (Hosea 11:1; Matthew 2:15).

The purpose of this easy-to-read, non-technical, layman's book is to assist you in studying the Bible with an open mind, and to discern what God's inspired and infallible Word teaches regarding such questions. *There is no quick answer.* To derive the greatest benefit from this volume, the chapters should be read consecutively, for each chapter is based on the previous one. Then form your own conclusions.

This book is only an introduction to the study of last things. It doesn't answer all the questions you may have. But I pray that this volume may be the means whereby you'll fall in love with Christ and His teachings all over again, trust the whole Bible again, and look forward to being with Him in His own appointed time, at death, or in the air.

But please note! Some of the men mentioned in this volume, with whom I passionately disagree, are my *blood brothers* in the Lord. They are faithful, godly men, loved by God, and redeemed by the blood of Christ. It's primarily in the subject of eschatology (the doctrine of final things) that I'm at odds with them, strongly disagreeing with their interpretations of the prophetic portions of Scripture.

I want to offer a special thanks to my wife and partner in the gospel, Noelene, for her encouragement. As a God-given helpmeet, she has questioned my presuppositions as only a faithful wife can. I have appreciated the helpful and scholarly advice of Dr. Ken Gentry, who made me rewrite it and get some help, and others for their willingness to read an early draft, for Chet and Barb Little, and Mrs. Norma Cook, my secretary, for typing and retyping, and Arie and Lynn VanWingerden for helping to make this book possible. And, for those comments on the jacket from men smarter than I, I'm thankful.

I would also like to acknowledge Ross Blankley, whose various skills, encouragement, and helpful suggestions were invaluable. Also, I wish to thank my son-in-law, Stephen Rarig, an Old Testament scholar, and vice president of Westminster College in Perth, Australia, and David Nadeau, whose editing skills were paramount in finishing this book, and Bob Kelly, of WordCrafters, Inc., for final editing and encouragement.

Finally, you will discover that I'm more of a boat-rocking preacher than an accomplished writer. I'm attempting to respond to questions asked of me during forty-five years of ministry—questions that both concern and excite me. This is an outpouring of a pastor's heart, more than an orderly theological treatise.

Whatever you may have previously read or been taught regarding futuristic dispensationalism, and whatever you may read in this book, let these biblical truths sustain you as we all face a future of uncertainty—here and now—and a glorious eternity with God still to come.

This book is dedicated to our most glorious Savior, Jesus Christ, the Captain of our salvation, King of kings, and Lord of lords who will not return to this late small planet earth until all his enemies are a footstool for His feet (Psalm 110:1; Matthew 22:44; Mark 12:36; Luke 20:43; Acts 2:35; Hebrews 1:13, 10:13).

Introduction

✦⇒⇐✦

In the past God spoke to our forefathers through the prophets
at many times and in various ways,
but in these last days
he has spoken to us by his Son,
whom he appointed heir of all things,
and through whom
he made the universe.

The Son is the radiance of God's glory
and the exact representation
of his being,
sustaining all the things
by his powerful word.
After he had provided
purification for sins,
he sat down
at the right hand
of the Majesty in heaven.
(Hebrews 1:1-3)

Imaginary Ghost Riders in the Sky

At a local gas station in a city where I served as a pastor many years ago, the owner of the station and I had many discussions about the end times. This man was a convinced dispensationalist; that is, he believed the Bible teaches that history is divided into seven distinct time frames in which God's dealings with man differ, according to each particular dispensation.

He believed we were living in the sixth dispensation and that, at any moment, Christ would secretly return to take up into heaven all truly born-again Christians. He believed what he'd been taught, that the church's purpose is a temporary one. In this system of belief, the church is a *parenthesis*, not a part of Christ's completed work. He also believed the church age would culminate in the Rapture, as now novelized by books like the *Left Behind* series, by Tim LaHaye and Jerry Jenkins.

One day as I was waiting for him to fill my tank, he approached my car very slowly, looking into the sky, and carrying his Scofield Bible under his arm. "What are you looking at?" I asked, looking into the sky myself, trying to discover what he was gazing at. I could see nothing but a blue sky. He mumbled, more or less to himself, "I know He's coming back on the clouds soon, maybe today."

"Hold it! Time out!" I responded. "I, too, believe Christ will return some day to take us, if we're still alive, unto Himself, but right now, make sure the nozzle goes into the tank and refills my car. That, for now, is your Christian responsibility."

That incident happened more than thirty years ago, and dozens of books have been written since. I well imagine he's still looking; I further suppose he may be getting more and more frustrated, perhaps even disappointed. Worse, I fear he may even doubt the whole prophetic scheme of Scripture, and perhaps the very integrity of the Bible.

Let's first agree that Scripture teaches us that to be ready for the Lord's return doesn't mean keeping your eye to the *eastern* sky, but rather, your nose to the grindstone. It means we must continue to use every biblical means to live godly lives, by conforming to the image of Christ, which is God's original and primary purpose for the whole plan of salvation.

It means to be the salt of the earth (Matthew 5:13), to let your light shine before men (Matthew 5:17), to seek first the kingdom of God and His righteousness (Matthew 6:33), to expose the works of darkness (Ephesians 4:11), to do all things to the glory of God (1 Corinthians 10:31), all the while following the biblical directives which equip us for every good work (2 Timothy 3:17).

Despite much of the current dispensationalist teaching, Christ has, in recent years, stayed in heaven, and the antichrist has never appeared on the world scene. Yet, more and more end-times books and pamphlets have flooded the market, and have even made the best-seller lists. And again, many Christians have been let down and disappointed.

In 1988, Dr. Charles R. Taylor published a book titled *Watch 1988 – The Year of Climax*. Needless to say, 1988 came and went without any extraordinarily climactic events. However, that didn't stop publication of a plethora of alarmist books. Here's a sample of some recent titles:

Hal Lindsey, *Planet Earth—2000: Will Mankind Survive?*

Lester Sumrall, *I Predict 2000*

David Allen Lewis, *Prophecy 2000: Rushing to Armageddon*

Steve Terrell, *The 90's: Decade of the Apocalypse*

Dave Hunt, *How Close Are We? Compelling Evidence for the Soon Return of*
Christ

Charles C. Ryrie, *The Final Countdown*

Grant R. Jeffries, *Armageddon: Appointment with Destiny*

James McKeever, *The Rapture Book: Victory in the End Times*

Don McAlvanny et al., *Earth's Final Days*

Texe Marrs, *Storming Toward Armageddon: Essays in Apocalypse*

Roberts Liardon, *Final Approach: The Opportunity and Adventure of End-Times*
Living

David Webber and Noah Hutchins, *Is This the Last Century?*

Peter and Patti LaLonde, *The Edge of Time: The Final Countdown Has Begun*

Peter and Paul LaLonde, *2000 A.D.: Are You Ready?*

Jack Van Impe, *2001: On the Edge of Eternity*

Robert Van Kampen, *The Sign*

Ed Dobson, *The End: Why Jesus Could Return by A.D. 2000*

John Hagee, *Beginning of the End*
Ed Hindson, *Approaching Armageddon: The World
    Prepares for War with God*
William T. James, ed., *Foreshocks of Anti-Christ*
Grant R. Jeffrey, *Final Warning*
Tim LaHaye and Jerry Jenkins, the novelizing of
    Scripture with the *Left Behind* series

Obviously, something isn't working out. In dealing with this subject, my concern is for the benefit of the average person in the pew. It's by no means a comprehensive or technical work, but rather, a primer. It's a pastor's introduction to a subject around which there's much confusion in the evangelical world—to help the average Christian understand the biblical teachings regarding this subject. For the interested reader, a list of scholarly books recommended by me can be found at the end of the book.

First, the Bad News

The Bible is the only rule of faith and practice. The "Bible plus..." phenomenon is an identifying mark of every cult. Nor are newspapers part of God's special revelation, despite Taylor's advice in *Watch 1988*, where he wrote: "The evidence has been set before you. The newspapers give daily testimony to the fact that all things are being fulfilled preparatory to the coming-again of the Lord Jesus Christ." Now, there's certainly nothing wrong with reading newspapers, but to consult them for biblical insights is bad news indeed.

That Christians seek to formulate a theology from the behavior of people or nations is bad news. As incredible as some national situations may be, or as miraculous as the reappearance of Israel may seem, attempts to interpret Scripture through the lens of current events are constantly proven wrong.

The devil's clever, deceptive work in the world is bad news. Satan is the most incredible counterfeiter and liar in all creation (John 8:44). He has deployed his deceptive devices for at least 6,000 years, misleading well-meaning Christians by giving them counterfeit signs. Clarion calls for "The End" have rung with regularity throughout the history of Christianity.

Hearing of Christians pointing out key signs for the return of Christ has disappointed many believers. The physical reestablishment of a great number of Jews in Palestine has led a vast multitude of Christians down a very troublesome path. This historical event, if interpreted improperly, has caused much disappointment among believers.

The reappearance of the physical nation of Israel has been linked with Christ's return, but the stubborn fact is that even though Israel was reestablished as a nation more than a half-century ago, Christ has not returned. This is going to take some painful examination.

That many evangelicals set dates for Christ's return is bad news. On page 43 of *The Late Great Planet Earth*, Hal Lindsey informs us that he, as well as "many scholars," believe we can look for the Rapture "within 40 years," a generation or so from 1948, when Israel was reestablished as a nation.

The year 1988 came and went with no change in world circumstances. It's bad news. Nothing happened in 1988 and nothing has happened in the thirty or more years since Lindsey's book appeared. What's the answer to this?

Sign-seeking is the behavior of "a wicked and adulterous generation," and is, therefore, bad news. Christ declared, "A wicked and adulterous generation asks for a miraculous sign! But none will be given it except the sign of the prophet Jonah" (Matthew 12:39).

We also need to re-think the practice of painting particular ethnic groups as godless. This is not good news for them. In futuristic teaching, the Arabs always seem to be the bad guys. Yet, the Word of God specifically promises, "The LORD Almighty will bless them, saying, '*Blessed be Egypt my people, Assyria my handiwork, and Israel my inheritance*'" (Isaiah 19:25).

The Russians and the Chinese are also the bad guys in most futuristic books. This is an Old Testament view that nations exist which are one hundred percent pagan. There may be more Christians in China than in the United States. There are no more one hundred percent pagan nations in the world, since the days when the great commission was given (Matthew 28:19).

Believers have always had a continued fascination with Old Testament prophecies but, too often, a reluctance to receive the authority and words of Christ. Even God the Father had to intervene and rebuke Peter for wanting to share Christ's glory with Moses and Elijah on the Mount of Transfiguration: "This is my Son, whom I love; with Him I am well pleased. *Listen to Him!*" (Matthew 17:5b).

Moses had already had his say; Elijah had served his purpose. Both are important figures in the history of God's dealings with man. "But now, it is my Son's turn," declares God. Don't ignore Jesus' supreme authority. More about this later.

What does Jesus teach about the prominence and centrality of Israel as a physical nation in His plan?

That most worthy and deliberate attempt of some godly men in the mid-nineteenth century to counteract the dangerous development and snare of liberal theology has come back in the twenty-first century to bite us.

Motivated by love of God's infallible Word, they adopted a literal interpretation of prophetic biblical literature. This popular system is known as dispensationalism. Unfortunately, like the proverbial pendulum, it swings too far. Consequently, that serious concern for the truth of God's Word caused an unintentional but serious deviation from a unified revelation of Scripture between the twin trees: the tree of life in Eden, and the tree of life in the last paragraph of Revelation.

It's at that point in theological history that the system of dispensationalism entered the mainstream of many conservative and mostly independent churches. Eventually, this problematic procedure was adopted by a number of Bible colleges and some independent seminaries. The Bible and church history, however, have taught us that the smallest deviation from sound theology produces ultimately painful and disastrous ramifications.

I lay, in humility and very reluctantly, at the feet of dispensationalism, an unintentional partial blame for radical extreme Islamic terrorist attacks. It's obvious that after scrutinizing dispensationalism, one discovers the logical conclusion that, in spite of the great commission's mandate of Christ, God still loves Jacob and still hates Esau.

This represents Christianity to the misinformed Islamic mind; they've been taught that Christianity is Jewish, and Jews kill

Arabs, and Arabs kill Jews. When this teaching is relentlessly preached by most international television preachers, and embraced by prominent political leaders in the United States, inflamed radical Islamic religious madness follows. Islam again raises the "arm of flesh" and, rightfully so, the free world has to respond with organized military power.

Think this through carefully: is it possible that the birth of dispensationalism in the mid-1800s produced an unintentional covert spiritual crusade against Arab people in general? Many Arab Christians believe so. This has been communicated to me when preaching in Egypt. Any political power or nation has the right of choice or preference to support and build up one nation over against another. But since "the fulfillment of the nations has come" (1 Corinthians 10:11), there's absolutely no biblical mandate or support for that kind of decision.

Looking at worldly events from a biblical perspective, one will discover that it's a *fallen little planet earth* in which we live, surrounded by counterfeit miracles and lies. Our guidance comes from a complete and unified Bible. It's a catastrophe when bad things happen to good prophecies. It leads to great disappointment, anxieties, and real disaster in the lives of many godly people.

In his book, *How Long to the End?*, Philip Mauro wrote:

> "Against this "strange" doctrine, I'm constrained to enter a most earnest protest, and to raise a most solemn warning. For not only is it contrary to the Scriptures, and therefore to be opposed for that reason alone, but it also affects disastrously the foundation truth of the Gospel, in that it proclaims *another hope* and *another salvation*, different from gospel salvation, to be received and enjoyed by a section of the human race, *after this day of grace is ended.*
>
> "Moreover, the danger with which this new doctrine threatens the household of faith is enhanced greatly by the fact that it's taught—not by men of heretical views and doubtful orthodoxy, but—by those who

are distinguished for the most unquestionable loyalty to the Word of God. Therefore, in opposing the doctrine, I wish to affirm my esteem and affectionate regard for many who teach it."

Now, the Good News

The holy Trinity—Father, Son, and Holy Spirit—in eternity past decreed a perfect plan of salvation for the whole world, for every race, as long as the world lasts. It was first communicated to Adam and Eve, and others, then clearly to Abraham (John 8:56). The Father is the originator of that plan; the Son is the executor of that plan; the Holy Spirit is the applicator of that plan.

First Peter 1:20 teaches that Jesus and His church are no unfortunate afterthought. There is no Plan A or Plan B with God. Everything is right on target; that's the good news. "He was chosen before the creation of the world, but was revealed in these last times for your sake." This eternal plan of salvation can never be fouled up, for man has no say in it. This is good news!

The news gets better all the time. Believe it or not, God is in charge of all history; it is literally *His story*. God's redemptive purpose in history is to gather together a people for Himself, to populate heaven for eternity. Before the world began, in timeless and spaceless eternity, Christ's death was foreordained. Abraham learned about the grace of God before Moses received the law of God. That is good news.

Let's carefully examine and see if the Abrahamic covenant is now being fulfilled through the body of Christ, the church of both Jew and Gentile. We know Christ perfectly fulfilled the requirements of the covenant. Believing Jews, Arabs, Africans, Americans, and people from every tribe and nation, are now included through the finished work of Christ by faith in Him alone (Galatians 3:28). This is very good news. The Bible is the *only* source of God's revelation to man, not the newspaper or the evening news. That's why the gospel is called the Good News.

The good news is that for a very loving, divine reason, Jesus has not as yet returned as a final act. As believers in Christ, we've been given the job description to disciple the whole world. "Thank You,

Lord, for delaying Your coming" should be every Christian's prayer. There are billions of people who've never heard the Good News.

Not ever hearing the Good News of Christ would be bad news for those who've spent their whole lives without it. The Good Shepherd is still continuing to complete His fold. It's not over until the last of His sheep have been found. The good news doesn't get any better than that.

The purpose of this layman's book is to take our eyes off this upside down, sinful world, and examine the confusing signs that have reappeared with every earthquake and war for the last 2,000 years, to see what the Bible says about them. We must look to Jesus and not to the Middle East, and be faithful in the areas where God, by His sovereign plan, has placed us, whether Christ comes again tomorrow or a thousand years from now.

Below are listed items which will be discussed throughout this book.

1. Who really are God's original people?
2. How can God punish sinners before the Ten Commandments were given?
3. Does the Bible support fulfilled prophetic reruns?
4. Are there any conditions attached to God's covenant with people?
5. What, and who, are Gog and Magog?
6. Are clouds celestial spacecrafts for Christ to travel on?
7. Is the Rapture a one-time or daily occurrence?
8. Why would Paul wish himself to be accursed for the sake of the conversion of the Jews, when he said in the same letter that they all are going to be saved?
9. Why are gold and precious jewels so important in the city of God, when Peter was proud that he didn't have any of those things?
10. Did the church in Jerusalem have a copy of Revelation before the fall of Jerusalem?
11. Are earthquakes in Scripture always ground-shaking events?
12. Is Jesus excited about coming back for a thousand-year reign?

13. Why does the Bible so often use typological and symbolic terminology?
14. What happens when a star falls on your head?
15. Did the gates of hell really block the church?
16. What is replacement theology?

Let's begin and let the Bible tell the story of God's revelation of Himself to man.

CHAPTER 1

God's Original Introduction to Man

-+=⊃⊂=+-

The Spirit of God was hovering over the waters. **(Genesis 1:2)**

God said let there be light and there was light. **(Genesis 1:3)**

Jesus said I am the light of the world.
Whoever follows me will never walk in darkness,
but will have the light of life.
(John 8:12)

God Consciousness

The hidden "Intelligent Designer" of the whole universe entered time and space He had purposefully created and introduced himself to Adam, making communication with him possible. I am your Almighty, Good, Holy Creator, and your God. Purposefully I have made you in Our image and likeness, including your wife and all your descendants after you. I am establishing a covenant of works with you, and give you authority over every living creature, except yourself. The earth and everything in it belongs to Me, including you. You do not belong to yourself. I keep the right to make laws and deal with its violations. And so painfully the history of self-rule contempt of God, and God's plan of salvation unfold.

Here's a quote from a faithful nineteenth century man of God.

> The gospel was of an eternal resolution, though of a temporary revelation; according to the revelation of the mystery, which was kept secret since the world began. It is an everlasting gospel; it was a promise "before the world began" (Titus 1:2). It was not a

new invention, but only kept secret among the arcana, in the breast of the Almighty. It was hidden from angels, for the depths of it are not yet fully made known to them; their desire to look into it, speaks yet a deficiency in their knowledge of it (1 Peter 1:12). It was published in paradise, but in such words as Adam did not fully understand; it was both discovered and clouded in the smoke of sacrifices: it was wrapped up in a veil under the law, but not opened till the death of the Redeemer: it was then plainly said to the cities of Judah, "Behold! Your God comes!" ... No traditions of men, no inventions of vain wits, that pretend to be wiser than God, should have the same credit as that which bears date from eternity. (Stephen Charnock, *Discourses upon the Existence and Attributes of God*)

The Mysterious Church

But the Lord came down to see the city and the tower that the men were building. The LORD said, "If as one people speaking the same language they have begun to do this, then nothing they plan to do will be impossible for them. Come, let us go down and confuse their language so they will not understand each other." So the Lord scattered them from there over all the earth, and they stopped building the city. That is why it was called Babel—because there the LORD confused the language of the whole world. From there the LORD scattered them over the face of the whole earth. (Genesis 11:5-9)

The struggle against God because of man's insistence on self-rule continued without end or mitigation.

From the words of the only mediator between God and man, our Lord Jesus Christ Himself: "No one comes to the Father except through me" (John 14:6).

From the Holy Spirit's inspired Word of God, through a converted dangerous religious fanatic, Paul the apostle, writing to Titus: "... a faith and knowledge resting on the hope of eternal life, which God, who does not lie, promised before the beginning of time..." (Titus 1:2).

It's a most humbling, but incredibly gracious fact that the eternal gospel involved God Himself, beginning with one married couple who rebelled against God. Oh, "How great is the love the Father has lavished on us, that we should be called the children of God!" (1 John 3:1).

We know that all breaking of the law of God is a sin (1 John 3:3); it's rebellion against and contempt of the triune God's infinite holiness. Sin against God is never dealt with unless God Himself is involved, responding either with judgment or with mercy.

The sin of Adam was a sin against the Father, the Son, and the Holy Spirit.

The insidious invitation that came to Eve to taste the forbidden fruit came from the one who was cast out from the presence of God. Jesus saw all this! He was there!

The gospel of the Lord Jesus Christ was first preached to Adam and Eve in paradise by God Himself (Genesis 3:15). Afterward, it was preached by Christ to both Jews and Samaritans. And finally, the great commission was to be executed by the universal church to the entire world, in response to the declaration of our victorious Christ.

Consequently, Christianity is the first, the original, the only true religion in the world.

We meet this situation in the beginning pages of the Bible. In Genesis 4, Abel offered unto God a blood sacrifice; at this point, the only sacrifice acceptable to God. Cain, for his part, offered vegetables. Since God did not accept Cain's offering, Cain was devastated and angry. God did not welcome Cain, and plainly told him to do it right next time. He also told him to watch out, "sin is crouching at your door" (Genesis 4:7). Cain had become the founder of his own religion, opening the door for the entrance of Satan.

On the other hand, God accepted Abel's offering. For within or by that specific offering of a choice lamb, the eternal gospel was included and proclaimed. It pictured the Lamb of God slain before

31

the foundation of the world.

By faith Abel offered God a better sacrifice than Cain did (Hebrews 11:4). Note that Abel wasn't saved and accepted by God because of this offering. Offerings of animals had no power to save and cleanse from sin. Rather, Abel was saved by what the offering represented; it was a shadow of the sacrifice of the Son of God on a hill called Calvary. All God-appointed blood sacrifices point to Christ's offering of Himself as a blood sacrifice.

This is truth, so basic that the little children's catechism, a steppingstone to the Westminster Shorter Catechism, plainly states:

66. Q. Before Christ came, how did believers show their faith?
    A. By offering the sacrifices God required.
67. Q. What did these sacrifices represent?
    A. Christ, the Lamb of God, who would come to die for sinners.

Cain's offering of produce was meaningless and rebellious. It was totally unacceptable to God. At that time, it represented nothing. It was a man-made pseudo-religious activity. It was a repeat of Adam's effort to clothe himself with leaves. From that unacceptable man-made offering of Cain's, all religions other than Christianity find their origin.

All of this begs at least eleven questions:

1. How did Abel know what was right? (Genesis 4:4)
2. How could Cain be punished for not doing right? (Genesis 4:6)
3. How did people manage to call on the name of God? (Genesis 4:26)
4. How on earth did Enoch manage to walk with God for 300 years? (Genesis 5:22)
5. How did Enoch disappear? (Genesis 5:24)
6. How could God judge sin before the Ten Commandments were given? (Genesis 6:5)
7. How did Noah manage to become blameless? (Genesis 6:9)
8. How did Ham know that what he had done was wrong?

(Genesis 9:22)

9. How is it that God called Abraham when he (Abraham) was a worshipper of other gods? (Joshua 24:2)
10. How did Job know about God and Jesus? (Job 19:25)
11. Where on earth did Melchizedek come from? (Hebrews 7:1)

Pre-Bethlehemic Christianity

It seems that the answers to these questions are in the words of the first condemned, murderous criminal, talking with the Lord when he said: "My punishment is more than I can bear. Today, you are driving me from the land, and I *will be hidden from your presence*; I will be a restless wanderer on the earth, and whoever finds me will kill me.

"But the LORD said to him, 'Not so; if anyone kills Cain, he will suffer vengeance seven times over.' The LORD put a mark on Cain so that no one who found him would kill him" (Genesis 4:13-15).

Note that the mark put on Cain was not a mark of condemnation; it was only a mark of protection.

Obviously, after the ejection of Adam and Eve from the Garden of Eden, they were not cast away from the care and presence of God. God communicated with Cain before, and even after, the murder of his brother. *Cain was terrified of losing the privilege of being in God's presence.*

Take note, and time to concentrate on this often overlooked fact that God is a covenant-making God, covenanting Himself to his chosen in this first revelatory period. A covenant in Scripture is not just a proverbial handshake, a well-wish from God to Adam and Noah, or a verbal blessing or a smile of approval from the Creator. No, it is thousands of times more significant and wonderful.

In his 1980 seminary text book, *The Christ of the Covenant,* Dr. O. Palmer Robertson wrote:

> Clearly any definition of the term "covenant" must allow for as broad a latitude as the data of Scripture demands. Yet the very wholeness of the biblical history in being determined by God's

covenants suggests an overarching oneness in the concept of the covenant.

What then is a covenant? How do you define the covenantal relation of God to his people?

A covenant is a *bond in blood sovereignly administered.* When God enters into a covenantal relationship with men, he sovereignly institutes a life-and-death bond.

A covenant is a bond in blood, or a bond of life and death, sovereignly administered.

This mysterious presentation and representation of the Son of God continued. People continued calling upon Him. There were blameless people whose sins would be laid on Christ at Calvary. People were walking with God. If Job existed before Abraham (and many scholars believe he did), then we have yet another example of God communicating with people before the call of Abraham. Abraham himself introduced and honored another mysterious personality who lived before Abraham's call—Melchizedek.

This, of course, fits biblically with the words of Moses, written before the establishment of the Jews as a nation, "Lord, you have been our dwelling place *throughout all generations*" (Psalm 90:1).

The answer to the above eleven questions is simply this: God the Father, God the Son, and God the Holy Spirit, in a mysterious way, made Their will and ways known to the inhabitants of the world long before the call of Abraham. Hebrews 11 tells us about God's gift of faith to Abel, to Enoch, and Noah, and many others.

Unfortunately, in this first revelational, pre-Abrahamic period, "Men loved darkness instead of light because their deeds were evil" (John 3:19). Consequently, they were destroyed. "Death reigned from the time of Adam to the time of Moses" (Romans 5:14). God's judgment continued, and is continuing until the last sheep is found, and the fold of Christ is full.

Genesis 1–11 is a description of God's mysterious working and presence among His children. Obviously, His law was communicated, for where there is no law, there is no sin (see Romans 5:13). In other words, it's impossible to do wrong if there's no law against it.

If an interstate highway has no speed limit, then the motorist can drive 100 miles per hour without fear of getting a ticket for speeding.

In these first eleven chapters of God's Word, we're introduced to the Lamb of God, who takes away the sin of the world (John 1:29). Christ, who appeared as an angel, or as the Lord, was involved in the plan of salvation from day one. There has never been any other way by which sin can be taken away, or covered, but by Christ alone.

We know of no other means by which that can happen. The work of the second person of the Godhead in any other period is still the ministry of Christ, and the beginning and perpetuation of Christianity. Thousands of years of this ministry went on before Abraham, or before the second stage of revelation.

The Messiah had been promised to Adam and Eve, the One who would save His people from their sin, and ultimately and completely destroy Satan (1 John 3:8).

We know from Scripture that by God giving faith to Abel, he offered a better sacrifice than Cain. By God giving faith to Enoch, he joined God in heaven. By God giving faith to Noah, he built an ark. *None of these people were Jews.* The establishment of the Jewish nation came at least two thousand years later. Faith was at work in the hearts of God's original people centuries before Abraham.

Here are some quotes from *The Christian's Reasonable Service*, the momentous four-volume work of the seventeenth century Dutch theologian, Wilhelmus a Brakel:

> *"The Old Testament Administration of the Covenant of Grace Begins in Paradise."*

> The Old Testament or Covenant encompasses the entire period from the gospel declaration in Paradise until Christ. During this entire time frame there was no diversity in its manner of administration—an administration which functioned during this entire period by way of promises and figures. However, relative to the subjects of this administration, we can make a chronological distinction between the church

35

prior to Abraham and *thereafter*. Prior to Abraham the church consisted of various nationalities—as is also true in the New Testament era. However, God took Abraham and his seed to be His church. Thus, subsequent to Abraham's time, other nations rapidly became estranged from true religion. This pure religion was preserved, however, among the descendants of Abraham. Therefore, when speaking of a national covenant, it must be understood as the covenant of grace established with that particular nation. The term does not imply more than that.

Not much has been recorded concerning the condition of the church from Adam to Abraham. What has been recorded, however, is sufficient to show us that *the gospel and true religion were as well-known and practiced then as was the case thereafter*. It was by way of that generational line that the Lord Jesus descended from Adam. His descent from Adam was necessary in order to His being the Mediator. It was necessary that this be known in order to acknowledge Him as such. The time frame from Adam to Abraham encompasses about two thousand years and has been recorded in the first chapters of the first book of Moses...

After Adam and Eve had transgressed the covenant of works, the Lord announced a new covenant, a covenant of grace, with the following words: "And I will put enmity between thee and the woman, and between thy seed and her Seed; it shall bruise thy head, and thou shalt bruise His heel" (Gen. 3:15) ... The words are few, but they encompass the great work of redemption of the sinner, the overthrow of the devil's tyranny over the elect; the enmity and warfare between God's children and the children of the devil—and they point to the Person through whom this would be accomplished, who is called the *Seed of the Woman* (and thus not seed of the man). This Person is Christ...

All sacrifices point to Christ. Apart from that purpose they were neither instituted, nor were they pleasing to God, who is not pleased with external service. Thus, the sacrifices prior to Moses also looked forward to Christ, and it is for that reason that Christ is called "the Lamb which was slain before the foundation of the world" (Rev. 13:8). Moreover, they sacrificed in faith, which always points to Christ. Therefore, the sacrifices prior to Moses typified Christ...

All the sacrifices were a remembrance again of sins to the humbling of those who sacrificed. All sacrifices declare that the guilt of sin had not been satisfied, but would be satisfied by the substitutionary Surety, Jesus Christ. All sacrifices declare that neither he who sacrifices nor the sacrifice itself can remove sin, but point to the substance of those shadows. All this is characteristic of a sacrifice; otherwise a sacrifice is not a sacrifice. Consequently, all sacrifices point to sins and their removal. This is to be observed in Leviticus 1:4: "And he shall put his hand upon the head of the burnt offering; and it shall be accepted for him to make atonement for him". Thus also the sacrifice of Job—, who did not descend from Abraham and who, in all probability, lived prior to Moses—pointed to sin and atonement. When offering a burnt offering, he said, "It may be that my sons have sinned" (Job 1:5). All sacrifices are of an identical nature. Nowhere is a distinction made between the sacrifices before and after Moses. There is no argument that the sacrifices after Moses pointed to sin and atonement; therefore, this is equally true prior to Moses." (*The Christian's Reasonable Service*, pages 374-375; italics his)

This is the mysterious church: Christ was busy; sinners were forgiven and punished. Adam's sin was laid on Christ; people called upon God; men were made holy; God was at work; His presence was experienced. God's plan was unfolding during this first stage of revelation. An unwritten law, verbally communicated, was known.

There was no temple, and that's all we know about the original church. The foundation was laid, and development continued through the second stage, and continues through the final stage, from Adam till the end of the world.

Here then is an unbroken historical link from Adam to Calvary. The ministry of Christ began in Eden. Jesus' testimony about Himself stated clearly that His recorded ministry began, not by a prophetic birth announcement, but by Christ's own testimony, "Before Abraham was born, I am" (John 8:58).

This begs at least five more serious questions:

1. Is it consistent with Scripture and the nature of YAHWEH that He created these God-breathed pre-Abrahamic praying souls purposeless? Of course not! Pre-Noahic and post-Noahic man continued to call on the name of the Lord (Genesis 4:26b). Earnest calling on the name of God is never an effort in futility.

2. Did the rebellion of Adam and Eve so totally destroy the souls of their descendants that further relationship with God (YAHWEH) was impossible? Of course not! Before and after Noah, sin increased over a long period of time. Romans 1:20, however, tells us, "Since *the creation of the world* God's invisible qualities—His eternal power and divine nature have been clearly seen, being understood from what has been made, so that men are without excuse."

3. Did that first knowledge that YAHWEH was a covenant-making God appear by the call of Abraham? Of course not! God made a covenant with Noah. He was declared righteous by God. Noah's wife and three married sons were saved

under that covenant, *and a greater, wider covenant followed:* "and with your descendants after you" (Genesis 9:8-9). That is, the whole human race began again with one God-fearing covenant family.

4. Were the Jews God's original people? Of course not! Throughout this long-lasting period, in a mysterious way, all the benefits of the eternal gospel were applied to various God-conscious people, by that only means of salvation: "the Lamb slain before the creation of the world."

5. Is the call of God to Abraham more important than the call of God to Noah? Of course not! What Noah was commanded by God to do was a hundred times more difficult, painful, ridiculed, and necessary. Both calls were absolutely indispensable. That the call and covenant with Noah and his descendants has been almost totally ignored is most unfortunate and troublesome.

Typical dispensationalism continually put into the background this first most important revelatory period. Modern-day Israel would never have come alive as a theological issue if it had been clearly understood that the faith of Abraham was to be a channel of divine truth for a certain period, and not a foundation of that truth.

The twelve tribes were never to be regarded as the root of Christianity. Christianity has its divine origin in the triune Godhead and her human origin in Adam, not Abraham. *Christ is the second Adam, not the second Abraham. However, to be a true child of Abraham is to possess the faith of Abraham. "So those who have faith are blessed along with Abraham the man of faith"* (Galatians 3:9).

Our sinful nature is in Adam, our regenerated souls are in Christ. "For as in Adam all die, so in Christ all will be made alive" (1 Corinthians 15:22). The first Adam became a living being; the last Adam, a life-giving spirit (1 Corinthians 15:45).

This first mysterious period had a biblical and historical beginning and ended with the call of Abraham.

A very bad thing has happened to the most fundamental prophecy in Scripture; the first

prophecy from the mouth of Jehovah that Christ would crush the head of Satan. The announcement by God that the ministry of Christ in the world would start from day one is almost totally ignored. *Consequently, dispensationalism is built on a faulty foundation,* because dispensationalism divides the Bible into seven unique periods.

CHAPTER 2

The Hidden Church

❖⟹⟸❖

Joshua said to all the people, "This is what the Lord, the God of Israel, says: 'Long ago your forefathers, including Terah the father of Abraham and Nahor, lived beyond the River and worshiped other gods.'"
(Joshua 24:2)

Simon has described for us how God at first showed his concern by taking from the Gentiles a people for himself.
(Acts 15:14)

By faith Moses, when he had grown up, refused to be known as the son of Pharaoh's daughter. He chose to be mistreated along with the people of God rather than to enjoy the pleasures of sin for a short time. He regarded disgrace for the sake of Christ as of greater value than the treasures of Egypt, because he was looking ahead to his reward.
(Hebrews 11:24-26)

God's Revelation of Himself, from Abraham to Christ, the True Parenthesis

Although God was at work in the lives of individuals, of which we have fantastic, but limited accounts in Scripture, there was great need for a chronological, systematized, unique revelation of God's plan for the nations of the world. This is clearly evidenced in God's choosing Abraham and his descendants to be a channel of objective truth about the triune God and fallen mankind.

God therefore determined, in time and space, an historical end to that first revelatory period. He would now communicate, through

41

His chosen and inspired prophets, priests, and kings, his unalterable and infallible Word, to the Jews first, and then to the whole world.

His plan of salvation for billions of believers, however, was not in the process of development. In other words, it was not changing, enhanced or fine-tuned. It was accomplished and applied before the creation of the world. Consequently, that truth can only be seen by eyes that have been opened by the Holy Spirit.

In Psalm 119:18, the writer prays: "Open my eyes that I may see wonderful things in your law." The Apostle Paul, that formerly blind persecutor of the church, said, "The man without the Spirit does not accept the things that come from the Spirit of God, for they are foolishness to him, and he cannot understand them, because they are spiritually discerned" (1 Corinthians 2:14).

> The Scriptures of the Old Testament verify the substance of the New, and the New doth evidence the authority of the Old, by the Scriptures of the prophets made known. The Old Testament credits the New, and the New illustrates the Old. The New Testament is a comment upon the prophetic part of the Old. The Old shows the promises and predictions of God, and the New shows the performance. What was foretold in the Old, is fulfilled in the New; the predictions are cleared by the events. The predictions of the Old are divine, because they are above the reason of man to foreknow; none but an infinite knowledge could foretell them, because none but an infinite wisdom could order all things for the accomplishment of them. *The Christian religion hath, then, the surest foundation, since the Scriptures of the prophets, wherein it is foretold, are of undoubted antiquity, and owned by the Jews, and many heathens, which are and were the great enemies of Christ.* The Old Testament is therefore to be read for the strengthening of our faith. Our blessed Saviour himself draws the streams of his doctrine from the Old Testament: he clears up the promise of eternal

life, and the doctrine of the resurrection, from the words of the covenant, "I am the God of Abraham," &c. (Matthew 22:32). And our apostle clears up the doctrine of justification by faith from God's covenant with Abraham (Romans 4). It must be read, and it must be read as it is writ: it was writ to a gospel end, it must be studied with a gospel spirit. The Old Testament was writ to give credit to the New, when it should be manifested in the world. It must be read by us to give strength to our faith, and establish us in the doctrine of Christianity. How many view it as a bare story, an almanac out of date, and regard it as a dry bone, without sucking from it the evangelical marrow! Christ is, in Genesis, Abraham's seed; in David's psalms and the prophets, the Messiah and Redeemer of the world. (Stephen Charnock, *Discourses upon the Existence and Attributes of God*, page 103)

And now a very clear word from God's communication to Moses: "...This is what you are to say to the house of Jacob and what you are to tell the people of Israel: 'Now, if you obey me fully and keep my covenant, then out of all nations, you will be my treasured possession. Although the whole earth is mine, you will be for me a kingdom of priests and a holy nation.' These are the words you are to speak to the Israelites" (Exodus 19:3b-6).

This is a bird's eye view of Judaism. The second stage of God revealing His plan of salvation to the world was "both discovered and clouded in the smoke of sacrifices: it was wrapped up in a veil under the law" (Charnock, page 103). This period is the true historical drama of an unbelievably gracious God and a rebellious, stiff-necked people.

It began with the call of God to an imperfect man, Abraham, who, by the grace of God, became a friend of God. This period ended, once and for all, with God's judgment as manifested by the destruction of the temple in Jerusalem in A.D. 70. Having fulfilled its divine purpose, this stage had a very clear beginning and a very anti-climactic end. The subject here is the physical nation of Israel as it relates to the Lord Jesus Christ. There will be much more about this subject in following chapters.

The modern, physical state of Israel no longer has any more significance than any other nation as far as Christianity is concerned. At risk of being accused of anti-Semitism, let us say that Israel is in the same category, as far as the church is concerned, as America, Bolivia, China, Denmark, Egypt, Finland, Greenland, Holland, India, and the rest of the alphabet, right up to Zimbabwe.

However, during the second stage of God's revelation of Himself, Israel was the only nation in the world whose God was *Jehovah*. All other nations were more or less without hope and without God. They were under the wrath and curse of God. That's why it was difficult for converted Jews to share the gospel with other nations at the beginning. Jehovah had been their unique possession, but under the gospel, they had to share Him, losing their uniqueness among the nations.

But the divine plan, however, was much bigger, for Israel had the privilege and responsibility to be obedient to the mandate, handed down by God, to Abraham, that *through him, not by him,* all nations of the world would be blessed.

The Bible makes it very clear that the use of the nation Israel, as far as Christianity is concerned, would have a limited time period. In reality, Israel was a divinely appointed *parenthesis*, with a divine beginning and a divine end. The equalization of all nations began with Christ's final words to His followers: "Therefore go and make disciples of all nations" (Matthew 28:19a).

Every nation now has a most-favored-nation status with God. He is the God of the nations. This is not an insult to the Jews, nor is it anti-Semitism, for—and let's be up front about this—physical Israel, in the past and now, could not care less about Christ or His church.

Israel had a special role to play in the second stage of God's revelation, for several reasons:

1. It was a God-produced nation, carefully chosen and graciously developed, and populated with holy men and women of God.

44

2. Abraham, Isaac, Jacob, and the patriarchs were nothing short of a biblical illustration of a merciful God. Throughout Scripture, God has used great sinners, saved by His amazing grace, to fulfill His sovereign purpose.
3. Through the Israelites, God would show, for the benefit of the nations yet to be born, how gracious, loving, forgiving, longsuffering, just, and righteous He is.
4. There needed to be a people who would receive the messages of the various prophets who, hidden in their divinely inspired utterances, were preparing the birthplace and land for the God-man to be revealed. Thus it was imperative to put an end to the random revelations of God in the first mysterious period, and develop through the means of Abraham and his descendants, a more precise way to God—by means of a second period, with a specific end (John 4:21-24), according to the words of Jesus.
5. The giving of the law, lessons learned, and psalms sung would be the guidelines of faith for all people as a directory of worship and means to know Christ and to increase in the knowledge of God, to the end of the world. The book of Deuteronomy is regarded to be the constitution of the Administration of the whole plan of salvation. The Bible is made complete only by the Old Testament and the New Testament until the end.
6. The original and only true way to God (Christ) needed clear and decisive means to communicate to the rest of the nations. That's why the prophets prophesied, and apostles recorded the acts of God to the world. "Men spoke from God as they were carried along by the Holy Spirit" (2 Peter 1:21b).
7. Moses, like Paul, participated in the sufferings of Christ. "He regarded disgrace for the sake of Christ as of greater value than the treasures of Egypt, because he was looking ahead to his reward" (Hebrews 11:26).
8. Christ was constantly among them—hidden in messages of the prophets—and present in all kinds of symbols: water from a rock; a serpent on a pole; a cloud to protect them from the pursuing Egyptian armies (Exodus 14:19, 24).

However, the holiness of God and the sinfulness of man reigned without mitigation or end throughout this whole period of God's revelation.

> The Israelites are a wonderful example of this contempt of Divine goodness; they had been spectators of the greatest miracles, and partakers of the choicest deliverance: he had solicited their redemption from captivity; and when words would not do, he came to blows for them, musters up his judgments against their enemies, and, at last, as the Lord of hosts and God of battles, totally defeats their pursuers, and drowns them and their proud hopes of victory in the Red Sea. Little account was made of all this by the redeemed ones; "they lightly esteemed the rock of their salvation," and launch into greater unworthiness, instead of being thankful for the breaking (of) their yoke: they are angry with him, that he had done so much for them: they repented that ever they had complied with him, for their own deliverance, and had a regret that they had been brought out of Egypt: they were angry that they were freemen, and that their chains had been knocked off: they were more desirous to return to the oppression of their Egyptian tyrants, than have a God for their governor and caterer, and be fed with his manna. "It was well with us in Egypt: Why came we forth out of Egypt?" which is called a "despising the Lord" (Numbers 11:18, 20). They were so far from rejoicing in the expectation of the future benefits promised them, that they murmured that they had not enjoyed less; they were so sottish, as to be desirous to put themselves into the irons whence God had delivered them: they would seek a remedy in that Egypt, which had been the prison of their nation, and under the successors of that Pharaoh, who had been the invader of their liberties; they would snatch Moses

from the place where the Lord, by an extraordinary providence, had established him; they would stone those that minded them of the goodness of God to them, and thereupon of their crime and their duty (Numbers 16:3, 9-11); they rose against their benefactors, and "murmured against God," that had strengthened the hand of their deliverers; they "despised the manna" he had sent them, and "despised the pleasant land" he intended them (Psalm 106:24): all which was a high contempt of God and his unparalleled goodness and care of them. All murmuring is an accusation of Divine goodness. (Charnock, *Discourses upon the Existence and Attributes of God*, page 318, Vol. II)

This attitude toward God is the black cloud without a silver lining hovering over Israel's history, climaxed by the opening verses of Daniel: "In the third year of the reign of Jehoiakim, king of Judah, Nebuchadnezzar king of Babylon came to Jerusalem and besieged it. *And the Lord delivered Jehoiakim king of Judah into his hand*, along with some of the articles of the temple of God. These he carried off to the temple of his god in Babylonia and put in the treasure house of his god" (Daniel 1:1-2).

And then came the unabated tears of a great lamentation: "How deserted lies the city, once so full of people! How like a widow is she, who once was great among the nations! She who was queen among the provinces has now become a slave" (Lamentations 1:1).

That is not, of course, the end of the story. They did come back to the land, according to God's promise. The last two verses of the Old Testament make an incredible promise: "See, I will send you the prophet Elijah before that great and dreadful day of the Lord comes. *He will turn the hearts of the fathers to their children*, and the hearts of the children to their fathers; or else I will come and strike the land with a curse" (Malachi 4:5-6).

This was followed by about 400 years of silence.

Enter John the Baptist, the last Old Testament prophet, on the pages of the New Testament: "Many of the people of Israel *will he bring back to the Lord their God.* And he will go on before the Lord, in the spirit and power of Elijah, *to turn the hearts of the fathers to their children* and the disobedient to the wisdom of the righteous— to make ready a people prepared for the Lord" (Luke 1:16-17).

Then Christ came, and indeed, many returned to the Lord. But of course, Christ knew He would not have the full support of all, for Isaiah the prophet had already seen the result:

> Who has believed our message, and to whom has the arm of the LORD been revealed? He grew up before him like a tender shoot, and like a root out of dry ground. He had no beauty or majesty to attract us to him, nothing in his appearance that we should desire him. He was despised and rejected by men, a man of sorrows and familiar with suffering. Like one from whom men hide their faces, he was despised and we esteemed him not. (Isaiah 53:1-3)

The attitude toward Christ had been one of continual rejection. "But his subjects hated him and sent a delegation after him to say, 'We don't want this man to be our king'" (Luke 19:14). Christ actually taught the parable in Luke 19 about His own rejection.

> The Old Testament is an administration during which it was promised that the Surety and Savior would come. Thus, the time from Adam to Christ was the age of promise, wherein the Savior was typified in His natures, suffering and death—the purpose being that the people of Israel would be better acquainted with and believe in Him. This was accomplished by way of many sacrifices, which the apostle denominates as *figures*. They clearly depicted Christ; and thus the people, so to speak, with their physical eyes daily witnessed and beheld Christ in His suffering and death". Wilhelmus a Brakel, *The Christian's Reasonable Service*, page 394 (emphasis his)

Rachmiel Frydland, a Jewish convert to the Messiah, Jesus Christ, in his incredible book: *When Being Jewish Was a Crime*, makes this wonderful observation.

> Many Christians today realize the deep significance of Passover, from which is taken the Lord's Supper. It was only many years later that I began to see that the three matzos represented the Trinity, and that it was the middle one, the Son, which was broken for us. I watched my father solemnly wrap it in white linen, "bury" it, and then bring it out again—resurrected—at the time of the third cup of wine. Truly the Lord had said that this piece of pure, unleavened, and broken bread was His body. We all partook of it at the Passover table along with the third cup, which we called the Cup of Redemption. (page 43)

However, the real and living Broken One came, fulfilling all the hidden ceremonies in the Old Testament.

Israel has fulfilled its national fleshly purpose—*the clear parenthesis*—in Scripture. In other words, if you must have a parenthesis, Israel fits the bill, and the church does not. For, from the time Genesis 3:15 was given, the increase of His kingdom has not ended (Isaiah 9:6). But as far as the gospel is concerned, "Israel of the flesh" has served her divine purpose with a clear beginning and a clear end. "When the power of the holy people has been finally broken, all these things will be completed" (Daniel 12:7).

This, of course, doesn't mean God is finished with the Jews or Israel as a whole. It would be an incredible blessing if Israel would turn to Christ, the true Messiah, and turn around and be like South Korea where approximately thirty percent of the people have become Christians. "God's gifts and call are irrevocable" (Romans 11:20). In other words, just because you are born in Israel, or born in New York in a Jewish family, doesn't shut the door to you becoming a Christian.

But the Old Testament's hidden church has long ago slowly marched through the God-appointed one-way Jewish tunnel. That tunnel pulled together the various random and individualistic opinions and revelations of God before Abraham's call, confirming and confining God's truth through the Fathers and prophets by the Holy Spirit (Hebrews 1:1).

That purposeful discipline of that hidden revelatory period came to completion by that eternal light at the end of the tunnel—Christ the light of the world—fulfilling all promises and prophesies of Scripture (Psalm 24:25-27). Christ said so!

Unfortunately, the stubborn, faithful Jewish traditionalists' refusal to acknowledge Jesus of Nazareth as God's promised Messiah keeps Judaism stuck in that dark, redundant, deteriorating tunnel like resigned prisoners, millennium after millennium, with backs turned to that Light.

Consequently, it's high time that the frequently superfluous term, "Judeo-Christian," is dropped altogether, as a valid or legitimate terminology. The fact is that it denotes a permanent attachment to a fulfilled revelatory system, which has served its divine prophetic purpose. Unintentionally, Christian writers and preachers are giving biblical legitimacy to a hopeless, stagnant religion without Christ, when they constantly use the term Judeo-Christian.

The truth jumps from the pages of the Old and New Testaments that Jesus Christ was sent to the entire world. It was never God's purpose to continue any saving relationship, apart from the gospel, with anybody or any nation, till the end.

"Whoever believes in him is not condemned, but whoever does not believe stands condemned already because he has not believed in the name of God's one and only Son. This is the verdict: Light has come into the world, but men loved darkness instead of light because their deeds were evil" (John 3:18-19).

Paul said: "None of the rulers of this age understood it, for if they had, they would not have crucified the Lord of glory. However, as it is written: 'No eye has seen, nor ear has heard, no mind has conceived what God has prepared for those who love him.'"

CHAPTER 3

The Visible Church

⊷≡◍⊜≍⊷

...in the last days He has spoken to us by his son. Whom he
appointed heir of all things,
and through whom he made the universe.
The Son is the radiance of God's glory
and the exact representation
of His being...
(Hebrews 1:2-3)

God's Revelation of Himself, from Christ to Eternity

We begin with the words of the Son of God: "I say to you that many will come from the east and the west, and will take their places at the feast with Abraham, Isaac and Jacob in the kingdom of heaven. But the subjects of the kingdom will be thrown outside, into the darkness, where there will be weeping and gnashing of teeth" (Matthew 8:11-12).

The same emphasis of Gentile conversions is repeated without mitigation by the apostle Paul, who said:

> I have become its [the church's] servant by the commission God gave me to present to you the word of God in its fullness—the mystery that has been kept hidden for ages and generations, but is now disclosed to the saints. To them God has chosen to make known among the Gentiles the glorious riches of this mystery, which is Christ in you, the hope of glory (Colossians 1:25-27).

In the passage that follows, God's truth, as revealed throughout

51

Scripture, is explained by Dr. Jack Scott:

> God, before creation, purposed to have a people who would spend eternity with him, with whom he would share the blessings of eternity in his presence. This concept alone is staggering to us and beyond our full comprehension. It speaks of a God of love who in love included us in his eternal purpose. He specifically chose us to be with him forever. He purposed to accomplish our inclusion in his family by his Son, Jesus Christ. Here is implied the whole plan of salvation as Scripture unfolds it for us. The point is that God did the choosing in Christ *before* he created heaven and earth. Thus we see how God's prior purpose affects all that he begins to do in creation of the world and man in it. (*God's Plan Unfolded*, page 18)

It's always wise to go first to Scripture and then to the age-old faithful documents of the church universal. The *Westminster Confession of Faith* is such a document. In just three paragraphs, these great theologians laid the groundwork and gave clear answers to what is now a troublesome issue with respect to opinions on what will happen in the last days.

They wrote hundreds of years before Darby, Scofield, Walvoord, Pentecost, Hagee, Tim LaHaye, etc., etc., etc. It seems the confessions of the Church *leave no room* for another age after the here and now:

> *Westminster Confession of Faith*
> Chapter VIII; of Christ the Mediator
> IV. This office the Lord Jesus did most willingly undertake; which that he might discharge, he was made under the law, and did perfectly fulfill it; endured most grievous torments immediately in his soul, and most painful sufferings in his body; was crucified and died, was buried, and remained under

the power of death, yet saw no corruption. On the third day, he arose from the dead, with the same body in which he suffered, with which also he ascended into heaven, and there sitteth at the right hand of his Father, making intercession, and shall return, to judge men and angels, *at the end of the world.*

Chapter XXV; of the Church
III. Unto this catholic [universal] visible church Christ hath given the ministry, oracles, and ordinances of God, for the gathering and perfecting of the saints, in this life, *to the end of the world*: and doth, by his own presence and Spirit, according to his promise, make them effectual thereunto.

Chapter XXVIII; of Baptism
1. Baptism is a sacrament of the new testament, ordained by Jesus Christ, not only for the solemn admission of the party baptized into the visible church; but also, to be unto him a sign and seal of the covenant of grace, of his engrafting into Christ, of regeneration, of remission of sins, and of his giving up unto God, through Jesus Christ, to walk in newness of life. Which sacrament is, by Christ's own appointment, to be continued in his church *until the end of the world.*

The *Westminster Confession of Faith* denies any other age of salvation following the one we're living in right now. And let's not forget the Scot's Confession, chapter V:

The Continuance, Increase and Preservation of the Kirk [*Kirk* is Scottish for *church*]

We must surely believe that God preserved, instructed, multiplied, honored, adorned, and called from death to life his Kirk in all ages *since Adam until the coming of Christ Jesus in the flesh.* For he called Abraham from his father's country, instructed him, and multiplied his seed; he marvelously preserved him, and more marvelously delivered his seed from the bondage and tyranny of Pharaoh; to them he gave his laws, constitutions, and ceremonies; to them he gave the land of Canaan; after he had given them judges, and afterwards Saul, he gave David to be king, to whom he gave promise that of the fruit of his loins should one sit forever upon his royal throne. To this same people from time to time he sent prophets, to recall them to the right way of their God, from which sometimes they strayed by idolatry. And although, because of their stubborn contempt for righteousness he was compelled to give them into the hands of their enemies, as had previously been threatened by the mouth of Moses, so that the holy city was destroyed, the temple burned with fire, and the whole land desolate for seventy years, yet in mercy he restored them again to Jerusalem, where the city and temple were rebuilt, and they endured against all temptations and assaults of Satan till the Messiah came according to the promise.

Chapter XVI; of the Kirk

As we believe in one God, Father, Son, and Holy Ghost, so we firmly believe that from the beginning, there has been, now is, and to the end of the world shall be, one Kirk, that is to say, one company and multitude of men chosen by God, who rightly worship and embrace him by true faith in Christ Jesus, who is the only head of the Kirk, even as it is the body and spouse of Christ Jesus. This Kirk is catholic, that is, universal, because it contains the chosen of all ages, of all realms, nations, and tongues, be they of the Jews or be they of the Gentiles, who have communion and society with God the Father, and with his Son, Christ Jesus, through the sanctification of his Holy Spirit. It is therefore called the communion, not of profane persons, but of saints, who, as citizens of the heavenly Jerusalem, have the fruit of inestimable benefits, one God, one Lord Jesus, one faith, and one baptism. *Out of this Kirk, there is neither life nor eternal felicity.* Therefore we utterly abhor the blasphemy of those who hold that men who live according to equity and justice shall be saved, no matter what religion they profess. For since there is neither life nor salvation without Christ Jesus, so shall none have part therein but those whom the Father has given unto his Son Jesus Christ, and those who in time come to him, avow his doctrine, and believe in him. (We include the children with the believing parents.) This Kirk is invisible, known only to God, who alone knows whom he has chosen, and includes both the chosen who are departed, the Kirk triumphant, those who yet live and fight against sin and Satan, and those who shall live hereafter.

These timeless confessions can't be improved upon. For me to say any more would be like taking a paintbrush and trying to improve a Rembrandt.

This then concludes a very important, most crucial truth. We have three distinct historical revelatory periods—the mysterious, the hidden, and the visible period—through which that gracious red line of redemption flows with ever-increasing volume.

In chapters 21 and 22 of Revelation, John, in the midst of a great tribulation, was very much in need of some real encouragement, and so were all the churches. He received an elaborate, magnificent description of the church, here described as the new, or renewed, Jerusalem, which originates in heaven. It is definitely not a description of eternity, where the saints dwell with God, for that is forbidden to talk about this side of eternity (2 Corinthians 12:4).

All the blessings described in these two chapters are now

available to the church. This is the gospel age. In Revelation 21:12-14, we read about that incredible city (church):

> It had a great, high wall with twelve gates and with twelve angels at the gates. On the gates were written the names of the twelve tribes of Israel. There were three gates on the east, three on the north, three on the south and three on the west. The wall of the city had twelve foundations, and on them were the names of the twelve apostles of the Lamb.

The city and the misunderstanding of its being will be dealt with later; here is just a hint. Now here is a New Testament description that the foundation of the church, or the origin of the church, did not begin with Israel; Israel was cradled in the already active environment of the gospel of grace.

The *foundations* of the bride, the city, the church are the *apostles of Jesus*. The pearly gates are the sons of Jacob. Is there any clearer example of the grace of God applied to the sons of Jacob, that they're represented as the gates of the city? They were thieves, liars, adulterers, murderers, kidnappers, and assassins, and repented sinners.

If Christianity had her origin in Judaism, then the foundation of the city should have been the twelve sons of Jacob, and the gates should be the twelve apostles, but that's not how it is. Praise God from whom all blessings flow! (Revelation 21:9-14).

Christianity Is Not Fundamentally Jewish

Consequently, the church, or Christianity, did not find its origin in Judaism, or Israel. Rather, Israel, or Judaism, came to life in the outstretched hands of the Lamb slain before the foundations of the world. Therefore, physical Israel has served her divinely appointed purpose, and, like the first stage of revelation, there is no need of a temple anymore—now or in the future.

The Promised Land, or cities, have no spiritual value anymore. Unfortunately, Jews and Palestinians will fight to the death over stones which were pronounced by Jesus as worthless rubble (Matthew 24:2).

The first recorded sacrifice pointing to Calvary occurred when the triune God slaughtered an animal, shed blood, and clothed Adam and Eve. That first divinely acceptable sacrifice of Abel, as has been stated before, pointed to the final sacrifice of Christ.

There has been no break, but instead, there has been a historical, spiritual, unbroken, uninterrupted link from Abel's shadow to the substance, even Jesus Christ our Lord.

Bad things continue to happen to good prophecies if it is preached that "Israel of the flesh" (the physical Israel as reestablished in 1948) has any bearing on the success or the failure of the gospel of the Lord Jesus Christ, His return or His kingdom. No, God's original plan for His people is a thousand times more wonderful.

In these first three chapters, we looked at three distinct but unified progressive periods in which God created an awareness of Himself to great multitudes. One could say it even better biblically:

- The first period is the day of the fathers.
- The second period is the day of the prophets.
- The third period is the day of the Son (Hebrews 1:1-2).

The Bible is God's revelation about one unified plan from the first Adam to the last Adam. One Savior, one completed task by that one Savior, one judgment, one way, one final dwelling place for glorified saints, one holy nation, one gospel, one tree of life, one universal church, one spiritual nation under God with grace, mercy and love.

When Will They Ever Learn?

When God wanted Abraham and his offspring to stay in the purposeful Promised Land, they kept running back and forth faithlessly to Egypt for help, and finally stayed and felt at home.

But God had an evangelical purpose for them and used "a pharaoh who did not know Joseph" to reduce them to slaves. Thus life in Egypt became intolerable and finally they went into the Promised Land after kicking and screaming.

Then when God wanted the greater and new Israel out of the land, after the "Great Commission" had been mandated by Christ, they stayed.

So God used evil stiff-necked, uncircumcised, unbelieving, ruling Jews to murder Stephen and finally we read:

> Now those who had been scattered by the persecution in connection with Stephen traveled as far as Phoenicia, Cyprus and Antioch, telling the message only to Jews. Some of them, however, men from Cyprus and Cyrene, went to Antioch and began to speak to Greeks also, telling them about the Lord Jesus. The Lord's hand was with them, and a great number of people believed and turned to the Lord (Acts 11:19-21).

The Word of God and the Testimony of Jesus Christ

In the first chapter of the last Book in the Bible, John connects the "Word of God and the testimony of Jesus Christ" twice in the same chapter. This concept is repeated six times: in 6:9; 12:11; 17; 15:3; 19:10 and 20:4. Since the resurrection of Jesus Christ, all Scripture has to be interpreted in the light of the "WORD OF GOD AND THE TESTIMONY OF JESUS CHRIST."

In the Old Testament, we have the song of Moses (Exodus 15). In the New Testament, we have the song of Moses and the Lamb (Revelation 15:3). Obviously, the Testimony of Jesus (the Lamb) has made that song evangelical.

In the New Testament, Jesus speaks. The Second person in the Godhead, the "I Am" of the Old Testament, the Completer of the old word, has the final divine word.

The Son of God did not come to perpetuate some kind of reformed Judaism with renewed interest in earthly paraphernalia. For example: take Psalm 122:6: "Pray for the peace of Jerusalem,

May those who love you be secure."

Although this is part of God's revelation, standing by itself it has served its purpose. It's incomplete; the testimony of Jesus doesn't fit here.

Compare this with the angelical message the shepherds received at Christ's birth announcement: "Peace on earth."

In the Gospel of John, we have, of course, the testimony of Jesus throughout. "God so loved the world" is very familiar, but even the non-Jewish Samaritans acknowledged: "We know that this man really is the Savior of the world" (John 4:42).

One example will suffice. It has the full support of the testimony of Jesus. In Psalm 2, we read: "Ask of me and I will make the nations your inheritance, the end of the world your possession."

The Old Testament is full of the testimony of Jesus. However, I've come to the conclusion that no New Testament theology or system is legitimate or sound if the testimony of Jesus cannot support it, be included, or appended to it.

Consequently, this writer's opinion is that the overall and various systems of futuristic dispensationalism fundamentally lack the Word of God and the testimony of Jesus Christ.

CHAPTER 4

Go South, Old Man!

⋅⊱≡⊰⋅

The Scripture foresaw that God would justify the Gentiles by faith, and announced the gospel in advance to Abraham. "All nations will be blessed through you."
(Galatians 3:8)

[Jesus said] "Your father Abraham rejoiced at the thought of seeing my day; he saw it and was glad."
(John 8:56)

The Big Surprise

Abram, by now an old man, hurried into his house. Out of breath and flustered, he called to his wife, "Sarai! Sarai! Where are you? You're not going to believe this. A god who claims to be the only living and true God just spoke to me. He claims to be the God of the whole universe—this world, the sun, the moon, and all the stars. Can you imagine that? I'm still shaking!"

"No, I can't imagine it! You're out of your mind!" said Sarai, and she tried to get out of the house. Mumbling under her breath, she said, "What next?"

"Listen," exclaimed Abram as he followed her outside. "He told me to destroy and burn all our handmade gods, and from now on, to only listen to Him and obey Him, no matter what!"

"Abram, you don't know what you're saying. Don't you understand how dangerous that will be? What would happen if our gods got angry? There would be no end of trouble for us. These gods have been good to us. Destroy them? Too dangerous!"

"Yes, Sarai, I know, but we'll just have to find out. I believe this God is who He says He is because He's the only God who has ever spoken to me. Our gods don't talk to us. You know that. You know how frustrating it is."

"Abram, let me smell your breath. Have you been in the wine again? We're supposed to be saving it for Lot's wedding."

"No, Sarai, I haven't touched any wine. I was sitting in my favorite spot under the tree, thinking about life, the death of my father, and our future, when I heard His voice. It was strange and terrifying."

"Well, what did He say?"

"Let me put it to you gently, and please, don't interrupt, because what He said scares me to death. But, at the same time it makes me burst with excitement! I don't know how to handle it. We've got to move again, and go to someplace in Canaan. Where, I don't know, but He will show us. He has chosen us to become parents of a great new nation, and guess what? You're going to get pregnant!"

"Moving *again*? I'm not moving again! Look at the sorrows we've endured since we left Ur. Your father died, and now you want to anger our gods even more? And PREGNANT! You're mocking me and I'll listen to no more of this nonsense. You know I haven't been able to get pregnant, and now it's too late. So stop it."

"Sarai! Listen to me. I think it's true what I heard. My name is going to be known in all the world as long as the world shall last. Are you ready for this? He said that through me, all the nations of the world would be blessed. Then He said that those who would bless me would be blessed by Him, and those who would curse me would be cursed by Him. I wish you'd been there.

"That's not all, Sarai. When we obey Him and go south as far as Canaan, He's going to give that land to me. I have no idea why God chose me, but when we get there, wherever the land is, He's going to give that land to me. He must own that land. Can you imagine that? I don't know what this is all about; I don't understand all of it; but our offspring are going to be impossible to number, that's how many we'll have. We're going and that's it!" (Genesis 11:27–12:9).

Abraham's Obedience

Of course, we have no idea how Abraham actually communicated this unbelievable information to Sarah, but we can imagine it was difficult to get his wife to buy into it immediately without some serious questions, fears, and tears. From the time they had left their homeland of Ur, which today can be found in Iraq, they had moved time and time again, and now she was being told that, at ninety, she was going to have a baby. It's no wonder she was upset. But Abraham obeyed God and moved from the first stage of God's mysterious revelation into the second stage of revelation.

This second period of revelation is what I call in this book, the *hidden church*. The Spirit of Jesus Christ entered Abraham's soul. Unbeknownst to Abraham and all the prophets, they were, in essence, Christians. They were equipped by the Spirit of Christ in them to prophesy about Christ.

Let's look carefully at how the apostle Peter describes it:

> Concerning this salvation, the prophets, who spoke of the grace that was to come to you, searched intently and with the greatest care, trying to find out the time and circumstances to which the *Spirit of Christ in them* was pointing when He predicted the sufferings of Christ and the glories that would follow. It was revealed to them that they were not serving themselves, but you, when they spoke of the things that have now been told you by those who have preached the gospel to you by the Holy Spirit sent from heaven. Even angels long to look into these things. (1 Peter 1:10-12)

This incredible call and divine assignment given to Abraham lays the foundation of the plan of salvation for all people who fear the Lord. Throughout the history of the whole world, a proper understanding of the call, and purpose of God's call to Abraham, is what's needed to avoid doing bad things to this good prophecy.

From Abraham to Today

First, the triune God is proactive in the plan of salvation for the whole world. He is the original covenant maker and the one who fulfills that eternal covenant.

Second, it's of fundamental importance to understand that this promise from our sovereign God to Abraham that "all nations will be blessed through you" is still in effect today! Billions of believers have become, and are still in the process of becoming, true children of Abraham, through his seed, the Lord Jesus Christ (Galatians 3:7).

Third, the Old Covenant was replaced by the New Covenant, and thus became redundant. God found fault with the people and said:

> "The time is coming," declares the LORD, "when I will make a new covenant with the house of Israel and with the house of Judah. It will not be like the covenant I made with their forefathers when I took them by the hand to lead them out of Egypt, because they did not remain faithful to my covenant, and I turned away from them, declares the LORD. This is the covenant I will make with the house of Israel after that time, declares the LORD. I will put my laws in their minds and write them on their hearts. I will be their God, and they will be my people. No longer will a man teach his neighbor, or a man his brother, saying, 'Know the LORD,' because they will all know me, from the least of them to the greatest. For I will forgive their wickedness and will remember their sins no more." (Jeremiah 31:31-34)

In other words, it's in the church, among converted believers, that it's not necessary to say, "I want you to know God," for that happened when they were saved. They may sing, "More about Jesus would I know," but not "I need to know Jesus."

"By calling this covenant new, He has made the first one obsolete; and what is obsolete and aging will soon disappear" (Hebrews 8:13).

It did disappear, just before Jerusalem was destroyed in A.D. 70. Notice here (Hebrews 8:8-12) that Jeremiah is quoted almost verbatim in the New Testament *to the church*, the new Israel and the new Judah.

This has to do with the conditional promise of real estate for the

Jews, the physical Jews. Obviously, the total possession of Palestine isn't possible. The Jews lost it; possession of it required obedience. However, the children of Israel, throughout their history, were disobedient.

Look what happened right after the death of Joshua: "After that whole generation had been gathered to their fathers, another generation grew up, *who knew neither the LORD nor what He had done for Israel*" (Judges 2:10).

The innumerable children of Abraham and Sarah, from the very first utterance of God to Abraham, were a promise to the nations, the whole world. Abraham was God's vehicle by which this original promise and call to him would bless the whole church of Christ till the end.

The promise that Abraham's children would be like the sand on the seashore or stars in the sky cannot, and has never been intended as, an ethnic, isolated promise to Abraham's physical descendants only, but to the great universal church, the seed of Christ. God planned it that way.

Because of unbelief, God would ultimately reduce the number of physical Jews. "In those days the LORD began to *reduce the size of Israel*. Hazael overpowered the Israelites throughout their territory east of the Jordan…" (2 Kings 10:32). Yet the numberless children of Abraham, through belief in Christ, continue to increase. "Of the *increase* of his government and peace there will be no end" (Isaiah 9:7).

This needs to be contrasted with chapter 19 of 1 Kings, where Elijah was ordered by God *to anoint a pagan king, Hazael, king of Aram, to reduce Israel,* and to anoint Elisha, the servant of God, to warn Israel and pray for them. Consequently, God's warning to Abraham that He would curse those who would curse Israel (Genesis 11:3) cannot be to physical Israel, for He, God, anointed Hazael to reduce Israel by the sword.

CHAPTER 5

The Purpose-Driven God

❖⇒◉⇐❖

"The scepter will not depart from Judah.
Nor the ruler's staff from between
his feet, until he comes to whom
it belongs and the obedience
of the nations is his."
(Genesis 49:10)

The Original Temporary Purpose of the Possession of the Land

God's chosen people needed to possess the land for the unique sovereign plan of God to provide a home for the Messiah. Consequently, there needed to be a couple who were direct descendants of Abraham and King David—Joseph and Mary. There needed to be the prophesied birthplace, Bethlehem, and a cradle for the "Word to become flesh." He needed to be seen by those who, because of prophecy, were expecting Him, as was the case of Simeon and Anna, and an immoral Samaritan woman (John 4:25).

To this land came John the Baptist, who prophetically linked the Old Testament with the New Testament, to be history's unique forerunner of Jesus Christ.

There needed to be a mountain on which God would provide the last sacrifice, as portrayed by Abraham's willingness to sacrifice Isaac.

There needed to be a city from which the Holy Spirit would flow as prophesied by Ezekiel, and fulfilled on the day of Pentecost, after which believers from all over the world, filled with the Holy Spirit, would go back to the uttermost parts of the world, so that, at the end of Paul's prison epistle to the Philippians, he could send his greetings to those of the household of Caesar.

Christ could not have been born in Rome or Cairo or any other city. Jerusalem, full of people, was God's appointed place to pour out His Holy Spirit like a river from there.

> On the last and greatest day of the Feast, Jesus stood and said in a loud voice, "If anyone is thirsty, let him come to me and drink. Whoever believes in me, as the Scripture has said, streams of living water will flow from within him." By this he meant the Spirit, whom those who believed in him were later to receive. Up to that time the Spirit had not been given, since Jesus had not yet been glorified. (John 7:37-39)

That's why, when Joshua took over from Moses, God said to him, "Moses my servant is dead, now then you and all these people get ready and cross the Jordan River into the land I am about to give to them" (Joshua 1:1-2).

Furthermore, that's why they had to be returned to the land after the Babylonian captivity (2 Chronicles 36:21-22; Ezra 1:2-4):

> The land enjoyed its Sabbath rests; all the time of its desolation it rested, until the seventy years were completed in *fulfillment* of the word of the LORD, spoken by Jeremiah. In the first year of Cyrus, king of Persia, in order to *fulfill* the word of the LORD spoken by Jeremiah, the LORD moved the heart of Cyrus, king of Persia, to make a proclamation throughout his realm and to put it in writing:
>
> "This is what Cyrus king of Persia says: "The LORD, the God of heaven, has given me all the kingdoms of the earth and he has appointed me to build a temple for him at Jerusalem in Judah. Any one of his people among you—may the LORD his God be with him, and let him go up to Jerusalem in Judah and build the temple of the LORD, the God of

Israel, the God who is in Jerusalem. And the people of any place where survivors may now be living are to provide him with silver and gold, with goods and livestock, and with freewill offerings for the temple of God in Jerusalem.'"

This then, once again provided a place of prophetic fulfillment for the Savior of the world to preach the good news of salvation and to be the "Lamb of God slain before the foundation of the world." After the divinely pronounced great commission (Matthew 28:18-20) and the Day of Pentecost, there was no further need for *Bethlehem* or *Jerusalem, or for a temple or animal sacrifices.*

There is no further need for the beggarly perishing physical things. The Ten Commandments are no longer chiseled in rock, but are to be engraved on the hearts of Christians, so that the earth will be filled with the glory of God by living stones.

The Dreadful Day of the Lord

We usually think of the birth of Christ as peace on earth to those on whom God's favor rests. All the participants of Christmas think that applies to everybody. But the last stern warning of the Old Testament is that Elijah would come before that *"dreadful day of the LORD"* (Malachi 4:5-6). What is the dreadful Day of the Lord?

The passage in Malachi quoted above is a clear reference to John the Baptist. In Luke 1, an angel of the Lord appeared to John's father, Zechariah, and promised him that he and his wife Elizabeth would have a son. Speaking of that son, John, the angel said, "And he will go on before the Lord, in the spirit and power of Elijah, to turn the hearts of the fathers to their children and the disobedient to the wisdom of the righteous—to make ready a people prepared for the Lord" (Luke 1:17).

So, according to Malachi and Luke, John would come and prepare the way for the Lord (see also Isaiah 40:3; Mark 1:2-3) before the dreadful Day of the Lord would come.

John identified the Lord as Jesus of Nazareth, and also describes the dreadful Day of the Lord: "I baptize you with water for repentance. But after me will come one who is more powerful than I, whose sandals I am not fit to carry. He will baptize you with the Holy Spirit and with fire. His winnowing fork is in his hand, and he will clear his threshing floor, gathering his wheat into the barn and burning up the chaff with unquenchable fire" (Matthew 3:11-12).

The dreadful Day of the Lord was also prophesied by Simeon in the temple, when he told Mary, the mother of Jesus, "This child [Jesus] is destined to cause the falling and rising of many in Israel, and to be a sign that will be spoken against, so that the thoughts of many hearts will be revealed" (Luke 2:34-35).

So then, the dreadful Day of the Lord would be a day of judgment, administered by Christ Himself, *in Israel*. Historically, a judgment upon Israel occurred in A.D. 70 when the Roman general Titus destroyed the temple and the city of Jerusalem. The period of time between the death and resurrection of Christ, and the destruction of Jerusalem was about forty years, and was a time of transition from the Old Testament church to the New Testament church.

The disciples were explicitly warned by Jesus about the dreadful Day of the Lord as recorded in Matthew 24:

> Jesus left the temple and was walking away when his disciples came up to him to call his attention to its buildings. "Do you see all these things?" he asked. "I tell you the truth, not one stone here will be left on one another; every one will be thrown down." [Stones and mortar were of no real importance to Jesus.]

> As Jesus was sitting on the Mount of Olives, the disciples came to him privately. "Tell us," they said, "when will this happen, and what will be the sign of your coming and of the end of the age?" Jesus answered: "Watch out that no one deceives you. For many will come in my name, claiming, 'I am the Christ,' and will deceive many. You will hear of wars and rumors of wars, but see to it that you are not alarmed. Such things must happen, but the end is still to come. Nation will rise against nation, and kingdom against kingdom. There will be famines

and earthquakes in various places. All these are the beginning of birth pains.

"Then you will be handed over to be persecuted and put to death, and you will be hated by all nations because of me. At that time many will turn away from the faith and will betray and hate each other, and many false prophets will appear and deceive many people. Because of the increase of wicked-ness, the love of most will grow cold, but he who stands firm to the end will be saved. And this gospel of the kingdom will be preached in the whole world as a testimony to all nations, and then the end will come." (Matthew 24:1-14)

The disciples took Jesus seriously and together with all the members of the Christian synagogue, left Jerusalem before the destruction of the city in A.D. 70. The dreadful Day of the Lord had come and confirmed Simeon's words, "The rising and falling of many in Israel" (Luke 2:29-32).

Some might object that the dreadful Day of the Lord cannot happen until the gospel has gone out to every nation (Matthew 24:14), the assumption being that it hasn't happened yet. However, please consider what the Scriptures say about this matter: "Now there were staying in Jerusalem God-fearing Jews *from every nation* under heaven" (Acts 2:5). This happened at Pentecost, and we know that many of these people accepted the gospel and took it back to their homes with them.

Note also the testimony of the apostle Paul in Colossians 1:6, "...All over the world this gospel is bearing fruit and growing, just as it has been doing among you since the day you heard it and understood God's grace in all its truth." Both of these passages have been dated well before A.D. 70.

The destruction of Jerusalem happened as predicted by the Scriptures that there would be an end to the physical usefulness and purpose of real estate, which is erroneously called Israel. The purpose has been fulfilled. After the return from the Babylonian exile, there is no other Scripture that speaks of another return to the Holy Land. There is nothing about 1948 in the Bible. What? Wait, there's more.

The Second Most Important Prophecy

An important prophetic scene takes place as Jacob's eventful life nears its end. Having been a father of what we may surely say was a very dysfunctional family, his sons now tearfully kneel before his deathbed eagerly waiting for his trembling hand upon their heads.

As the fourth son, Judah, kneels before him, Jacob pronounced that most significant prophetic word from God by the Spirit of Christ within him (I Peter 1:10-12).

> Judah, your brothers will praise you; your hand will be on the neck of your enemies; your father's sons will bow down to you. *You are a lion's cub*, O Judah; you return from the prey, my son. Like a lion he crouches and lies down, like a lioness—who dares to rouse him? *The scepter will not depart from Judah, nor the ruler's staff from between his feet, until he comes to whom it belongs and the obedience of the nations is his.* (Genesis 49:8-10)

Take note that Jacob understood by divine inspiration that Israel of the flesh would have temporary participation in the spreading of the universal everlasting gospel of Jesus Christ. We'd have no idea what he meant, if the Holy Spirit hadn't told John in the last book of the Bible: "Then one of the elders said to me, 'Do not weep! See, the *Lion of the tribe of Judah*, the *root of David*, has triumphed. He is able to open the scroll and its seven seals.' Then I saw a Lamb, looking as if it had been slain..." (Revelation 5:5-6).

Finally, and very seriously, the promise of real estate was conditional; it was based on obedience. Through Abraham, the vehicle of eternal blessing to all nations was fulfilled. God's promise to the nations was never in jeopardy because of the disobedience of the Jews, but according to Paul, it was enhanced by their faithlessness and the faithfulness of God. Hallelujah!

A bad thing will happen to a good prophecy when emphasizing a minor point out of context, and overlooking or ignoring the core element of a divine proclamation.

Once a Dispensationalist, Not Always a Dispensationalist

In closing this chapter, I want to quote from a 1927 publication, *How Long To the End?* It is by Philip Mauro who, like the world-famous preacher and expositor, Dr. G. Campbell Morgan, at one time was an ardent supporter of dispensational teaching and supported Christian Zionism. Here is his testimony:

> "My study of the prophecies of Scripture had been carried on under the domination of a system of interpretation which has for its cardinal principles that "the church is not the subject of prophecy"; that "when Israel was laid aside the prophetic clock stopped"; that this gospel dispensation is a "parenthesis"; and that hence we have no light of prophecy whereby we may check our course and determine our whereabouts.

> That system of interpretation I had accepted wholeheartedly and without the least misgivings, for the reason that it was commended by teachers deservedly honored and trusted because of their unswerving loyalty to the Word of God. But I had eventually to learn with sorrow, any modern system of 'dispensationalism', or 'futurism' (or so-called 'rightly dividing the word of truth') to which I had thoroughly committed myself, *not only was without scriptural foundation, but involved doctrinal errors of serious character.*

> What is especially to the present purpose I found that the effect of this latter-day 'dispensationalism' which makes 'Israel after the flesh' to be the central subject

of prophecy, was virtually to extinguish the light thereof, or at least to bring upon it such a pall of obscurity as to render it useless for its intended purpose. For there is evidently a flat contradiction between the system of teaching referred to and what the New Testament prophecy is. That system of teaching affirms that the Jewish nation is the subject of prophecy and that this present dispensation lies outside its scope; whereas the Holy Spirit in the New Testament plainly declares (to cite one passage out of many) that the theme of the prophets was the salvation and grace that should come unto us by them that have preached the gospel unto us with the Holy Ghost sent down from heaven. (1 Peter 1:10-11)

And not only so, but modern dispensationalism has made the political affairs of the Jews to be a sign (indeed, "the sign") of the coming of Christ; and this notwithstanding that (in the language of Dr. Campbell Morgan) "there are no signs whatever available, or intended to be, as to the nearness or distance of our Lord's Second Advent." (See Matthew 24:36-42; Luke 17:23-30.)

As a specimen of the way the Scriptures are construed in the interest of modern dispensational-ism, take our Lord's parable of the fig tree, which, by the putting forth of its leaves, gives a sure sign that summer is nigh. Teachers of dispensationalism commonly declare (though without the slightest scriptural warrant) that our Lord here uses the fig tree as a type of natural Israel; and that he means us to understand that, when that scattered people begin to manifest the stirrings of national life, then the Lord's second advent is at hand, "even at the doors." But this forced interpretation is palpably erroneous. For the context of the parable, in all three gospels that contain it (Matthew 24:32-33; Mark 13:28-30; Luke 21:29-32) makes it plain that the parable of the fig tree was spoken by Christ to his disciples for the purpose of impressing upon their minds the sign whereby *they were to be warned of the approaching destruction of Jerusalem and to save themselves by timely flight*; whereas in regard to His coming again, he is explicit and emphatic in teaching that "of that day and hour knoweth no man, no not the angels of heaven, but My Father only"; and that no signs of the approach of that day would be given." (Matthew 24:36-44) (Mauro, page 4-6)

Here then, is my position—that the writing of the apostles not only say nothing about a separate word or future for ethnic Jews, *but they say the very opposite*! It's a bad thing that has happened to a good prophecy. Particularly when, in futuristic, dispensational writings and songs, they speak of nothing but that "signs of the times are everywhere."

CHAPTER 6

Prophetic Reruns?

❖⇒◎⇐❖

And beginning with Moses and all the Prophets,
he explained to them what was said
in all the Scriptures concerning Himself.
(Luke 24:27)

Prophecy Turned Into History

If God had not revealed to us something about Himself, if He had not prepared and instructed the fathers and prophets with truths about Himself, about His ways and His Word, we would still be religious beings, but we would worship ancestors, trees, mountains, crocodiles, etc., and practice religious ceremonies accompanying such varied objects of worship. But, as we read in Scripture: "...prophecy never had its origin in the will of man, but men spoke from God as they were carried along by the Holy Spirit" (2 Peter 1:21).

So we have God's message available to us, but this message didn't come all at once. The Bible didn't fall out of heaven complete, maps and all. It was written in time and space over a period of approximately 1500 years by some 40 different writers. A major portion deals with recorded history, primarily about God's rebellious chosen people.

Consequently, much of that faithfully recorded history is fulfilled and has served its literal purpose. However, many things that have been fulfilled in the past history of the Jews are of vital importance today because of their spiritual significance and eternal ramifications (1 Corinthians 10:1-13).

Creation or Evolution?

Without spending too much space on this subject, it's a fact that all of Scripture, the whole foundation and validity of the gospel, rests on the basic fact that *God created all things.* "In the beginning, God created the heavens and the earth" (Genesis 1:1).

The psalmist echoes this: "When I consider your heavens, the work of your fingers, the moon and the stars, which you have set in place" (Psalm 8:3).

And: *"By the word of the LORD* were the heavens made, their starry host by the breath of his mouth" (Psalm 33:6).

Although this happened long ago, fulfilled and declared "good" by God, it's impossible to have the good news of the gospel without God being the creator, for the following reasons:

If God is not our creator, and we are cosmic accidents, then:

1. God can lay no claim of ownership on any of us.
2. He has no claim or interest in our redemption, for redemption presupposes previous ownership.
3. It follows that Christ was a fake and died for nothing.
4. Eternal life is a fantasy, a pipe dream.
5. There is no such thing as right or wrong.
6. It's all over at the grave.
7. And finally, and logically, a spotted owl is more valuable than an unborn child.

The teaching of evolution as a science in our public schools is a very clever scheme of Satan, for it robs God of His creatorship, and makes soulless monkeys out of mankind. Although creation happened long ago, and is not repeated, all of life (and eternal life) is built upon it.

There are, of course, other main events faithfully recorded in the Old Testament which lay the groundwork, once and for all, for the gospel, and thus for mankind in every age. Here I mention a few:

- Casting Satan down out of heaven upon the earth.
- God's pre-creative purpose, making man in His own image.
- The creation of Adam and Eve.
- The tree of life in paradise.
- The entrance of sin.

- The eternal covenant introduced by the promise of one who would destroy Satan.
- God's covenant with Noah and his descendants.
- God's redeemed people before Abraham.
- The call of Abram.
- God's covenant with Abraham.
- God's chosen people of the church in the Old Testament.
- The Ten Commandments.
- God's grace in dealing with His people from day one.
- The punishment for sin.
- All kinds of messianic hints and prophecies.
- The dispersion of God's people because of their disobedience.
- The fulfilled promises of their return.
- Preparation for the coming Messiah.
- A man named John the Baptist.
- The birth of the Son of God fulfilled literally hundreds of messianic prophecies.
- All nations blessed through Abraham. This has been fulfilled, and is being fulfilled in His church.

Remember Not to Forget

The purpose of this book is to discuss why Christ refuses to show up here on earth the way some writers want Him to show up, and particularly, why the "Rapture" didn't occur during Y2K, as millions believed. Each chapter will hopefully clear up misunderstandings about the end times, the Rapture, the second coming, and the end of the world. We also want to show that it's very difficult to prove, biblically, any connection between these events and the reestablishment of Israel as a nation in 1948.

When Will a Virgin Give Birth?

Isaiah prophesied during troublesome days in Israel, and proclaimed: "The virgin will be with child and will give birth to a son, and will call him Immanuel" (Isaiah 7:14).

This is clearly prophesied in Scripture. When this will happen is, of course, a silly question, for all of us know that it has already happened in Bethlehem over 2,000 years ago. Christ was born. A virgin gave birth. *A prophecy became history within the pages of Scripture.* This is the first and foremost message this writer is very emphatically trying to get across.

Particularly, consider the following situation: What would one say if today, an unmarried pregnant girl in Bethlehem would claim to have been impregnated by God? Her claim would be as unfounded as the claim that the 1948 reestablishment of Israel is based on Scripture. She might say something like, "The Bible says a virgin will give birth and I'm that virgin."

Nonsense? No! There are many people who read the Bible, which clearly states: "The promise of the Jews returning to the promised land" has been fulfilled, and yet believe that it refers to 1948. But that promise was fulfilled *within Scripture* as surely as the Virgin Mary has already given birth. There's no more scriptural warrant for believing the Bible speaks about the 1948 Jewish return to the Holy Land than there is for believing the Bible speaks about Dutch people immigrating to Australia.

> *There are, within the pages of the Bible, prophecies that have their fulfillment in Bible times, prophecies that are now histories, never to be repeated. There are hundreds of literally fulfilled prophecies about Christ, which find their literal fulfillment within the pages of Scripture.*

Once again, there isn't another virgin waiting somewhere to give birth to a messiah. In other words, *not everything in the Bible is futuristic.* Not many will argue with this, but it has led millions astray when things that have been fulfilled are looked upon as still needing fulfillment, or having been fulfilled very recently.

This throws out of sequence the whole progressive history of redemption and loses sight of God's message and meaning to the original recipients of the prophets' message to them. This, then, is a very important element often ignored by futuristic proclaimers.

Daniel: the Passive Lion Tamer

Here is God's promise to the Jewish people. Take special notice of God's conditions attached to these gracious promises.

> If you *fully obey* the LORD your God and *carefully follow all his commands* I give you today, the LORD your God will set you high above all the nations on earth. All these blessings will come upon you and accompany you *if you obey the LORD your God*:

> You will be blessed in the city and blessed in the country. The fruit of your womb will be blessed, and the crops of your land and the young of your live-stock—the calves of your herds and the lambs of your flocks. Your basket and your kneading trough will be blessed. You will be blessed when you come in and blessed when you go out.

> The LORD will grant that the enemies who rise up against you will be defeated before you. They will come at you from one direction but flee from you in seven.

> The LORD will send a blessing on your barns and on everything you put your hand to. The LORD your God will bless you in the land he is giving you. (Deuteronomy 28:1-8).

> However, *if you do not obey the LORD your God* and *do not carefully follow all his commands* and decrees I am giving you today, all these curses will come upon you and overtake you:

> You will be cursed in the city and cursed in the country. Your basket and your kneading trough will be cursed. The fruit of your womb will be cursed, and the crops of your land, and the calves

of your herds and the lambs of your flocks. You will be cursed when you come in and cursed when you go out.

The LORD will send on you curses, confusion and rebuke in everything you put your hand to, until you are destroyed and come to sudden ruin because of the evil you have done in forsaking him. The LORD will plague you with diseases until he has destroyed you from the land you are entering to possess. The LORD will strike you with wasting disease, with fever and inflammation, with scorching heat and drought, with blight and mildew, which will plague you until you perish. The sky over your head will be bronze, the ground beneath you iron. The LORD will turn the rain of your country into dust and powder; it will come down from the skies until you are destroyed. (Deuteronomy 28:15-24)

In Deuteronomy 28, Moses reported to Israel God's encouraging words regarding blessings (verses 1-14), and His dreadful words regarding curses (verses 15-68—notice that there were only fourteen verses of blessings, but fifty-four verses of curses). Blessings would come as the result of obedience, but curses as the result of disobedience.

We know, of course, from the Scripture, that the Israelites forsook God and ran after other gods. Consequently, after passionately repeated pleas by God to repent through His prophets, they turned a deaf ear to Him, and were carried off to Babylon.

Now listen to the passive lion tamer turned prime minister of Babylon in his passionate, heart-rending intercessory prayer: "Therefore the curses and sworn judgments written in the law of Moses, the servant of God, have poured out on us, because we have sinned against you. You have *fulfilled the words spoken against us and against our rulers by bringing upon us great disaster.* Under the whole heaven nothing has ever been done like what has been done to Jerusalem" (Daniel 9:11b-12).

In his book, *The Millennium,* published in 1957, the late theologian Dr. Loraine Boettner wrote:

> There is a little known prophecy in Leviticus 26:27-33, in which God speaking through Moses says that, if after being punished for her sins Israel does not repent, her punishment will be increased seven times longer. It apparently was with this warning in mind that Daniel gave the remarkable prophecy of the "70 weeks," which generally are understood to mean weeks of years, 7 times 70, or 490 years (9:24-27). Daniel was the prophet with the exiles in Babylon at the end of the 70 years exile that had been foretold by Jeremiah (25:11,12; 29:10). When understood from the Scriptures that the 70 years were at an end (Daniel 9:2), he earnestly besought God for the deliverance of his people. However, Israel as a nation did not repent as a result of the Babylonian captivity. Only a small remnant had faith enough to return to Jerusalem with Ezra and Nehemiah, and the Jews who were reestablished in Palestine had only a very precarious existence, successively under Persian, Greek, and Roman rule, and were under such kings or governors as Antiochus Epiphanes, Herod, and Pilate, until the coming of Christ. Daniel's prophecy, we believe, was fulfilled some 400 years later in the later history of Israel, extending from that time until the coming of the Messiah, the accomplishment of His work of redemption on Calvary, and ending in the destruction of the city of Jerusalem—extending "even unto the full end (Dan. 9:27).
>
> The role assigned to Israel in the Divine plan, reached the end of the tunnel upon the refusal of Israel to embrace Him who is the Light of the world at the end of that God- appointed parenthesis.

It may seem harsh to say that, "God is through with the Jews." But the fact of the matter is that He is through with them as a literal, physical or, as a unified national group having anything more to do with the evangelization of the world.

Here then, is another example of fulfilled prophecy within the pages of Scripture. Daniel realized God means what He says. These curses no longer apply today, for they've already been applied. God carried out His warnings. Conversely, the physical blessings no longer apply either, for now the blessings are applied through belief and obedience to Christ.

The lesson of Deuteronomy 28 for physical Israel is that those blessings and curses served their divine purposes at that time. It is a biblical bygone. Once again, prophecy has become history.

It's horrible to think that 6,000,000 Jews lost their lives in World War II; however, it can't be related to Deuteronomy 28, for more than 60,000,000 non-Jews lost their lives, including millions and millions of innocent little children, adults, pagans, and Christians.

CHAPTER 7

The Last Prophesied Biblical Return

❖➤≡◦⊂≡❖

"... I tell you that the kingdom of God will be taken away from
you and given to a people [nation]
who will produce its fruit."
(Matthew 21:43)

The Prophets to the Nations

When Jesus told His disciples to go out into the fields that were ready for harvest, He told them others had done the hard work: "I sent you to reap what you have not worked for. Others have done the hard work, and you have reaped the benefits of their labor" (John 4:38).

He must have been thinking of Jeremiah as one example among many. What a man, what a task, and what horrible frustration he endured for the gospel's sake. Remember, the gospel was already begun in Genesis 3:15, and also that Abraham knew the gospel (Galatians 3:8). The Pulpit Committee that prepared and called Jeremiah consisted of the Trinity, so all he could do was obey.

Jeremiah served the Lord courageously. He was the Lord's messenger in days of darkness, despair, and disaster; all of which were consequential because of Israel's rebellion against God. The people were exiled into Babylon, and although Ezekiel finished up in Babylon with them, and prophesied from that foreign land, Jeremiah stayed behind in the fulfilled Promised Land.

The point I want to make is that, in the midst of gloom and despair, God gave Jeremiah many divine promises that His people would return from exile. Here are just two examples:

"So then, the days are coming," declares the LORD,

"when people will no longer say, 'As surely as the LORD lives, who brought the Israelites up out of Egypt', but they will say, 'As surely as the LORD lives, who brought the descendants of Israel up out of the land of the north and out of all the countries where he had banished them.' Then they will live in their own land" (Jeremiah 23:7-8).

The "out of Egypt" had been accomplished by Moses and is prophecy turned history. The next deliverance was about to take place shortly after Jeremiah's days. There is nothing in the Bible regarding a third deliverance.

"Hear the word of the LORD, O nations; proclaim it in distant coast lands: he who scattered Israel will gather them and will watch over his flock like a Shepherd" (Jeremiah 31:10).

A bad thing happens to a good prophecy when it has already been literally fulfilled in Scripture, yet people look for it to be literally fulfilled again! Prophetic reruns?

Here is the fulfillment:

"The land enjoyed its Sabbath rests; all the time of its desolation it rested, until the seventy years were completed in *fulfillment* of the word of the LORD spoken by Jeremiah. In the first year of Cyrus king of Persia, *in order to fulfill* the word of the LORD spoken by Jeremiah, the LORD moved the heart of Cyrus king of Persia to make a proclamation throughout his realm and to put it in writing" (2 Chronicles 36:21-22).

Surely if two or more synonymous words or expressions are found in the same passage, it's generally safe to conclude that their special signification requires special attention.

Not only does 2 Chronicles mention fulfillment twice but, now turn one page in your Bible and again, in case you missed it the first two times, it is repeated by Ezra. "In the first year of Cyrus king of Persia, *in order to fulfill* the word of the LORD spoken by Jeremiah..." (Ezra 1:1a).

All the promises of restoration to the scattered people of God by the word of Jeremiah were fulfilled, just like the promise of a virgin to give birth to the Messiah. We look for no other God-directed plan of Israel's physical restoration as a fulfillment of divine prophecy.

> **The promise of restoration and return to the Promised Land was made to the dispersed Jews of that day, over 2,500 years ago, to that generation! It applied to those living at that time and was fulfilled during their lifetime!**

As has been said in chapter 2, and is worth repeating: God needed them back in the land. There needed to be a Bethlehem for the promised Messiah to have a cradle, an Old Testament environment, a city, a people, a Jerusalem from which the church would cover the world. Israel has always been, in the mind of God, the original evangelists! Jesus said: "You Samaritans worship what you do not know; we worship what we do know, for salvation is of the Jews" (John 4:22).

The same applies to Ezekiel's prophecies. He was among the exiles by the Kebar River when God gave him all those incredible visions and *promises of the return to the land: The land before and during Christ's physical ministry was totally indispensable.*

"In the thirtieth year, in the fourth month on the fifth day, while I was among the exiles by the Kebar River, the heavens *were opened* and I saw visions of God" (Ezekiel 1:1).

Remember, Christ could not have been born in Babylon or Cairo. It was through Abraham that all the world would be blessed, so God had to get His people back in the land. *And to the land they returned.*

"...who says of Cyrus, 'He is my shepherd and will accomplish all that I please'; he will say of Jerusalem, 'Let it be rebuilt,' and of the temple, 'Let its foundations be laid'" (Isaiah 44:28).

> This is what the LORD says to his anointed, to Cyrus, whose right hand I take hold of to subdue nations before him and to strip kings of their armor, to open doors before him so that gates will not be shut: "I will go before you and will level the mountains; I will break down gates of bronze and cut through bars of iron. I will give you the treasures of darkness, riches stored in secret places, so that you may know that I am the LORD, the God of Israel, who summons you by name. For the sake of Jacob, my servant, of Israel my chosen, I summon you by name and bestow on you a title of honor, though you do not acknowledge me. I am the LORD and there is no other; apart from me there is no God. I will strengthen you, though you have not acknowledged me, so that from the rising of the sun to the place of its setting men may know there is none besides me. I am the LORD, and there is no other. I form the light and create darkness, I bring prosperity and create disaster; I, the LORD do all these things." (Isaiah 45:1-7)

And now look at these amazing words of the Son of God, as quoted from Isaiah 61:

> "The Spirit of the Lord is on me, because he has anointed me to preach good news to the poor. He has sent me to proclaim freedom for the prisoners and recovery of sight to the blind, to release the oppressed, to proclaim the year of the Lord's favor."
>
> Then he rolled up the scroll, gave it back to the attendant and sat down. The eyes of everyone in the synagogue were fastened on him, and he began by saying to them, *"Today, this scripture is fulfilled in*

your hearing." (Luke 4:18-21, emphasis mine)

A bad thing happens to a good prophecy when it is insisted that there are additional promises in the Bible regarding the 1948 return of the Jews to the land. Israel, as a corporate, physical, fleshly nation, is no longer an exclusive part of God's plan: salvation is no longer available under the national ethnic umbrella of modern day Israel, or any other nation.

"Yet to all who received him, to those who believed in his name, he gave the right to become the children of God—children born not of natural descent, not of human decision or a husband's will, but born of God" (John 1:12-13). Can this be any clearer?

This, no doubt, is a surprise statement for many—for great multitudes have been convinced, just like Hal Lindsey, who states emphatically in *The Late Great Planet Earth* on his preface page, "The Jew is the most important sign to the generations" (1972). Is this what Christ tells us? "Keep your eyes on the Middle East." Is this what Hebrews 12:2 tells us? This, then, should be looked upon as a reason why predictions about Christ's return are so disappointing.

> *"Let us fix our eyes on Jesus*, the author and perfecter of our faith, who for the joy set before him endured the cross, scorning its shame, and sat down at the right hand of the throne of God" (Hebrews 12:2).

"Keep your eyes upon the development of the riches in the Dead Sea" (Lindsey, 1972). Where does it say that in the Scriptures? Are we not instructed to do the very opposite, and *not* look at the fallen world, the sinful world, the confused world, the condemned world?

This futuristic kind of supposition constitutes a Bible-plus-*Time*-magazine theology. No wonder millions of Christians are confused and disappointed about all those false predictions concerning the so-called Rapture, which is supposedly linked with Israel's reestablishment as a nation. It not only lacks the testimony of Jesus Christ, but blatantly contradicts the testimony of Jesus Christ.

We Have a Busy Devil

What we know from the Bible is that the devil is a dirty fighter, a liar, a schemer, a devious slanderer, and that we need to be aware of his schemes.

His most effective tool has been to lead Christians astray by misuse of Scripture, by majoring on the minors and minoring on the majors. Pick a few unrelated symbolic verses, ignore biblical chronology, interpret them literally, and build a whole theology on it to confuse and divide the body of Christ. What a scheme!

You will never establish sound biblical theology if you hop, skip, and jump through the Bible, "here a verse, there a verse, everywhere a verse, verse," ignoring chronology, as well as prophetic and historical situations.

From Promise to Possession

Did God fulfill His promise to Abraham? Yes, but not fully! God's promise first came to a heathen named Abram from Ur. Why did He do it? For His divine purpose and hidden reasons (God only knows). "It is the glory of God to conceal a matter..." (Proverbs 25:2).

God gave Abram this *command*:

> The LORD had said to Abram, "Leave your country, your people and your father's household and go to the land *I will show you. I will make you* into a great nation and *I will bless you*; I will make your name great, and you will be a blessing. I will bless those who bless you, and whoever curses you *I will curse*; and all peoples on earth will be blessed through you" (Genesis 12:1-3).

> The LORD said to Abram after Lot had parted from him, "Lift up your eyes from where you are and look north and south, east and west. All the land

you see *I will give to you and your offspring forever.* I will make your offspring like the dust of the earth, so that if anyone could count the dust, then your offspring could be counted. Go, walk through the length and breadth of the land, for *I am giving it to you*" (Genesis 13:14-17).

Let the Scriptures speak for themselves. God said, *"I will give it to you,"* not *"I will give it ultimately, in the next thousands of years, to your descendants."* At the request, and harboring understandable doubts, Abram had the promise renewed with an additional ceremony and illustration. Please read the whole of Genesis 15. Here's just a little part of it:

"After this, the word of the LORD came to Abram in a vision: "Do not be afraid, Abram. I am your shield, your very great reward.""

But Abram said, "O Sovereign LORD, what can you give me since I remain childless and the one who will inherit my estate is Eliezer of Damascus?" And Abram said, "You have given me no children; so a servant in my household will be my heir." Then the word of the LORD came to him: "This man will not be your heir, but a son coming from your own body will be your heir." He took him outside and said, "Look up at the heavens and count the stars—if indeed you can count them." Then he said to him, "So shall your offspring be."

Abram believed the LORD, and he credited it to him as righteousness. The Lord also said to him: , "I am the LORD, who brought you out of Ur of the Chaldeans to give you this land to take possession of it" (Genesis 15:1-7).

The promise was reiterated in response to the fact that, at that time, Abram had no descendants. That's why God pressed into his heart that he would have a son. Did Abraham and his descendants receive what God had promised, that his descendants would be impossible to count, like the stars or the sand on the seashore? Yes! Take note of the words of Moses, the servant of God:

> The LORD our God said to us at Horeb, "You have stayed long enough at this mountain. Break camp and advance into the hill country of the Amorites; go to all the neighboring peoples in the Arabah, in the mountains, in the western foothills, in the Negev and along the seacoast, to the land of the Canaanites and to Lebanon, as far as the great river, the Euphrates. *See, I have given you this land.* Go in and take possession of the land that the LORD swore he would give to your fathers, to Abraham, Isaac and Jacob, and to their descendants after them. At that time I said to you, 'You are too heavy a burden for me to carry alone. The LORD your God *has increased your numbers so that today you are as many as the stars in the sky.* May the LORD, the God of your fathers, increase you a thousand times and bless you as he has promised!'" (Deuteronomy 1:6-11).

Those were the words of Moses, the primary prophet and lawgiver in the Old Testament. The same statement is picked up again by Joshua:

> "So the LORD gave Israel *all the land he had sworn to give their forefathers, and they took possession of it and settled there.* The LORD gave them rest on every side, just as he had sworn to their forefathers. Not one of their enemies withstood them; the LORD handed all their enemies over to them. *Not one of the LORD's good promises to the house of Israel failed; every one was fulfilled.*" (Joshua 21:43-45).

Under King Solomon, the same fact became clear:

The people of Judah and Israel were as *numerous as the sand on the seashore*, they ate, they drank and they were happy. And Solomon ruled over all the kingdoms from the River to the land of the Philistines, as far as the border of Egypt. These countries brought tribute and were Solomon's subjects all his life (1 Kings 4:20-21).

In addition, Solomon blessed the people in a loud voice saying:

"Praise be to the LORD, who has given rest to his people Israel just as he promised. Not one word has failed of all the good promises he gave through his servant Moses (1 Kings 8:56)."

And finally, Nehemiah records the great prayer of repentance before the people:

"You gave them kingdoms and nations, *allotting to them even the remotest frontiers.* They took over the country of Sihon king of Heshbon and the country of Og king of Bashan. You made their sons as *numerous as the stars in the sky* and you brought them into the land that you told their fathers to enter and possess. Their sons went in and *took possession of the land.* You subdued before them the Canaanites, who lived in the land; you handed the Canaanites over to them, along with their kings and the peoples of the land, to deal with them as they pleased. They captured fortified cities and fertile land, they took possession of houses filled with all kinds of good things, wells already dug, vineyards, olive groves and fruit trees in abundance. They ate to the full and were well-nourished; they reveled in your great goodness." (Nehemiah 9:22-25)

Futuristic dispensationalist writers, blatantly inconsistent with their own system of interpretation, refuse to believe the clear statements of Scripture in these passages just quoted. *But the answer is yes! They did receive and owned all the land God had promised Abraham.* Please note the difference between God's original promise of Abrahamic possession and the post-exilic repossession of the land. Both have been fulfilled. *God fulfilled His earthly promise to Abraham. The Israelites did inherit, and they did possess the land.*

God's promise to Abraham: "No longer will you be called Abram; your name will be Abraham, for *I have made you a father of many nations*" (Genesis 17:5).

The promise was fulfilled literally, "And so from this one man, and he as good as dead, came descendants as numerous as the stars in the sky, and as countless as the sand on the seashore" (Hebrews 11:12). This verse was written, most likely, before the fall of Jerusalem.

"I have made you a father of many nations" is fulfilled spiritually. In reality, the Jews are one ethnocentric people, not many nations. A Jew may be a descendant without any mixed blood since Abraham. The spiritual Israel involves many nations.

The answer is that Abraham is the father of many nations *within* the body of Christ. The true children of the promise of God are included in that one great nation, the church, the living temple, and the peculiar people of God. Christians are impossible to count, like counting dust.

"There is neither Jew nor Greek, slave nor free, male nor female, for you are all one in Christ Jesus. If you belong to Christ, then you are Abraham's seed, and heirs according to *the promise*" (Galatians 3:28-29).

What other promise is there apart from "the promise"? The original fulfillment of God's promise to Abraham does not fit the modern theology of those who connect Israel with the Rapture; this has caused all kinds of false information regarding the *end times.* If you have been misled, it is because you have looked in the wrong direction. You have read the wrong books. The answer is not in a *crisis of the nations* but in *the Christ of the nations.*

94

CHAPTER 8

Unconditional Covenants?

⊹⊱═⊰═⊱⊰⊹

After that whole generation
had been gathered to their fathers,
another generation grew up,
who knew neither the Lord
nor what he had done for Israel.

Then the Israelites did evil
in the eyes of the Lord
and served the Baals.
(Judges 2:10-11)

To Be or Not to Be Obedient, That's the Answer

Where the dispensational system makes a number of serious mistakes is in its claim that God made the chronologically developing covenant with Abraham unconditional. In the dispensational system, it's necessary that the nation of Israel remain an heir to the covenant. That's why they fight for *unconditional covenants to the bitter end.*

Here's an example I picked up randomly from sermons and reading dispensational books, pamphlets, and TV programs:

> No conditions were made with Abraham. Except for the original condition of leaving his homeland and going to the Promised Land, the covenant is made with no condition whatever. God just made a declaration and God would fulfill by His own sovereignty.

Think about this strange paragraph for a moment. In effect,

dispensational teachings relentlessly claim that no obedience is required, but is that biblical? Leave your modern town, your family, live in tents, be among strangers. *No obedience?* The whole covenant to Abram was based on his unswerving obedience!

Is it possible that when the call first came to Abraham it included Terah, his father, as well? Genesis 11:31-32 tells us that *Terah took Abram* to go to Canaan. However, Terah only went halfway and died in Haran. I'm not saying this is exactly what happened, but it's certainly interesting to speculate about the possibility that there was disobedience right at the beginning, and that Terah was judged for it. Notice that the call of Abram in Genesis 12:1 was a repeat of the original call, "The LORD *had said* to Abram…"

Yet it is true that, at the first observation of God's declaration to Abram, there seem to be no conditions attached to these generous promises of the land that God gave to him and his offspring. Now of course, God had the right to do so, for "The earth is the LORD's, and everything in it, the world, and all who live in it" (Psalm 24:1).

This land was no ordinary piece of real estate. The land was God's choice for God's people to receive and obey God's plan, for ultimately the whole earth was to be flooded with the glory of God.

God did not make any promise to Abraham that did not require his absolute obedience.

Please consider the following observations:

1. "Leave your country." Abram did.

2. Abram, the former heathen, left idols behind and worshiped the true and living God (Joshua 24:2-3).

   > So Abram moved his tents and went to live near the great trees of Mamre at Hebron, where he built an altar to the LORD (Genesis 13:18).

3. Abram recognized the priest of the most high God and paid his tithe to him.

   > Then Melchizedek king of Salem brought out bread

and wine. He was priest of God Most High, and he blessed Abram, saying, "Blessed be Abram by God Most High, Creator of heaven and earth. And blessed be God Most High, who delivered your enemies into your hand." Then Abram gave him a tenth of every-thing (Genesis 14:18-20).

4. Abram believed God.

    Abram believed the LORD, and he credited it to him as righteousness (Genesis 15:6).

5. Abram provided, in obedience to God, all the animals for a special ceremonial sacrifice and was busy keeping the vultures away all day. The major obedient work was done by Abram that day and night.

    So the LORD said to him, "Bring me a heifer, a goat and a ram, each three years old, along with a dove and a young pigeon." Abram brought all these to him, cut them in two and arranged the halves oppo-site each other; the birds, however, he did not cut in half. Then birds of prey came down on the carcasses, but Abram drove them away (Genesis 15:9-11).

6. Abram was told "...walk before me and be blameless."

    When Abram was ninety-nine years old, the LORD appeared to him and said, "I am God Almighty; walk before me and be blameless" (Genesis 17:1).

7. God *did* require continued obedience to Him.

    Then God said to Abraham, "As for you, you *must keep my covenant, you and your descendants after you for the generations to come*" (Genesis 17:9).

Abraham did keep the covenants. *His descendants did not.*

8. All the male members of Abram's household, in obedience to God, were circumcised.

> Abraham fell facedown; he laughed and said to himself, "Will a son be born to a man a hundred years old? Will Sarah bear a child at the age of ninety?" And Abraham said to God, "If only Ishmael might live under your blessing!" Then God said, "Yes, but your wife Sarah will bear you a son, and you will call him Isaac. I will establish my covenant with him as an everlasting covenant for his descendants after him. And as for Ishmael, I have heard you: I will surely bless him; I will make him fruitful and will greatly increase his numbers. He will be the father of twelve rulers, and I will make him into a great nation. But my covenant I will establish with Isaac, whom Sarah will bear to you by this time next year." When he had finished speaking with Abraham, God went up from him. On that very day Abraham took his son Ishmael and all those born in his household or bought with his money, every male in his household, and circumcised them, as God told him (Genesis 17:17-23).

9. Abraham was told to teach his whole household in order for the blessing to be fulfilled.

> For I have chosen him, so that he will direct his children and his household after him to keep the way of the LORD by doing what is right and just, *so that* the LORD will bring about for Abraham what he has promised him (Genesis 18:19).

10. After Abraham's horrible nightmare of being tested by God, the Bible makes very clear that obedience was required.

"...and through your offspring all nations on earth will be blessed, *because you have obeyed me"* (Genesis 22:18).

11. Isaac was told by the Lord that his father Abraham had obeyed God's requirements, commands, decrees, and laws.

"...because Abraham obeyed me and kept my requirements, my commands, my decrees and my laws" (Genesis 26:5).

12. The writer to the Hebrews emphasizes all of this when he wrote, "By faith Abraham, when called... *obeyed."*

By faith Abraham, when called to go to a place he would later receive as his inheritance, obeyed and went, even though he did not know where he was going (Hebrews 11:8).

If no conditions were laid down, why would God punish Israel, and send them into captivity? Why would Jesus (God's final revealed Word) tell unbelieving Jews that the kingdom of God will be taken away from them and be given to a nation producing the fruits thereof? "Therefore I tell you that the kingdom of God will be taken away from you and will be given to a people who will produce its fruit" (Matthew 21:43). There is nothing here about an additional restored kingdom in the future.

Why would God give Israel a bill of divorce? (Jeremiah 3:8). Obviously, writers of dispensational books, who maintain that God's promise of the inheritance of real estate was unconditional and thus today's reestablishment of physical Israel is in fulfillment of Scripture, are very confused and mistaken.

Numerous, No Longer Numberless

As already mentioned in chapter 2, in 2 Kings 10:32, God reduced the size of Israel: "In those days the LORD began to reduce the size of Israel. Hazael overpowered the Israelites throughout their territory."

Take careful note of the big change God made. In Ezekiel 36:37-38, Israel is made as numerous as sheep, no longer as stars or sand:

> This is what the Sovereign LORD says: "Once again I will yield to the plea of the house of Israel and do this for them: I will make their people as numerous as sheep, as numerous as the flocks for offerings at Jerusalem during her appointed feasts. So will the ruined cities be filled with flocks of people. Then they will know that I am the LORD" (Ezekiel 36:37-38).

In Ezekiel 39:23, they all died by the sword:

> "And the nations will know that the people of Israel went into exile for their sin, because they *were unfaithful to me.* So I hid my face from them and handed them over to their enemies, *and they all fell by the sword*" (Ezekiel 39:23).

If you're consistent and take this as literal, then there's not a true Jew left on a fallen great planet earth. So then, to those writers who obviously have been wrong and have discouraged millions of Bible-believing Christians, conditional clauses in God's covenants with His people are very troublesome, because the conditions were not kept, hence no Mosaic covenantal promise remains.

For the sake of argument, let's say that the covenant with Abram *is* unconditional. But the gospel is conditional. Why? Because repentance toward God, and faith in the Lord Jesus Christ is *necessary* for salvation. Then the Old Covenant is superior to the New Covenant! Then the gospel should fade away, but that's not what the Bible teaches:

> For if there had been nothing wrong with the first covenant, no place would have been sought for another. *But God found fault with the people and*

said: "The time is coming, declares the Lord, when *I will make a new covenant* with the house of Israel and with the house of Judah. It will not be like the covenant I made with their forefathers when I took them by the hand to lead them out of Egypt, *because they did not remain faithful to my covenant, and I turned away from them, declares the Lord*" (Hebrews 8:7-9).

a) Apart from the new covenant of grace, what new covenant according to Hebrews do Israelis have?
b) How can God find fault with the people if there's no condition?

If the first Abrahamic covenant was supposed to be unconditional, what can be better than that? Hebrews 8:6-7 talks about a superior covenant, because something was wrong with the first, so a place was made for a second covenant in Hebrews 8:13: "But the ministry Jesus has received is as superior to theirs as the covenant of which he is mediator is superior to the old one, and is founded on better promises. For if there had been nothing wrong with the first covenant, no place would have been sought for another" (Hebrews 8:6-7). "By calling this covenant 'new', he has made the first one *obsolete*; and what is obsolete and aging will soon disappear" (Hebrews 8:13).

The destruction of Jerusalem was just around the corner. This prophetic announcement by the author of Hebrews (probably written between A.D. 60–69) was soon fulfilled, for *soon* means *soon*! (see Revelation 1:1).

CHAPTER 9

Those Troublesome Conditional Clauses

⊰⇌⇋⊱

"But if you [all of you] turn away and forsake the
decrees and commands I have given you and go off
to serve other gods and worship them, then I
will uproot Israel from my land,
which I have given them,
and will reject this temple I have
consecrated for my Name."
(2 Chronicles 7:19-20)

"Do you see all these things?" He asked.
"I tell you the truth, not one stone here
will be left on another;
every one will be thrown down."
Matthew 24:2

The Road to Holocaust

Here is a classic example of how dispensational teaching refuses to acknowledge the fact that there are conditions to God's covenant with Israel. Hal Lindsey accused and belittled a Christian group called postmillennialists in his book, *The Late Great Planet Earth*. In essence and in order to prove his point, he accuses Martin Luther and postmillennialists of a major part of the blame for the Holocaust.

Although I don't wholly endorse the postmillennial viewpoint, let me make a number of defensive observations in support of this legitimate system of theology.

1. The postmillennialists are still here and growing, particularly

among reformed and charismatic groups.
2. They never taught that they could bring in the kingdom by their own efforts; that is not correct.
3. They do not believe in the inherent goodness of man.
4. Christian influence is not declining in the world. Never before in the history of the world has the influence of Christianity been greater. (Of the *increase* of His kingdom, there will be no end. Isaiah 9:7).
5. Looking at the world's changing conditions, and mixing and integrating biased observations with theological concepts, is a Bible-plus theology, which is the error of all the cults.
6. No self-respecting scholar looks at the world condition and then forms his theology from mistaken observations.

The point is: Hal Lindsey's book has now been contradicted because this group of postmillennialists has been growing so fast, and giving his theology fits.

The futuristic dispensational theology, like Lindsey's, will not use all of available Scripture. Conditional clauses and, it seems, the words of Christ, don't fit their system.

Here, then, is Hal Lindsey's own classical example to prove that the Jews who have not received Christ are still God's people. On this he built the foundation for his book, *The Road to Holocaust* (page 1). This is how he wants you to read it, *omitting all the conditional clauses*. He begins by quoting half of Deuteronomy 28:63. (The first part of verse 63 doesn't fit Lindsey's theology.)

> ...you will be uprooted from the land you are entering to possess. Then the LORD will scatter you among the nations, from one end of the earth to the other... Among those nations you will find no repose, no resting place for the sole of your foot... You will live in suspense, filled with dread both night and day, never sure of your life...
>
> ...When all these blessings and curses I have set before you come upon you and you take them to

heart wherever the LORD your God disperses you among the nations... The LORD your God will restore your fortunes and have compassion on you and gather you again from the nations where he scattered you... And the LORD your God will put all these curses on your enemies who hate and persecute you (Deuteronomy 28:63-66; 30:1, 7).

Here's what the Bible says. *The italicized are the conditional clauses Hal Lindsey omitted to make you believe God made no conditional clauses.*

You who were as numerous as the stars in the sky will be left but few in number, because you did not obey the LORD your God. Just as it pleased the LORD to make you prosper and increase in number, so it will please him to ruin and destroy you. You will be uprooted from the land you are to possess. Then the LORD will scatter you among the nations, from one end of the earth to the other. *There you will worship other gods—gods of wood and stone, which neither you nor your fathers have known.* Among those nations you will find no repose, no resting place for the sole of your foot. *There the LORD will give you an anxious mind, eyes weary with longing, and a despairing heart.* You will live in suspense, filled with dread both night and day, never sure of your life (Deuteronomy 28:61-66).

Obviously, Israel was at one stage as numerous as the stars in the sky, which is clearly God's fulfilled promise to Abraham.

When all these blessings and curses I have set before you come upon you and you take them to heart wherever the LORD your God disperses you among the nations, *and when you and your children return to the LORD your God and obey him with all your heart and with all your soul according to everything I command you today,* then the LORD your God will restore your fortunes and have compassion on you and gather you again from the nations where he scattered you. *Even if you have been banished to the most distant land under the heavens, from there the LORD your God will gather you and bring you back. He will bring you to the land that belonged to your fathers, and you will take possession of it. He will make you more prosperous and numerous than your fathers. The LORD your God will circumcise your hearts and the hearts of your descendants so that you may love him with_all your heart and with all your soul, and live. The LORD your God will put all these curses on your enemies who hate and persecute you. You will again obey the LORD and follow all his commands I am giving you today. Then the LORD your God will make you most prosperous in the work of your hands and in the fruit of the womb, the young of your livestock and the crops of your land. The LORD will again delight in you and make you prosperous, just as he delighted in your fathers, if you obey the LORD your God and keep his commands and decrees that are written in this Book of the Law and turn to the_LORD your God with all your heart and with all your soul.* (Deuteronomy 30:1-10).

The Bible makes it very clear that they did not return to the Lord. Left out are the very clear conditions laid down that were ignored and disobeyed by physical Israel. It can't be an innocent oversight, for here's another example by another dispensational teacher. In a book titled *The Sign*, Robert Van Kampen does exactly the same thing. On page 82 of that book, he also quotes Deuteronomy 30 and prints out verse 1, then jumps to verse 5. Please note that he omits verses 2 and 3, as emphasized below:

> *...and when you and your children return to the LORD your God and obey him with all your heart and with all your soul according to everything I command you today, then the LORD your God will restore your fortunes and have compassion on you and gather you again from the nations where he scattered you.*

Now, look at how the Israelites had broken and violated those very conditions God, through Moses, laid out before them. The verse below needs to be repeated again. This was the situation just after Joshua.

> After that whole generation had been gathered to their fathers, another generation grew up, who knew neither the LORD nor what he had done for Israel. Then the Israelites did evil in the eyes of the LORD and served the Baals (Judges 2:10-11).

"In those days Israel had no king; everyone did as he saw fit" (Judges 21:25; the KJV translates the last clause as, "...everyone did what was right *in his own eyes*").

The Restoration of David's Fallen Tent

One final word about conditional clauses. The argument is often used that, in a particular passage, no condition is mentioned. The dispensationalists jump on that argument, and say there is no condition mentioned for this particular covenant. But how many times does God have to remind them of His conditions? Amos 9:11-15 is an example of a missing conditional clause:

> "In that day I will restore David's fallen tent. I will repair its broken places, restore its ruins, and build it as it used to be, so that they may possess the remnant of Edom and all the nations that bear my name," declares the LORD, who will do these things. "The days are coming," declares the LORD,

"when the reaper will be overtaken by the plowman and the planter by the one treading grapes. New wine will drip from the mountains and flow from all the hills. I will bring back my exiled people Israel; they will rebuild the ruined cities and live in them. They will plant vineyards and drink their wine; they will make gardens and eat their fruit. I will plant Israel in their own land, never again to be uprooted from the land I have given them," says the LORD your God. (Amos 9:11-15)

But of course, this is a promise related to the greater universal spiritual Israel. Unbeknownst to Amos, who was a faithful prophet during the hidden church period, his apocalyptic words of prophecy confirmed the universality of the body of Christ. Amos, of course, did not know that the spirit of Christ was in him (1 Peter 1:10-11).

The apostles and elders met to consider this question. After much discussion, Peter got up and addressed them: "Brothers, you know that some time ago God made a choice among you that the Gentiles might hear from my lips the message of the gospel and believe. God, who knows the heart, showed that he accepted them by giving the Holy Spirit to them, just as he did to us. He made no distinction between us and them, for he purified their hearts by faith. Now then, why do you try to test God by putting on the necks of the disciples a yoke that neither we nor our fathers have been able to bear? No! We believe it is through the grace of our Lord Jesus that we are saved, just as they are."

The whole assembly became silent as they listened to Barnabas and Paul telling about the miraculous signs and wonders God had done among the Gentiles through them. When they finished, James spoke up: "Brothers, listen to me. Simon has described for us how God at first showed his concern by taking from the Gentiles a people for himself. The words of the prophets are in agreement with this, as it is written:

"'After this I will return and rebuild David's fallen tent. Its ruins I will rebuild, and I will restore it, that the remnant of the men may seek the Lord, and all the Gentiles who bear my name, says the Lord, who does these things' that have been known for ages.

"It is my judgment, therefore, that we should not make it difficult for the Gentiles who are turning to God. Instead we should write to them, telling them to abstain from food polluted by idols, from sexual immorality, from the meat of strangled animals and from blood. For Moses has been preached in every city from the earliest times and is read in the syna-gogues on every Sabbath." (Acts 15:6-21)

God only needs to establish His condition once; any repeat of His covenantal condition is sheer grace.

No Payday Someday

Here's an example: a mother promises her son a new CD. Great! The condition is: "First, do these jobs."

"What jobs?"

"Clean your room; empty the wastebasket and the big trash can; take the clean dishes out of the dishwasher; and sweep the garage. Understood?"

"Yes, ma'am."

She has gone over this for a week and he understands it very clearly. Now, as she backs up her car to go shopping, she calls out to him, "Son, I'm going to get that CD for you because I love you. Bye."

"WOW! Oh, major Wow!" the boy says to himself. "She never mentioned the jobs again. I'm getting the CD and she hasn't mentioned work again. Wow! She hasn't mentioned the conditional obligation. I'm off the hook. Wow!"

When his mother returned and the jobs she'd given him weren't done (or the clear conditions weren't fulfilled), he did *not* get his CD.

Here's one more example: Jesus said: "Come to me, all you who are weary and burdened, and I will give you rest" (Matthew 11:28).

He said nothing about turning from sin in this particular invitation, before coming to Him. It's simply understood by what He has said before regarding proper repentance.

We've looked at the subject of a prophecy turned history as far as the physical promise is concerned. But that's not all.

God's promise to Abraham was both physical and spiritual, fulfilled and yet in the process of being fulfilled.

To the original questions asked there's the second answer to the question, "Did God fulfill His promises to Abraham?" Yes, and not yet fully. Therefore, we need to deal briefly with the "not yet fully" answer.

God promised that through Abraham, Isaac, and Jacob: "I will bless those who bless you, and whoever curses you I will curse; and all peoples on earth will be blessed through you" (Genesis 12:3).

This obviously is not as yet fulfilled or completed, for it is a *prophecy in progress.* All Christians—Jews and Gentiles alike—are benefiting from this promise now and until the end of the age. It is being fulfilled in the great universal church of God.

> Consider Abraham: "He believed God, and it was credited to him as righteousness." Understand, then, that those who believe are children of Abraham. The Scripture foresaw that God would justify the Gentiles by faith, and announced the gospel in advance to Abraham: "All nations will be blessed through you." So those who have faith are blessed along with Abraham, the man of faith (Galatians 3:6-9).

> You are all sons of God through faith in Christ Jesus, for all of you who were baptized into Christ have clothed yourselves with Christ. There is neither Jew nor Greek, slave nor free, male nor female, for you are all one in Christ Jesus. If you belong to Christ,

then you are Abraham's seed, and heirs according to
the promise (Galatians 3:26-29).

Dr. Walvoord, in his book, *The Millennium Kingdom* (page
145), maintains, however, that there are three different senses in
which one can be a child of Abraham:

1. First, there is the natural lineage, or natural seed.
2. Second, there is the spiritual lineage within the natural for
   obedient law keepers.
3. Third, there is the spiritual seed.

First category: where are they now? At one stage, there were
only 7,000 men left who had not bowed the knee to Baal (1 Kings
19:18).

And what about Walvoord's second category? Who are the
people who kept the law? Where are they?

> Therefore no one will be declared righteous in his
> sight by observing the law; rather, through the law
> we become conscious of sin (Romans 3:20).

Dr. Walvoord does not mention this verse in his whole comprehensive textbook.

Paul warned the Galatian Christians who were intimidated by
Judaizers, who passionately tried to make non-ethnic church
members adopt Jewish traditions in order to be acceptable to God,
with the following:

> You are all sons of God through faith in Christ Jesus,
> for all of you who were baptized into Christ have
> clothed yourselves with Christ. There is neither Jew
> nor Greek, slave nor free, male nor female, for you
> are all one in Christ Jesus. If you belong to Christ,
> then you are Abraham's seed, and heirs according to
> the promise (Galatians 3:26-29).

One People Under God

There are no such things as simultaneous covenants of God with different peoples. The Bible makes very clear that there is no such thing as an additional covenant for spiritual children of Abraham, but only an original covenant for the faithful Jews. Scripture speaks of an old covenant that has been superseded by one new covenant.

Let the writer of Hebrews clear this up forever and for all, *once again.* "By calling this covenant 'new,' he has made the first one obsolete, and what is obsolete and aging will soon disappear" (Hebrews 8:13).

This disappearance was just around the corner at the fall of Jerusalem in A.D. 70. A major problem I see with "end times" theologians is that they maintain God has one plan for Israel, and a different one for the rest of the converted Gentiles. It divides the Bible and robs the prophets of being part of the whole history of redemption.

The second problem is that they believe the existence of modern day Israel is fulfilled prophecy and is connected with the future so-called Rapture of the church.

However, a large percentage of Israelis living in Israel are either traditionalists, agnostics, or atheists and enemies of the cross.

The third problem is that much of Scripture must be ignored in order to prove that God made unconditional promises to Israel. Even the eternal covenant between the Father and the Son was subject to the obedience of Christ. "Not my will, but your will be done," Jesus said. Thus He fulfilled perfectly and singularly the will of the Father.

If God still has plans for Israel of the flesh, then all His warnings and the inspired words of the faithful prophets are empty threats. It follows that the false prophets who said, "Peace, peace, when there is no peace," are right. Even hell itself has no fear in it. God's integrity becomes questionable.

Bad things happen to good prophecy when God's warnings are ignored and only blessings are forwarded. God has been demoted to a weak father who yells his threats but lacks the courage to carry out His punishments. God was never serious about His curses so very clearly recorded

in Deuteronomy 28, where we find fourteen bless-ings and fifty-three verses of curses.

The fourth problem is that they say the church is *the great parenthesis*, and is not part of the Israel of God. The church, they say, is the parenthesis between the sixty-ninth and seventieth weeks of Daniel's prophecy. How on earth can anything that lasts 2000 years be between sixty-nine and seventy weeks? Particularly since no amount of creativity or sound exegesis of Scripture yields the slightest hint of such a possibility. If, however, you want a parenthesis, then the nation of Israel fits the description, and that can be shown from both Scripture and history.

The fifth problem is that these questionable premises are commonly regarded as a sound biblical foundation, and dispensationalism is built upon it. Anyone who doesn't agree with it, more or less, is looked upon as a heretic or a liberal, or Roman Catholic.

In the following chapters, we'll discover the very sovereign, gracious work of God to discontinue the old Mosaic covenant with His own blood for all who believe. This covenant was communicated to Adam, rejoiced over by Abraham, believed by Moses, and echoed throughout Scripture. Dispensationalism fails because God made His covenant develop *chronologically*—from the mysterious first church to the hidden second church to the final visible church (1 Corinthians 10:11).

The salvation of the world, the redemption of a great multitude of people from all nations, has never depended upon the obedience or disobedience of Abraham or his descendants, but on the obedience of Christ and the faithfulness of God! The one and only God of the whole universe.

Hallelujah!

CHAPTER 10

Bible Talk

◆⟫◯⟨◆

Bear in mind that our Lord's patience means salvation,
just as our dear brother Paul also wrote you
with the wisdom that God gave him.

He writes the same way in all his letters,
speaking in them of these matters.

His letters contain some things
that are hard to understand,
which ignorant and unstable people distort,
as they do the other Scriptures,
to their own destruction.
(2 Peter 3:15-16)

All's Well That's Understood Well

Long my imprisoned spirit lay
Fast bound in sin and nature's night;
Thine eye diffused a quick'ning ray,
I woke, the dungeon flamed with light.
My chains fell off; my heart was free.
I rose, went forth and followed thee.
(from Charles Wesley's hymn, *And Can It Be?*)

This magnificent verse is written in Bible-talk style. It's called apocalyptic language, and is used throughout Scripture, especially in Ezekiel, Daniel, and Revelation. All Charles Wesley was saying is: "I was a non-Christian, a sinner. Christ was presented to me, and offered salvation. I became saved, and became a follower of Christ."

This is simply what happened to him, but this poetic example of this style of writing is one of the most glorious expressions of eternal salvation that has been preserved for us.

Now watch! If the erroneous dispensational method of relentlessly interpreting everything as being literal is insisted upon and applied to this verse, then the verse becomes a series of absurdities:

> Charles Wesley must have been insane, and an imprisoned criminal.
> He suffered from severe spiritual depression.
> He was tied up with chains to the wall in a windowless, pitch-dark dungeon.
> Something woke him up—perhaps an earthquake.
> Lightning struck, and fire broke out in the dungeon.
> By some strange miracle, his chains magically fell off.
> He got up, ran out of the dungeon and escaped.
> He saw Jesus and pursued Him.

Now imagine that someone who has just immigrated to the U.S., and has managed to learn a few hundred words of English, encounters this verse. That person knows the meaning of words like prison, spirit, lay, sin, night, dungeon, chains, follow, etc. Therefore, in this case, to interpret the hymn *literally* is understandable, and would probably happen. It takes some time to understand the poetic use of words. (More about this in chapter 14.)

Look at the symbolism of this great hymn the international church has been singing for over two hundred years. No one in his right mind interprets this song literally. *Charles Wesley was no more bound with literal chains than is the devil* (Revelation 20:1-3). But what an incredible means it is to communicate in apocalyptic terms the conversion of a soul from death to life.

Here's another example: Two women were talking across the back fence when a hyperactive three-year-old son of one of them kept interrupting by constantly trying to get her attention. "Please go away and play. I'll be with you in a minute," she said. Turning back to her friend, exasperated and irritated, she said, "That kid is driving me up the wall."

The next day, she was talking to another neighbor and the same thing happened. Her son was demanding her attention and pulling her skirt. "If you don't go away and let me talk, I'll get the wooden spoon." He got the message and walked away. Continuing her conversation, she said, "That hyperactive kid is driving me crazy."

Here's the point. The *first* statement of the mother is understood symbolically and cannot be interpreted literally. He can't literally drive her up the wall. It's everyday language that everyone understands isn't literal.

The second statement is also understood symbolically, *although it can be fulfilled literally,* as stated on a bumper sticker I saw: "Insanity is hereditary; you can get it from your kids."

Just because a biblical or prophetic statement can be interpreted literally doesn't mean it has to be. It can be, and most often is interpreted literally, but it doesn't always have to be, as is insisted upon by dispensationalist teachers.

This becomes extremely crucial when we open the pages of the Bible. The Bible is read, and should be understood differently than, say, the local newspapers. Prophetic books especially require great care in understanding.

This book will only deal briefly, and only as an introduction, with one aspect of interpretation, and that is: what kind of Scripture is to be understood as literal and what's to be understood as symbolic or spiritual. This is of crucial importance, for here the writers of futuristic, dispensational, and rapture books differ from this writer, or differ from the bulk of orthodox theologians throughout the whole history of redemption.

It's All in the Way You Handle It

When does *walk* not mean walk, and *stand* not mean stand, and *sit* not mean sit?

"Blessed is the man who does not walk in the counsel of the wicked or stand in the way of sinners or sit in the seat of mockers" (Psalm 1:1).

Here's the futuristic interpretation of Scripture. Across the board, the common denominator of dispensationalist use of Scripture is more or less this: the prophetic word is always interpreted literally, unless it's impossible. When the plain sense of Scripture makes common sense, seek no other.

Compare that with the orthodox and reformed interpretation:

> The Scriptures must be understood as they furnish their own interpretation in the light of the grammatical-historical circumstances of their impartation to man by the Sovereign God of the universe who is, at the same time, the covenanting redeemer of His people. The basis for an understanding of the coming of the Kingdom of God, therefore, centers in Jesus Christ (Herman Ridderbos, *The Coming of the Kingdom,* Introduction, page 9).

There are many premillennialists who would claim to believe the above quotation by Ridderbos, but they don't display any such belief in their writings.

When, for instance, the clearly fulfilled prophecies of Jeremiah are taken out of their historical circumstances and thrown into a context taking place thousands of years later, to be fulfilled before the so-called 1000-year reign of Christ, then violence has been done to biblical interpretation, in the light of their grammatical-historical circumstance of their impartation.

Hal Lindsey is not faithful to his own statement. I quote again, "When the plain sense of Scripture makes common sense seek no other sense." On page 43 of his book, he takes Matthew 24:34 out of its 2000-year-old context by just quoting that verse and adding that this will be "fulfilled in our generation." "I tell you the truth, this generation will certainly not pass away until all these things have happened" (Matthew 24:34).

Let's look at the context. The disciples had just asked Jesus about the destruction of the temple and the end of the age that belongs to the temple. The plain sense of Scripture here is that the disciples' generation would not all die until the temple had been destroyed (which occurred in A.D. 70).

In Matthew 24:4, Jesus says, "Watch out." In verse six, He says, "You will hear of wars and rumors of wars, but see to it that you are not alarmed." Why would Jesus say that if it didn't apply to them, but to whoever lives now or two thousand years from now?

Jesus answered, "Watch out that no one deceives you" (Matthew 24:4). "You will hear of wars and rumors of wars, but see to it that you are not alarmed. Such things must happen, but the end is still to come" (Matthew 24:6).

In Matthew 24:25, Jesus says, "See, I have told you ahead of time." We know from history that the Christians in Jerusalem escaped that terrible tribulation, because they believed what Jesus had warned them about and left town in time. The church escaped that great tribulation of A.D. 70 when Jerusalem was destroyed.

Then, in Matthew 24:33, when Jesus tells them, "Even so, when *you see* all these things," He is talking to the living, inquiring followers of His day, who would and should know about the disaster Christ warned them about. "Even so, when you see all these things, you know that it is near, right at the door" (Matthew 24:33).

And then verse 34: "I tell you the truth, *this* generation will *certainly* not pass away until all these things happen."

From Matthew 24, Lindsey only quotes verse 34, and says that the generation reading his book are the recipients of verse 34. He violates his own principle of interpretation. For further study of the interpretation of Matthew 24, get a copy of *Matthew 24 Fulfilled,* by John Bray, a well-known Southern Baptist evangelist.

Run This by Me Again

To interpret a prophecy in its entirety in a spiritual or symbolic manner isn't discarding the prophecy, or spiritualizing it away, but giving it the fullest and most universal meaning intended by the Holy Spirit, in order to benefit the church until the end of the world.

In Bible language, there is incredible symbolism, which was never intended by God to be understood literally. For example:

This is what the LORD, the God of Israel said to me:

"Take from my hand this cup filled with the wine of my wrath and make all the nations to whom I send you drink it. When they drink it, they will stagger and go mad because of the sword I will send among them."

So I took the cup from the LORD's hand and made all the nations to whom he sent me drink it: Jerusalem and the towns of Judah, its kings and officials, to make them a ruin and an object of horror and scorn and cursing, as they are today; Pharaoh king of Egypt, his attendants, his officials and all his people, and all the foreign people there; all the kings of Uz; all the kings of the Philistines (those of Ashkelon, Gaza, Ekron, and the people left at Ashdod); Edom, Moab and Ammon; all the kings of Tyre and Sidon; the kings of the coastlands across the sea; Dedan, Tema, Buz and all who are in distant places; all the kings of Arabia and all the kings of the foreign people who live in the desert; and all the kings of the north, near and far, one after the other all the kingdoms on the face of the earth. And after all of them, the king of Sheshach will drink it too (Jeremiah 25:15-26).

How do we interpret this passage? Are we to be faithful to Scripture, and not spiritualize it into oblivion? (This is what non-dispensational believers are often accused of doing with Scripture.) If we take this passage *literally*, then:

God has a hand.
God has a cup.
God has wine in the cup.
Those who drink the wine will stagger and go mad.
God will send a sword to all of them.
Jeremiah touched the hand of God.
He took the cup.
He did not spill any of it.

> He traveled the world.
> He managed to get an audience with all the kings of
> the world.
> He made them drink the wine.
> All of them were ruined.

It would have been a very difficult assignment. Literally, it *is* possible to walk around with a cup in the hand, and make all the kings of the known world drink out of it.

Of course, the wine in the cup from the hand of God does not constitute physical liquid that can be drunk by a bodily act. The whole assignment is understood spiritually by Jeremiah, who courageously pronounced the alarming judgment of an angry God to the sinful nations described in this revelation.

The same understanding should be applied to similar references throughout Scripture to the cup of God's wrath. The book of Revelation must be studied in this way.

Jesus cried on His knees in unparalleled agony, pleading with His Father: "My Father, if it is not possible for this cup to be taken away unless I drink it, may your will be done" (Matthew 26:42).

But of course, the most incredible fact is that, for the benefit of all believers in Christ, our Lord and Savior drank the cup of God's wrath for them.

Note here that Jesus uses Jeremiah's Old Testament kind of Bible language in the most agonizing moment of His earthly life. Of course, we know there was no literal cup in the garden from which Christ drank.

Jesus Talk

> When they went across the lake, the disciples forgot
> to take bread. "Be careful," Jesus said to them. "Be
> on your guard against the yeast of the Pharisees and
> Sadducees." They discussed this among themselves
> and said, "It is because we didn't bring any bread."
> Aware of their discussion, Jesus asked, "You of little
> faith, why are you talking among yourselves about

having no bread? Do you still not understand? Don't you remember the five loaves for the five thousand, and how many basketfuls you gathered? Or the seven loaves for the four thousand, and how many basketfuls you gathered? How is it you don't understand that I was not talking to you about bread? But be on your guard against the yeast of the Pharisees and Sadducees." Then they understood that he was not telling them to guard against the yeast used in bread, but against the teaching of the Pharisees and Sadducees (Matthew 16:5-12).

Jesus loved to use Old Testament language. In describing the fall of Jerusalem and the destruction of the temple, Jesus sounded like an Old Testament prophet:

"Immediately after the distress of those days the sun will be darkened, and the moon will not give its light; the stars will fall from the sky, and the heavenly bodies will be shaken. At that time the sign of the Son of Man will appear in the sky, and all the nations of the earth will mourn. They will see the Son of Man coming on the clouds of the sky, with power and great glory. And he will send his angels with a loud trumpet call, and they will gather his elect from the four winds, from one end of the heavens to the other" (Matthew 24:29-31).

The language Jesus uses here seems to be nothing short of a catastrophic end of everything as we know it. But in reality, we must remember that Christ is using prophetic Bible language so familiar in the Old Testament.

The statement, "The sun, moon and stars fall down from the sky" needs to be looked at from something other than a literal interpretation. It cannot be anything else but symbolic.

A Clouded Issue

"He was taken up before their eyes, *and a cloud hid him from their sight*" (Acts 1:9).

Let's look at what is possibly the most misunderstood passage in the gospels: "At that time the sign of the Son of Man will appear in the sky, and all the nations of the earth will mourn. They will see the Son of Man coming on the clouds of the sky, with power and great glory" (Matthew 24:30).

A sign represents or points to something. For example, if I walk into the sanctuary of our church, the congregation doesn't say, "We see the *sign* of our pastor." Rather, they say, "We see the pastor." I don't need a sign if I'm there in real life. Think this through. If, however, I'm late entering the sanctuary but, through the window, someone sees my car in the parking lot, that's a sign I may be somewhere in the building.

First, in Matthew 24:30, Jesus says the *sign* of the Son of Man will appear. Second, it will not be a happy time. No! The nations will mourn! Why? It's judgment time!

Third, they will *see* the Son of Man coming on the *clouds*. The typical interpretation of this passage is, "Here He is—we can see Him. The sign is gone, we recognize Him." This agrees with Hal Lindsey's understanding of the passage: "Perhaps the sign of the Son of Man will be a gigantic celestial image of Jesus flashed upon the heavens for all to see" (Lindsey, page 173).

Not so fast! It doesn't say "in the middle of bright sunlight," but "on the *clouds*." Why clouds?

> **A bad thing will happen to a good prophecy when a particular term is met in Scripture and fantasized about in a fanciful way. That term is there for a reason. Search the Scriptures about the use and meaning of the term. Clouds in Scripture are never used as celestial spacecraft for Jesus to travel on, but are used to cover, to hide, or to make invisible.**

The use of clouds in the Scriptures appears some 160 times.

123

Here are some Old Testament examples:

> Praise the LORD, O my soul. O LORD my God, you are very great; you are clothed with splendor and majesty. He wraps himself in light as with a garment; he stretches out the heavens like a tent and lays the beams of his upper chambers on their waters. He makes the clouds his chariot and rides on the wings of the wind. He makes winds his messengers, flames of fire his servants (Psalm 104:1-4).

> Then the angel of God, who had been traveling in front of Israel's army, withdrew and went behind them. The pillar of cloud also moved from in front and stood behind them... (Exodus 14:19).

> During the last watch of the night the LORD looked down from the pillar of fire and cloud at the Egyptian army and threw it into confusion (Exodus 14:24).

> ..."I am going to come to you in a dense cloud, so that the people will hear me speaking with you and will always put their trust in you (Exodus 19:9).

Now, here are some New Testament examples:

> While he was still speaking, *a bright cloud enveloped them, and a voice from the cloud said*, "This is my Son, whom I love; with him I am well pleased. Listen to him!" (Matthew 17:5).

> After he said this, he was taken up before their eyes, *and a cloud hid him from their sight* (Acts 1:9).

> Look, he is coming with the clouds, and every eye will see him, even those who pierced him; and all

the peoples of the earth will mourn because of him.
So shall it be! Amen (Revelation 1:7).

Lindsey realizes the difficulty of the clouds, so he does away with the clouds and replaces them with a *gigantic celestial image.* But the Bible does *not* tell me so.

The general symbolic use of clouds in the Scriptures could be summed up in the following:

1. To hide God, or Christ, or angels.
2. To bring deliverance.
3. To show His glory.
4. To show God's protection.
5. To give direction.
6. To show His grace.
7. To bring judgment.
8. To block the enemies of God's people, etc.

Therefore, when Matthew 24:30 and Revelation 1:7 tell us Christ is coming on the clouds, and every eye shall see Him, then it's saying that Christ is coming in judgment on the peoples, and He will be seen with *perceived eyes, not naked eyes.* (See also 2 Kings 6:17.)

When Christ came in judgment upon Jerusalem in A.D. 70, He appeared in the clouds. The church in Jerusalem saw Him, perceived His judgment, and understood the sign of the Son of Man, and obediently left Jerusalem in a hurry.

CHAPTER 11

Typological Time Bombs

⊷══◉══⊷

"Just as Moses lifted up the snake in the desert,
so the Son of Man must be lifted up,
that everyone who believes in him
may have eternal life."
(John 3:14-15)

Declarable Dreams

From Genesis 37, we remember that Joseph had his dreams. The first dream dealt with sheaves bowing down. The second is recorded as follows:

> Then he had another dream, and he told it to his brothers. "Listen," he said, "I had another dream, and this time the sun and moon and eleven stars were bowing down to me." When he told his father as well as his brothers, his father rebuked him and said, "What is this dream you had? Will your mother and I and your brothers actually come and bow down to the ground before you?" His brothers were jealous of him, but his father kept the matter in mind (Genesis 37:9-11).

It's interesting to note that figuratively, Israel is here referred to as sun, moon, and stars. Marcellus Kik refers to Christ's description in Matthew 24 this way:

> God in his righteous wrath has removed the Jewish nation from his heavens to rule as a servant to win

the world for God. The sun of Judaism has been darkened; as the moon no longer reflects the light of God; bright stars, as the list of heroes in Hebrews 11, no longer shine in the Israel of the flesh. (Kik, *An Eschatology of Victory*, page 128)

Babylonian Blues

Israel was not the only one spoken of by the prophets in such a descriptive, symbolic way: "The stars of heaven and their constellations will not show their light. The rising sun will be darkened and the moon will not give its light" (Isaiah 13:10).

This whole chapter, referred to as *the burden of Babylon*, deals with the destruction of this leading nation, which politically shone like the sun, moon, and stars.

Furthermore, here's a passage that deals with the destruction of the nations, with particular reference to Edom (the descendants of Esau): "All the stars of the heavens will be dissolved and the sky rolled up like a scroll; all the starry host will fall like withered leaves from the vine, like shriveled figs from the fig tree" (Isaiah 34:4).

If we see how the Holy Spirit uses such vivid but figurative language with a lesser nation, it's not hard to figure out why He would use language like that for Israel, which for so long had a most-favored-nation status in the eyes of God.

Egypt didn't miss out either. "When I snuff you out, I will cover the heavens and darken their stars; I will cover the sun with a cloud, and the moon will not give its light" (Ezekiel 32:3).

The point to remember is simply this: these calamities did come upon these nations physically, but the *sun, moon, and stars* are still shining. That's Bible language for you! Obviously, one needs to look further than limited literal fulfillment only.

The Old in the New

In the Old Testament book of Joel, we read the following prophecy:

"And afterward, I will pour out my Spirit on all people. Your sons and daughters will prophesy, your old men will dream dreams, your young men will see visions. Even on my servants, both men and women, I will pour out my Spirit in those days. I will show wonders in the heavens and on the earth, blood and fire and billows of smoke. The sun will be turned to darkness and the moon to blood before the coming of the great and dreadful day of the LORD. And everyone who calls on the name of the LORD will be saved; for on Mount Zion and in Jerusalem there will be deliverance, as the LORD has said, among the survivors whom the LORD calls." (Joel 2:28-32)

Then, in the book of Acts, this passage from Joel's prophecy is quoted nearly verbatim by Peter on the day of Pentecost. Filled with the Holy Spirit in order to prophecy and be an infallible spokesman for God, he informs the bewildered and skeptical bystanders that what is happening in Jerusalem is in fulfillment of Joel's prophecy on the day of Pentecost!

No, this is what was spoken by the prophet Joel: "'In the last days, God says, I will pour out my Spirit on all people. Your sons and daughters will prophesy, your young men will see visions, your old men will dream dreams. Even on my servants, both men and women, I will pour out my Spirit in those days, and they will prophesy. I will show wonders in the heaven above and signs on the earth below, blood and fire and billows of smoke. The sun will be turned to darkness and the moon to blood before the coming of the great and glorious day of the Lord. And everyone who calls on the name of the Lord will be saved.'

"Men of Israel, listen to this: Jesus of Nazareth was a man accredited by God to you by miracles, wonders and signs, which God did among you through him, as you yourselves know" (Acts 2:16-22).

Literally, of course, none of this happened on the day of Pentecost. Symbolically or spiritually, the light went out for physical Israel. It was the beginning of the end, which was climaxed as Christ had warned them, when Jerusalem would be destroyed.

Dr. Milton S. Terry makes a statement in his *Biblical Hermeneutics* which is well to the point. He writes:

> We might fill volumes with extracts showing how exegetes and writers on New Testament doctrine assume as a principle not to be questioned that such highly wrought language as Matthew 24:29-31, 1 Thessalonians 4:16 and 2 Peter 3:10, 12, taken almost *verbatim* from Old Testament prophecies of judgment, and apocalyptic language and style, would seem to be the reason for this one sided exegesis. It will require more than assertion to convince thoughtful men that the figurative language of Isaiah and Daniel, admitted on all hands to be such in those ancient prophets, is to be literally interpreted when used by Jesus and Paul. (Quoted by Kik, *An Eschatology of Victory*, page 135.)

The prophet Amos is often quoted in support of a new and continued state of Israel. But read this passage carefully in the light of what has been said so far with regard to Bible language.

As a safe general principle, a prophecy is not interpreted correctly if the interpreter jumps back and forth from figurative into literal language to prove his point.

> "In that day I will restore David's fallen tent. I will repair its broken places, restore its ruins, and build it as it used to be, so that they may possess the remnant of Edom and all the nations that bear my name," declares the LORD, who will do these things.

> "The days are coming," declares the LORD, "when the reaper will be overtaken by the plowman and the

planter by the one treading grapes. New wine will drip from the mountains and flow from all the hills. I will bring back my exiled people Israel; they will rebuild the ruined cities and live in them. They will plant vineyards and drink their wine; they will make gardens and eat their fruit. I will plant Israel in their own land, never again to be uprooted from the land I have given them," says the LORD your God (Amos 9:11-15).

How much is symbolic here?

Verse 11   Restoring David's fallen tent.
             Repair, restore, and rebuild.

Verse 12   Possess the remnant of Edom.

Verse 13   The reaper overtaken by the plowman; if literal, that spells disaster.
             Wine dripping from the mountains and flowing down the hills.

Verse 14   The return of the exiled people in context is that they may evangelize and bless the whole world, e.g., Edom and all the nations that bear my name.

Verse 15   Replanting of Israel.
             The exiles returned to the land from 536 to 520 B.C. To be there forever can't be literal, for the earth will pass away (2 Peter 3).

First of all, you must understand that in the last days scoffers will come, scoffing and following their own evil desires. They will say, "Where is this 'coming' he promised? Ever since our fathers died, everything goes on as it has since the beginning of creation." But they deliberately forget that long ago by God's word the heavens existed and the earth was formed out of water and by water. By these waters also the world of that time was deluged and destroyed. By the same word the present heavens and earth are reserved for fire, being kept for the day of judgment and destruction of ungodly men.

But do not forget this one thing, dear friends: With the Lord a day is like a thousand years, and a thousand years are like a day. The Lord is not slow in keeping his promise, as some understand slowness. He is patient with you, not wanting anyone to perish, but everyone to come to repentance.

But the day of the Lord will come like a thief. The heavens will disappear with a roar; the elements will be destroyed by fire, and the earth and everything in it will be laid bare (2 Peter 3:3-10).

A bad thing happens to a good prophecy when the Holy Spirit's interpretation of His own particular Scripture in the New Testament is ignored in favor of forcing a literal interpretation of that Scripture.

Let's read on from the words of a converted fisherman:

"God, who knows the heart, showed that he accepted them by giving the Holy Spirit to them, just as he did to us. He made no distinction between us and them, for he purified their hearts by faith. Now then, why do you try to test God by putting on the necks of the disciples a yoke that neither we nor our fathers have been able to bear? No! We believe it is through the grace of our Lord Jesus that we are saved, just as they are."

The whole assembly became silent as they listened to Barnabas and Paul telling about the miraculous signs and wonders God had done among the Gentiles through them. When they finished, James spoke up, "Brothers, listen to me. Simon has described to us how God at first showed his concern by taking from the Gentiles a people for himself. The words of the prophets are in agreement with this, as it is written:

"After this I will return and rebuild David's fallen tent. Its ruins I will rebuild, and I will restore it, that the remnant of men may seek the Lord, who does these things that have been known for ages" (Acts 15:8-18).

Thus the general assembly of the church in Acts 15 was still not quite sure if the Gentiles had any place within the Jewish camp. Read the passage carefully. The Gentiles were given the Holy Spirit. He made no distinction between Jew and Gentile. And both people groups are saved through the grace of the Lord Jesus Christ alone. Then follows the fulfilled prophecy of Amos in the wider spiritual use to confirm to the church:

1) that born-again Jews and the church are now one and the same thing.
2) God's promise to Abraham is fulfilled in the great universal church which Christ, the branch, is building.

Here then is a further biblical example of the two-fold use of Old Testament prophecy from a temporal, literal fulfillment and secondly, a wider, eternal, spiritual fulfillment.

"When Israel was a child, I loved him, and out of Egypt I called my son" (Hosea 11:1). Here is a very clear description of a historical event, that is, Israel's exodus. Yet the Holy Spirit tells us in Matthew 2:15 that the greater fulfillment has to do with Christ's return out of Egypt: "...where he stayed until the death of Herod. And so was fulfilled what the Lord had said through the prophet: 'Out of Egypt I called my son'" (Matthew 2:15).

> *Many literal historical events and situations in the Old Testament have permanent value for the Church, not in a literal repeat of those events, but in a symbolic or spiritual outworking of those events during the rest of the history of the world.*

Typology is Explosive

That momentous epic movie, *The Ten Commandments*, a fantastic dramatization of a real time-and-space historic fact, misses the most vital point and purpose entirely. The producers were praised; Charlton Heston secured a permanent place among the greats of Hollywood. Exit comments by pleased moviegoers included: I want to see it again...Great acting...Wonderful special effects...I'm sorry it's over... etc. However, it's not over, for in that great Exodus is hidden divine typology, the seed of something so great it's almost like an explosion, a time bomb waiting to explode in the greatest divine blessing for the whole world.

> **Biblical typology is a divine, purposeful, historic event or thing in seed form of something millions of times greater than its original existence. It waits for the Holy Spirit to germinate it to its fullest purpose, and then, together with the Scripture, communicate its fullest truth to the awakened believer.**

The apostle Paul, in writing to new converts and members of the Colossian church said, "For he has rescued us from the dominion of darkness and brought us into the kingdom of the Son he loves, in whom we have redemption, the forgiveness of sins" (Colossian 1:13-14).

Every born-again believer, Arab, Jew, black, white, or other individual, has been the recipient of a divine, custom-made rescue drama, administered from heaven by Christ and snatched or uprooted from the illegal realm of Satan, and transplanted into the kingdom of the Son He loves! Never to leave it!

God, by His sovereign electing purpose, has engaged numerous invisible angels in protecting, controlling, and manipulating a potential convert and performing whatever it takes, and possibly much more than ten miracles, to execute His plan for the salvation of that one soul.

The Bible clearly promises: "Are not all angels ministering spirits sent to serve those who will inherit salvation?" (Hebrews 1:14). That's why the movie is not over, its purpose not finished. Exodus is nothing more than the type of glorious salvation. Abraham was never asked by God to fulfill God's covenantal promise that He would be the father of billions. God has to fulfill His own divine prophecy.

Of course, the participants of the Exodus under Moses were not aware of what was happening, other than getting away from Pharaoh. We know they constantly complained about their lot.

I can imagine the following:

1. The ark of the covenant: "What's all the fuss about?"
2. Animal blood sacrifice: "What a waste of healthy animals!"
3. Water from the rock: "It's about time!"
4. Serpent on a pole: "We asked for protection from poison snakes and Moses comes up with a ridiculous brass snake."
5. Manna: "Must be blowing over us from a distant forest."

It's extremely important to remember that the purpose for the believer is to glorify God and enjoy Him forever. So the Christian is a candidate for heaven, with mind and heart opened to God, making *the Word alive with the signs of the Messiah,* pronouncing confidence in God, encouragement from God, and commitment to God.

Obviously the futuristic theology of dispensationalism, so

preoccupied with earthly things—a new temple, the city of Jerusalem, 1000-year reign, rapture, the conversion of Israelis—has to leave the typology locked up, or close ended. *But all typology must open up to Christ and the Church.*

Why Did Good King Hezekiah Destroy the Serpent of Brass?

When a typological event or object has exploded or been fulfilled, the physical remains need to be discarded or destroyed; otherwise, they will become malignant idols, a real tool of Satan, and objects of worship (2 Kings 18:4). It would be as dangerous as an un-detonated bomb. The typological purpose was to communicate and apply eternal life for all who are led astray by Satan's poison, and look in faith to the cross of Christ.

The Holy Spirit enlightened the mind of Hezekiah that the serpent of brass had served its physical and typological purpose; and like Abraham, saw beyond it a greater purpose (John 3:14-15). That's why Jesus was not impressed by the physical temple—God did not oppose its destruction.

Why is God not fighting for the Jews to gain control of the unholy Holy Land? It has served its eternal purpose for the gospel, about which Abraham was so excited.

I wonder how many Christians visiting Israel have knelt down on Mount Calvary, thinking by doing so they were closer to Christ there than praying in the kitchen at home. Muslims need pilgrimages; Christians may visit Israel for historical reasons only. Christ told the disciples to leave it and evangelize the world. The land has fulfilled its usefulness for the sake of Christ.

To the Christian, it's sad to see faithful Jews praying and crying at the Wailing Wall. They don't realize the temple was only a type of the real temple, the *living* temple—the Lord Jesus Christ and the church, in fulfillment of God's promise to Abraham.

Think about this serious question. Apart from the universal church, in what possible other way have Abraham and his offspring been a blessing to all people for the last 2000 years?

Rejoice over the words of Jesus, and clarified by John, by means of the Holy Spirit, at the writing of his gospel many years later.

> On the last and greatest day of the Feast, Jesus stood and said in a loud voice, "If anyone is thirsty, let him come to me and drink. Whoever believes in me, as the Scripture has said, streams of living water will flow from within him." *By this he meant the Spirit, whom those who believed in him were later to receive. Up to that time the Spirit had not been given, since Jesus had not yet been glorified* (John 7:37-39).

And there are hundreds more real, historical, and literal events. This is what Paul says about the history of Israel recorded in Scripture: "These things happened to them as examples and were written down as warnings for us, *on whom the fulfillment of the ages has come*" (1 Corinthians 10:11). We have dealt with this in chapter 3, but it's worth repeating!

Note that it doesn't say Israel will have some future fulfillment. *But the fulfillment of the ages is now*. It has come; it began with Pentecost.

Let's go back to this verse and place it in its proper context:

> "For I do not want you to be ignorant of the fact, brothers, that our forefathers were all under the cloud and that they all passed through the sea. They were all baptized into Moses in the cloud and in the sea. They all ate the same spiritual food and drank the same spiritual drink; for they drank from the spiritual rock that accompanied them, *and that rock was Christ*. Nevertheless, God was not pleased with most of them; their bodies were scattered over the desert.
>
> "Now these things occurred as examples, to keep us

from setting our hearts on evil things as they did. Do not be idolaters, as some of them were; as it is written, 'The people sat down to eat and drink and got up to indulge in pagan revelry.' We should not commit sexual immorality, as some of them did, and in one day 23,000 of them died. We should not test the Lord, as some of them did, and were killed by snakes. And do not grumble, as some of them did, and were killed by the destroying angel.

"These things happened to them as examples and were written down as warnings for us, *on whom the fulfillment of the ages has come*" (1 Corinthians 10:1-11).

The first age is Adam to Abraham, the second age is Abraham to A.D. 70; the third age (in which we are now) is the fulfillment of the ages, symbolically the 1000-year reign of Christ, and then comes eternity.

Once again the Bible teaches in plain, symbolic, typological events and language, that God's dealing with Israel in the past had as its eternal object, the body of Christ, the church, in which the promise to Abraham found its complete fulfillment, "All nations will be blessed through you" (Genesis 12:3).

So then, Bible language and historical events among the twelve tribes had as their purpose to communicate God's Word to His original people, first by the prophets in language and historical events they could understand, and at the same time, speak to us today, thousands of years later. That is why symbolic language is such a useful vehicle of divine truth.

If, however, it's insisted that Scripture be interpreted literally, no matter what, then nothing but chaos is the result. Ask the bewildered, frustrated, angry Korean Christians, who when lied to about the Rapture in September 1992, gave away their possessions.

When I was a child, I told my mother I was very glad I hadn't lived in Old Testament days. "Why?" she asked.

I said, "How would you like to live in a land flowing with milk and honey? What if the milk gets sour and the honey sticks to your shoes?"

"You silly boy. That's not what it means," she said.

I soon learned that the Bible doesn't always mean what it says in a literal sense.

The fathers and the prophets were God's servants in time and space receiving and applying God's Word during times of sinful behavior in the covenant relation between God and His people. They spoke a language their contemporaries could understand and in forms suited to their audience.

However, they did not serve themselves; the Spirit of Christ in them pointed to the church. The prophets can be clearly understood by us, thousands of years later, without any diminishing eternal value, but with explosive possibilities.

Be assured and encouraged by the fact that God and His spiritual servants have battled for you, have possibly protected you thousands of times you're not aware of. One soul rescued from Satan and hell is of greater value and a greater victory than a million people physically escaping from Pharaoh (Hebrews 1:14).

Don't bother about some international event or rapture. Be aware of what God has done today, and will do for you personally. There are so many unimaginable things still waiting.

CHAPTER 12

The Big Announcement

❖⟹⟸❖

"I will raise up for them a prophet like you
from among their brothers;
I will put my words in his mouth,
and he will tell them everything I command him.

If anyone does not listen to my words that the prophet speaks in
my name, I myself will call him to account."
(Deuteronomy 18:18-19)

For Moses said, "The Lord your God
will raise up for you a prophet like me
from among your own people;
you must listen to everything he tells you.

Anyone who does not listen to him
will be completely cut off from among his people."
(Acts 3:22-23)

A Preacher Breaks a 400-Year Silence

The miraculous birth of John the Baptist took place six months before the birth of Christ. The prophet Isaiah had foretold that the Christ would have a divinely planned forerunner. "As it is written in the book of the Lord, make straight paths for him. Every valley shall be filled in, every mountain and hill made low. The crooked roads shall become straight, the rough ways smooth. And all mankind will see God's salvation" (Luke 3:4-6).

Now that you've read about Biblical language (chapter 11), you'll realize the value of the spiritualization of this passage. See if you can figure out the various significant permanent meanings.

First, there's the literal fulfillment of the birth of this forerunner. Then follows additional permanent spiritual significance:

- Straight paths
- Valleys filled in
- Mountains made low
- Crooked roads straightened
- Rough ways made smooth

John the Baptist was a special, miraculous, unique servant of God, and a most important person in the New Testament after Christ, as the forerunner of Jesus—"He was not that light." He realized his place and, when Jesus came onto the scene, John disappeared, having been murdered by Herod, and Jesus took His rightful place on center stage. When Jesus came, *the last prophet had to disappear immediately from center stage.*

From the Words of the last Old Testament prophet, John the Baptist: "He must become greater and greater and I must become less" (John 3:30). The murderous enemies of Christ took care of it.

From the words of Peter; look carefully at these divinely inspired and fulfilled verses he preached on the day of Pentecost, when Jews from all over the world had gathered for the feast.

> "But this is how God fulfilled what he had foretold through all the prophets, saying that his Christ would suffer. Repent, then, and turn to God, so that your sins may be wiped out, that times of refreshing may come from the Lord, and that he may send the Christ, who has been appointed for you—even Jesus. He must remain in heaven until the time comes for God to restore everything, as he promised long ago through his holy prophets. For Moses said, 'The Lord your God will raise up for you a prophet like me from among your own people, you must listen to everything he tells you. *Anyone who does not listen to him will be completely cut off from among his people.'*

"Indeed, all the prophets from Samuel on, as many as have spoken, have foretold these days. And you are heirs of the prophets and of the covenant God made with your fathers. He said to Abraham, 'Through your offspring all peoples on earth will be blessed.' When God raised up his servant, he sent him first to you to bless you by turning each of you from your wicked ways" (Acts 3:18-26).

My biggest problem by far with most of the futuristic teaching of this past century is the violence it does to the glory, exaltation, and the finished work of Christ. Christ is placed in the background. Dispensationalism is not *Christocentric*. Judge for yourself and see if these facts don't indicate that Christ has been marginalized by dispensational teaching.

From his popular best-seller, *The Late Great Planet Earth*, Hal Lindsey says the most authentic voices in the Bible are the voices of the Old Testament prophets. Therefore, the Jews are the most important people. He's stepping aside and letting the prophets speak.

I'm glad Lindsey is stepping aside, but he has the wrong persons on center stage. Jesus is God's final revelation and He has the final word on final things. That's final! Jesus is superior to all the prophets combined and, more importantly, is the only person in Scripture who did not look, unlike Moses and Paul, through a glass darkly.

Where Did You Get the Information?

A scriptural index gives us good information about the biblical base for a theological textbook. First, let's look at Dr. Walvoord's textbook, *The Millennial Kingdom*. In his book, he quotes over 300 verses from Isaiah, over 150 verses from Jeremiah, over 100 from Ezekiel, etc., *but only five verses from John's gospel!* Not one verse of John is exegetically expounded. But take note of the fact that the book of John alone has the word *Jew* in it *eighteen times*!

Let's consider those facts; if the word *Jew* is used eighteen times in John, does this mean Walvoord isn't interested in what Christ, the second person of the Godhead, had to say about the future of the Jews? If you carefully read the whole book of John, you'll have a very good understanding what He, who is the final Word of God, had to say about His own people who did not believe in Him.

If Christ were on earth today, He could be tried and found guilty of anti-Semitism. Are we to believe that Christ's teachings about the future of the Jews are not important, compared to Isaiah?

An unfortunate book by Robert Van Kampen (*The Sign*, Crossway Books 1992) has almost 500 quotes from Revelation, the most symbolic book in the New Testament. There are, by contrast, four quotes from Galatians, and three from Philippians. There are only thirteen quotes from Hebrews, but about 120 from Matthew 24 alone.

Dwight Pentecost, in his much larger textbook, *Things to Come*, has seven times more quotes from Isaiah than from the Gospel of John. Are futurists guilty of elevating the *fulfilled* words of the prophets above the words of Christ when dealing with end-times theology? *Does this explain why end-times books continually miss the mark?*

The Bible Tells Me So

> In the past [prophecy turned history] God spoke to our forefathers through the prophets at many times and in various ways, but in these last days he has spoken to us by his Son, whom he appointed heir of all things, and through whom he made the universe (Hebrews 1:1-2).

It's understandable that the disciples and all those following Jesus needed time to recognize who He really was. It took many lessons, many miracles, many personal conversations, and many rebukes for failure, in order to give Him the honor due Him. For instance, Jesus rebukes Philip by saying, "Don't you know me, Philip, even after I have been among you such a long time?" (John 14:9).

It's also understandable that in the minds of His companions whom Jesus was discipling, the Old Testament prophets were held in high regard – particularly so, Moses and Elijah. Poor Peter, there was another big lesson coming down the pike for him.

Peter, You and Your Big Mouth!

> Jesus took Peter, John, and James with him and went up onto a mountain to pray. As he was praying, the appearance of his face changed, and his clothes became as bright as a flash of lightning. Two men, Moses and Elijah, appeared in glorious splendor, talking with Jesus. They spoke about his departure, which he was about to bring *to fulfillment at Jerusalem.* Peter and his companions were very sleepy, but when they became fully awake, they saw his glory and the two men standing with him. As the men were leaving Jesus, Peter said to him, "Master, it is good for us to be here. Let us put up three shelters—one for you, one for Moses, and one for Elijah."
>
> While he was speaking, a cloud appeared and enveloped them, and they were afraid as they entered the cloud. A voice came from the cloud, saying, "This is my Son, whom I have chosen; listen to him." When the voice had spoken, they found that Jesus was alone. The disciples kept this to themselves, and told no one at that time what they had seen (Luke 9:28-36).

To look at this passage in context, Peter had acknowledged Jesus as the "Christ of God" eight days earlier. The disciples were then told not to be ashamed of Christ *and His words. Now they had to learn that Christ had the final authoritative word. He was the Word of God in the flesh.* Every prophecy in the Old Testament is either in the process of being, or has already been, fulfilled in Christ.

I can imagine that James and John were angry with Peter: *Peter, if you hadn't opened your big mouth, we could have enjoyed this extraordinary event much longer.*

If God wants to make something clear to His servants, He has unusual ways of doing so at His disposal, to make sure it sticks in their memories forever. This event, they remembered clearly.

What do we learn from this passage?

1. Both Moses and Elijah had asked God, during their life-times, to reveal His glory to them. They received the answer to their request when they met Christ, the glory of God.
2. Both had been faithful servants of God.
3. Both had faithfully proclaimed God's Word to His stiff-necked and sinful people.
4. Both left this earth in unusual ways.
5. Both now were put in their places, even though they were Old Testament superstars. However, they had no business being placed in the same category as Christ.
6. Both had their say in their day.
7. Now it's Christ's turn. *Listen to Him*! "This is my Son, whom I have chosen; listen to him." In Matthew's gospel, the account of this event finishes with these words: "When they looked up, *they saw no one except Jesus*" (Matthew 17:8).

This is the lesson of the New Testament—God's final word has become flesh. In futuristic, premillennial teaching, there's an obvious reluctance to listen to Christ, the one who has the first and final word about the beginning and the end of the world.

The Old Testament prophets must be interpreted in the light of, and consistent with, the teaching of Jesus. It's plain heresy to interpret the teaching of the prophets in a particular way, while contradicting the words of Christ.

A bad thing happens to good prophecy when it's not recognized that Abraham and his descendants were chosen by God to reveal Christ to the whole world. Like Cain did, heathen nations established unacceptable ceremonies and worshipped animals, ancestors, stars, etc. There was no hope for them to know the true God apart from Israel. For that all nations are thankful. The Glory of Israel, however, is Jesus Christ. Judaism has fulfilled her literal, unique, historical purpose—to bless all the nations of the world by Christ.

Thank You, Faithful Prophets

We should never ignore or disregard the Old Testament. The church would have no record of creative and redemptive history and, as already stated, we have all of it for our inspiration, prayer, warnings, hope, worship, etc. From the Old Testament, we discover the wonderful grace of Jesus.

Abraham and Moses knew about that grace. The Ten Commandments, as Calvin explained, give us a small reflection of the nature of God. And we could never do without the Psalms. When you read the Psalms, you're reading and praying at the same time.

However, as has been previously explained, the problem with dispensationalism causing all the confusion about the end times is that the physical reestablishment of Jews in Israel in 1948 is believed to be fulfilled prophecy and is inseparably connected with the Rapture, the seven-year Tribulation, the Second Coming, the Millennium, and eternity.

This is a wrong interpretation of Scripture. It doesn't fit. It's a bad thing to do to perfectly good prophecies.

If Jesus had never spoken to us, and if His words were only privately related to the apostles, even then, this system wouldn't fly. We honor and thank God for the prophets; we thank them for laying the groundwork that harmoniously, and without interruption, connects the old with the new.

However, there comes a time when God says, "Well done, good and faithful servants." There are mysteries that needed to be carefully revealed, a responsibility which belonged to the apostles. Look what Paul says to non-Jewish converted heathens:

> Remember that at that time you were separate from Christ, excluded from citizenship in Israel and foreigners to the covenants of the promise, without hope and without God in the world. But now in Christ Jesus you who once were far away have been brought near through the blood of Christ.
>
> For he himself is our peace, who has made the two one and has destroyed the barrier, the dividing wall of

hostility, its commandments and regulations. His purpose was to create in himself one new man out of the two, thus making peace, and in this one body to reconcile both of them to God through the cross, by which, he put to death their hostility. He came and preached peace to you who were far away (Gentiles) and peace to those who were near (Jews). For through him we both have access to the Father by one Spirit.

Consequently, you are no longer foreigners and aliens, but fellow citizens with God's people and members of God's household, built on the foundation (Revelation 21:14) of the apostles and prophets, with Christ Jesus himself as the chief cornerstone (Ephesians 2:12-20).

For this reason I, Paul, the prisoner of Christ Jesus for the sake of you Gentiles – Surely you have heard about the administration of God's grace that was given to me for you, that is, the mystery made known to me by revelation, as I have already written briefly. In reading this, then, you will be able to understand my insight into the mystery of Christ, which was not made known to men in other generations as it has now been revealed by the Spirit to God's holy apostles and prophets. *This mystery is that through the gospel the Gentiles are heirs together with Israel, members together of one body, and sharers together in the promise in Christ Jesus* (Ephesians 3:1-6).

This then is a somewhat comprehensive bird's eye view of what was divinely communicated to them. The prophets and apostles are inseparably linked throughout Scripture.

CHAPTER 13

A New Person Takes Center Stage

⊹⇥⊙⇤⊹

The Word became flesh
and lived for a while among us.
We have seen his glory,
the glory of the one and only Son,
who came from the Father,
full of grace and truth.
(John 1:14)

Enter the Final Prophet, the Exact Image of God

Simeon was a faithful old servant of God, one upon whom the Holy Spirit had come. The Holy Spirit was in the habit of revealing things to him, particularly things related to the coming Messiah. He was told he wouldn't die until he met the Lord's Christ. "Now there was a man in Jerusalem called Simeon, who was righteous and devout. He was waiting for the consolation of Israel, and the Holy Spirit was upon him" (Luke 2:25).

God, who is good at setting up divine appointments, created a situation that made Mary and Joseph and Simeon run into each other at the temple for Christ's circumcision. Simeon, inspired by the Holy Spirit, took baby Jesus in his arms and prayed a magnificent prayer of praise:

> "Sovereign Lord, as you have promised, you now dismiss your servant in peace. For my eyes have seen your salvation, which you have prepared in the sight of *all people*, a light for revelation to the Gentiles and *for glory to your people Israel*."

The child's father and mother marveled at what was said about him. Then Simeon blessed them and said to Mary, his mother, *"This child is destined to cause the falling and rising of many in Israel, and to be a sign that will be spoken against,* so that the thoughts of many hearts will be revealed. And a sword will pierce your own soul too"* (Luke 2:29-35).

Obviously, this Old Testament saint who happened to appear on New Testament pages realized, by the Holy Spirit, that the consolation of Israel, the salvation of all peoples and *the glory of Israel, is not real estate or a city or a temple, but Christ.* What a blessing this must have been for Simeon, this great Old Testament saint, to actually hold in his arms the baby he *knew* was the *consolation of Israel.* Israel's hope and consolation were never apart from the body of Christ.

Take note of a few more things that had come together prior to this glorious event at the temple.

The Absolutely Peerless Man

The unique difference between Jesus Christ and every other religious founder is that the virgin birth of Jesus had been prophesied for hundreds of years, climaxed and made visible by a forerunner who was divinely prophesied also in Scripture. Random religious founders around the world had no anticipated coming, but had to introduce themselves to the world cold turkey. Among these are Buddha, Muhammad, Joseph Smith, Mr. Moon. No living people or nations in the world were expecting Buddha, Muhammad, or any other self-appointed so-called enlightened ones.

There are three other distinctions between Christ and all other religious founders and self-proclaimed messiahs. First, every leader of every cult and false religion had to make sure they had as many converts at the time of their deaths as possible.

Christ, on the other hand, made no such frenzied attempt to gain converts, and at the time of His death, He was virtually alone. Only the apostle John, His mother, and perhaps a few other women were there to mourn His death. Christ was so certain about His resurrection, there was no need for a big crowd to attend His death.

Second, Christ had absolute confidence in the follow-up ministry of the Holy Spirit, who, in Christ's absence, would point people to Christ, and regenerate them by the millions.

Third, all self-appointed pretenders who claim divine authority need to make sure people remember their lives and actions. Not so with Christ. The last thing He said at the table to the disciples was, *"Remember my death until I come."*

> **A bad thing happens to a good prophecy when those prophecies are claimed and distorted by false teachers of new religions for the purpose of emphasizing their own lives. Christ only emphasizes His significant, purposeful, prophesied, redemptive, substitutionary death.**

It's very obvious to anyone reading the Bible that the great hatred the unbelieving Jews and Gentiles had for Jesus wasn't because of what He did, but because of what He said. One example is enough to understand the many eyeball-to-eyeball confrontations with unbelievers:

> "Abraham is our father," they answered. "If you were Abraham's children," said Jesus, "then you would do the things Abraham did. As it is, you are determined to kill me, a man who has told you the truth that I heard from God. Abraham did not do such things. You are doing the things your own father does." "We are not illegitimate children," they protested. "The only Father we have is God himself."
>
> Jesus said to them, "If God were your Father, you would love me, for I came from God and now am

> here. I have not come on my own; but he sent me. Why is my language not clear to you? Because you are unable to hear what I say. You belong to your father, the devil, and you want to carry out your father's desire. He was a murderer from the beginning, not holding to the truth, for there is no truth in him. When he lies, he speaks his native language, for he is a liar and the father of lies. Yet because I tell the truth, you do not believe me! Can any of you prove me guilty of sin? If I am telling the truth, why don't you believe me? He who belongs to God hears what God says. The reason you do not hear is that *you do not belong to God*" (John 8:39-47).

Those are fighting words, fearless words, loving words, for love rejoices in the truth. Jesus was not hated for healing people, but for piercing unbelieving Jews with the truth of God.

The Discriminating Shepherd

A similar situation developed between Jesus and unbelieving Jews when He claimed He was the shepherd of the Old Testament's Psalm 23. Christ tried to explain to them that it was no longer a private relationship between a special king and his God, but now He described that this relationship has to do with all those who follow Him: "My sheep listen to my voice; I know them, and they follow me. I give them eternal life, and they shall never perish; no one can snatch them out of my hand" (John 10:27).

Just prior to that, He said to those who did not follow Him: "...but you do not believe because you are not my sheep" (John 10:26).

In the eternal covenant between God the Father, the Son, and the Holy Spirit, the exact number and names of the sheep were sovereignly determined. These lost sheep, because of the Fall, needed to be brought back by Christ, and He redeemed them with His own blood. When Christ came to this world, judgment began: "This is the verdict: Light has come into the world, but men loved darkness instead of light because their deeds were evil" (John 3:19).

Here, then, is a vivid historical situation where Jesus judges, or differentiates, between those who are His sheep and those who are not.

This is partially what He focused on in His great high priestly prayer in John 17:

> After Jesus said this, he looked toward heaven and prayed: "Father, the time has come. Glorify your Son, that your Son may glorify you. For you granted him authority over all people that he might give eternal life to all those you have given him. Now this is eternal life: that they may know you, the only true God, and Jesus Christ, whom you have sent. *I have brought you glory on earth by completing the work you gave me to do.* And now, Father, glorify me in your presence with the glory I had with you before the world began" (John 17:1-5).

Now what do we learn from the prayer of this discriminating good shepherd?

1. He was given authority over all flesh. That is, every nation, Jew and Gentile alike.
2. He bestows eternal life to those the Father gave Him. Eternal life is an act of God, not an act of man. It's like birth.
3. Eternal life is equated with knowing the Father and the Son in a believing relationship.
4. Christ claims to have *completed* the work God gave Him to do. That's why the cover of this book states that Christ said, "It is finished," not, "So far, so good."

A bad thing happens to good prophecy when the purpose of Christ is divided into two categories; one for the Jews, and one for the rest of the world. From the overall teaching of Scripture, we learn that both Jew and Gentile were equally rejected because of unbelief and equally accepted because of faith and trust in Christ.

"Abraham believed God and it was credited to him as righteousness" (Romans 4:3).

"After Zacchaeus repented, Jesus said, 'Today salvation has come to this house, because this man, *too, is a son of Abraham*'" (Luke 19:9).

The belief of dispensationalism is simply this: that God has a different plan for Gentiles than for the Jews. The futurists have tried to prove this by careful manipulation of many different Bible passages, cutting out and putting together unrelated paragraphs, mostly from the Old Testament, and a few from the New Testament. They call this "rightly dividing the word of truth." But it's *wrongly* dividing the word of truth.

Rightly dividing the word of truth doesn't mean cutting up the Scriptures into thousands of literal and symbolic phrases, but making a clear distinction between the Old and New Testaments.

Keep in mind the historical situation and dates if possible. Don't make the books and prophesies meaningless to the original recipients. Such is obviously the habit of dispensationalism, with Daniel, Ezekiel, and especially the book of Revelation. We may ask what blessing the book of Revelation is to the seven churches when, according to Van Kampen, the antichrist is Hitler who will come to life again.

The Bible says: "He was in the world, and though the world was made through Him, the world did not recognize Him. He came to that which was His own, but His own did not receive Him. Yet to all who received Him, to those who believed in His name, He gave the right to become children of God; children born not of natural descent, nor of human decision or a husband's will, but born of God" (John 1:10-13).

We learn from this:

1. The world did not recognize Jesus.
2. The Jews, with few exceptions, rejected Him.
3. Belief in Christ is universal and international.
4. The legal right to belong to God as a son is worldwide.

5. Natural descent has nothing to do with it.
6. Belief in Christ is not based on a human decision.
7. It is a new birth, and that's God's business.

CHAPTER 14

God's Word: Handle with Care

⊷⟾⟽⊷

For the word of God is living and active.
Sharper than any double-edged sword,
it penetrates
even to dividing soul and spirit,
joints and marrow;
it judges the thoughts
and attitudes of the heart.

Nothing in all creation is hidden
from God's sight.

Everything is uncovered and laid bare
before the eyes of him
to whom we must give account.
(Hebrews 4:12-13)

When Bad Things Happen to Lonely Verses

One of the major characteristics of dispensational teaching is crisscrossing Bible verses. In other words, it's going from Old Testament to New Testament and back again – Ezekiel, Matthew, Daniel, Revelation, back and forth, one verse from here, one verse from there. "Rightly dividing the word of truth" becomes, in effect, cutting in pieces the revealed and systematic word of truth.

More importantly, when a verse or a paragraph is all by itself, an orphan with no support anywhere else in Scripture, like a lone ranger, don't build a theology on it. It's a foundation of one brick. Take, for example, the term "Great Tribulation," where a whole new theology is built on the adjective "great."

Conversely, some statements or verses are interpreted as if they're orphans or lonely verses when they're not. Romans 11:26 is one example. A verse looked upon or treated in isolation, and interpreted that way, may mean completely the opposite. We'll say more about that in the next chapter.

So grab a cup of coffee or tea, get comfortable in your favorite chair, take your Bible and let's read through the writings of Paul in First and Second Thessalonians, and John in the Revelation of Jesus Christ. You need to do this without jumping or skipping from one book to the other.

You must always ask the question: *"What was the meaning of the book for the first recipients of that book?"* For example, Christ's first words to John in Revelation 1:1 are "...what must soon take place." The word translated as *soon* also means with haste, quick, or without delay.

Things to Study from a Letter to the "Model" Church

Turn now to the book of 1 Thessalonians:

2:14-16	Strong words from a converted Jew about unconverted Jews. The wrath of God has come upon them. So much for being the apple of God's eye.
4:13-15	The final coming will be very noisy, very well orchestrated, and every Christian will recognize the voice of Christ. The righteous will join Him and be with the Lord forever (not just a thousand years).
4:16-17	Please take note again that this coming of Christ for believers will be listened to and heard by those who are familiar with His voice and will not be understood by unbelievers. (Is there another biblical example of this historical phenomenon? Yes, at the conversion of Saul of Tarsus, as described in Acts 9:7. Paul heard the voice of Christ, but the people around him heard thundering sounds only.)
4:18	Be encouraged by Christ's final coming.
5:2-3	His coming will be unexpected. Those left behind will not go through a tribulation period, but will be

158

	destroyed.
5:9	Salvation by Christ is the only means to escape God's wrath.
5:19-20	To be filled with the fire of the Spirit, you will treat God's Word with respect.

There is nothing here about the so-called Rapture.

Consider These Verses from a Letter to the Worried Model Church

Now let's look at 2 Thessalonians:

1:7-10	The Lord Jesus will be revealed from heaven in blazing fire. He will punish, with total destruction, those who don't know God and don't obey the gospel. There'll be no second chance in some sort of millennial kingdom here. There will be only believers left to perfectly glorify our Lord. Unbelievers will be taken or snatched away. This is the diametrical opposite of the so-called secret, silent Rapture.
2:1-14	This is a much quoted chapter. Let me give a few suggestions: (1) Verse 2: Don't get alarmed or excited. (2) Verse 3: No one knows exactly who or what this is. Is it secular humanism? Whatever he is or whatever it is, it's nothing new (verse 7). Christ will destroy him (or it) very easily by the breath of His mouth and the splendor of His coming. (3) Verse 4: The evil one will appeal to all those who delight in evil.
2:16-17	Learn these verses by heart.

The Left Behind *bestsellers are based on a questionable interpretation of those lonely verses found in First and Second Thessalonians, nowhere else.* Comparing Scripture with Scripture will avoid serious misunderstanding of God's holy and divinely inspired Word. Not to do so has good prophesies changing into bad and deceptive fantasies.

The last words of Christ to John were, "He who testifies to these things says, 'Yes, I am coming soon.' Amen. Come Lord Jesus" (Revelation 22:20).

If you read books by Tim LaHaye, who claims that Christ's words were meant for this day and climaxed in this age, then *how can John give comfort to the original recipients of the book of Revelation?* We know Christ did come in judgment on Jerusalem. Christ did come to receive His disciples as He promised He would in John 14. (This does *not* mean that Christ has already come again for His bride, the whole church.)

> "Do not let your hearts be troubled. Trust in God; trust also in me. In my Father's house are many rooms; if it were not so, I would have told you. I am going there to prepare a place for you. And if I go and prepare a place for you, I will come back and take you to be with me that you also may be where I am. You know the way to the place where I am going" (John 14:1-4).

Note: because these disciples of Jesus are no longer walking around Jerusalem, then Jesus fulfilled His promise to them and must have come for them. They have, *in effect*, experienced His second coming. We can even say that their rapture took place two thousand years ago.

The Revelation of Jesus Christ, a Book of Symbolism

The Book of Revelation of Jesus Christ is exactly what the introduction spells out (Revelation 1:1). It's the Revelation of Jesus Christ. It's primarily about Jesus, but in a totally different way than the Gospels. It's written in symbolic style but understood by the seven churches.

In the Gospels, we see Christ as the Son of God and the Son of Man – literally. The Gospels show Christ on earth, consequently the soil on which he walked became holy because of his presence. Just like the situation when the Lord met with Moses, he was told to take off his shoes, for that little spot had become holy, temporarily.

After Christ's ascension into heaven, the Holy Land became unholy, just like any other square foot of earthly soil.

The Book of Revelation of Jesus Christ deals with the ministry, the warfare, the judgment, the victory of Jesus Christ in the heavenly realms, hidden from our physical sight. But as Paul warned us, it is perceived spiritually.

> For our struggle is not against flesh and blood, but against the rulers, against the authorities, against the powers of this dark world and against the spiritual forces of evil in the heavenly realms (Ephesians 6:12)

Revelation therefore has to be handled differently than, for example, the Book of Acts. A further comparison may be helpful. For instance, look at the letter of Paul to the Corinthians, which is clearly addressed to Christians – past, present and future. Then look at the letter headed "Hebrews." It isn't addressed to Christians, but is a general message about Christ and, more or less, a sermon for believers and unbelievers full of promises, blessing and terrible warnings.

These two books are handled differently, for Hebrews 10:31, "It's a dreadful thing to fall into the hands of the living God," doesn't apply to born-again Christians. It's a warning to non-believers.

Now back to the Book of Revelation of Jesus Christ, which promises a blessing to believing readers, and yet stays on bookshelves gathering dust or is mostly wrongly interpreted. Why is that so?

There are three major difficulties, unique to Revelation, which need to be addressed.

1. Late dating.

Giving the book a late date, after the fall of Jerusalem, leaves a terrible void, a big gap, for the judgment of God upon Jerusalem to which Jesus referred as the "beginning of birth pains" (Matthew 24:5) is totally missing. Birth pains are the signs of new life, a new beginning. In those days, the death of the mother and life to an infant was an often painful common occurrence. It deals with the end of Judaism and the beginning of the third Revelation period.

Get a copy of Dr. Kenneth L. Gentry's book, "Before Jerusalem Fell," and be convinced and blessed.

2. Robbing the church of its relevance in every age.

The Revelation of Jesus Christ was written for the churches of that day and every church since that day. Right at the end, in Revelation 22:16, we're told: "I, Jesus, have sent my angel to give you this testimony for the churches. I am the Root and the Offspring of David, and the Bright Morning Star."

It speaks to all churches throughout the whole New Testament church age. For all churches in every age need a picture of the conquering Savior in or behind the clouds. Unfortunately, dispensationalism teaches that the book only deals with the seven churches mentioned, and only up through Chapter 3. The rest of Revelation's nineteen chapters are claimed to be about the future, including the Great Tribulation and the Thousand Year Kingdom.

This is where a major problem lies. In Chapter 4:1, we read: "After this I looked, and there before me was a door standing open in heaven. And the voice I had first heard speaking to me like a trumpet said, 'Come up here, and I will show you what must take place after this.'" It was only a vision; John never left Planet Earth.

Futuristic prophetic preaching is based on this very serious literal interpretation of Revelation 4:1. The argument is that when John is told, "Come up here," that is the Rapture of the church. This raises a very troublesome issue, and is totally without warrant, and void of normal interpretation of Scripture. One may ask, since when has the apostle John become the embodiment of the church, as a representative of all of Christendom?

Consequently, we're now faced with a whole new theological system, by which the whole message of the Revelation of Jesus Christ is taken away and withheld from two thousand years of Christendom until the Rapture. Obviously, it's erroneously built on three words: "Come up here."

3. Careless literal interpretation.

It's the result of a failure to investigate where strange things are first used and, rather than looking at them literally, one must understand them functionally and, most often, spiritually. For example: "The mystery of the seven stars that you saw in my right hand and of the seven golden lampstands is this: The seven stars are the angels of the seven churches, and the seven lampstands are the seven churches" (Revelation 1:20).

So then, very carefully and plainly, we learn about the key to interpret the Revelation of Jesus Christ. The seven stars aren't really stars, but messengers to each congregation. The seven lampstands aren't lampstands, but seven light-bearing congregations.

Look at Chapter 6:2 of Revelation, "I looked, and there before me was a white horse! Its rider held a bow, and he was given a crown, and he rode out as a conqueror bent on conquest."

To interpret this literally makes no sense. It should be interpreted symbolically or functionally. For He is our conquering Savior, the King of Kings and Lord of Lords, who doesn't need a physical white beast to get around. But to the church of the first century, a king sat on a white horse, and there was nothing that could move faster.

The Book of Revelation of Jesus Christ shouts to its readers: "Do not interpret me literally."

Failure to interpret Revelation symbolically where needed is very troublesome dogma, built on faulty interpretation of Scripture. And that's a major reason why the relentless promises of the imminent return of Jesus Christ prove to be wrong all the time.

CHAPTER 15

Those Confusing Pearly Gates

⊷══◯══⊷

I did not see a temple in the city, because the Lord God Almighty and the Lamb are its temple.

The city does not need the sun or the moon to shine on it, for the glory of God gives it light, and the Lamb is its lamp.

The nations will walk by its light, and the kings of the earth will bring their splendor into it.
(Revelation 21:22-24)

Crying for the Wrong Reason at the Wrong Time in the Wrong Place

You've destroyed the most important and exciting part of my Bible," said a tearful woman to her pastor as she was leaving the church after worship.

"My dear lady," he said, "what do you mean?"

"About the new Jerusalem and heaven and seeing Jesus," she said in obvious frustration.

"Please let me talk to you as soon as the last person who wants to greet me has left. If you'll take a seat in the back pew, I'll be with you in a moment."

After a few minutes, the pastor returned to her, sat down, and said, "I'm so sorry, but I have no idea how I could have hurt you so badly."

"Well," she said, "I've been a Christian, a Bible-believing Christian, since early childhood. The thing I've been most excited about is that at death, I'll go through the pearly gates, walk on streets of pure, solid gold, eat from the tree of life, drink from the river of living water, and enjoy the presence of Christ in the New Jerusalem.

"Now you're saying there's no such physical thing at all. I think this is a liberal church, for I don't see too many people upset the way I am. I'm sorry, sir, but I think I'll have to join a Bible-believing church, because all these things are clearly promised in the book of Revelation."

"Oh now, let's talk about this for a moment," said the pastor. "First of all, I'm a conservative Bible-believing fundamentalist, and so is all the leadership of this congregation."

"It doesn't sound like it," she said.

"Please let me explain and reassure you. I'm sure we'll agree that both of us have accepted many literally described things in Scripture in non-literal ways. Christians have readily accepted them in a metaphorical way, without fear of destroying the Bible, or being accused of liberalism."

"What things?" she asked.

"To illustrate my point, let me ask you a few questions."

"Are you and your garments washed in the blood?"

"Yes!"

"Are you in Christ?"

"Yes!

"Have you been crucified with Christ?"

"Yes!"

"Are you a sheep or a goat?"

"A sheep."

"Are you born again?"

"Yes!"

"Okay, now let's look at your answers. Will you agree that you've never been literally washed in blood, or crucified, and that you're not a sheep?"

"Yes, of course."

"Nevertheless, your answers were correct, because you realized that my questions, based entirely on Scripture, were meant to be taken metaphorically or symbolically."

"Now, I can see what you're getting at," she said.

"Now then," he continued, "at the end of your life, you'll enter the Father's house. This is the term Jesus gave to heaven where God dwells. The Father's house is *not* the New Jerusalem of Revelation. The New Jerusalem replaces the Old Jerusalem, of which some of the temple foundations still exist and are valued by many Jews. First, there's the physical Jerusalem of the Old Testament. Then there's the New Jerusalem of the New Testament.

"The New Jerusalem Abraham looked forward to is a spiritual one which Christ is building and came down from heaven. It's a biblical description of the church made up of born-again worshippers. It's called the body of Christ, the bride, the kingdom, where Christ is the light or the way.

"The Bible says *the Lamb is the Lamp.* Didn't Christ say plainly, 'I am the Light of the world, he that followeth me shall not walk in darkness'? He didn't say, 'I am the light of heaven.' It's a place of healing for the nations. There's no longer any need for healing in God's house in heaven. This New Jerusalem is the place where God is pleased to be, where He wipes tears from eyes.

"Now, dear lady, let's talk about the streets of pure gold and pearly gates. Don't you see that if streets are made of earthly gold, and if pearls are on the gates, it means those highly desired riches of the world have no spiritual value in the New Jerusalem. There is no spiritual value of things unconverted people outside the city will sell their souls for."

"It seems very strange to me. I've never heard this before, but it doesn't make any sense," she said.

With a reassuring smile the pastor said, "You *are* walking on streets of gold. You've already walked through the pearly gates. Christ is your light; you're a living temple in which the Lord dwells. You're constantly drinking the living water of God's Word, and you've eaten from the tree of life."

> Blessed are those who wash their robes, that they may have the right to the tree of life and may go through the gates into the city (Revelation 22:14).

"All this was so beautifully written in symbolic words two thousand years ago and up to today people have been part of that spiritual household. It was promised to the churches that existed when the book of Revelation of Jesus Christ was first received. Walking through the Pearly Gates happens at conversion, when Christ, the Spiritual Pearl of great price, is embraced. Worldly wealth, pearls and gold no longer have any spiritual value."

Amazed, she said, "Well, what do you know? It makes good sense. I've got to stop dragging earthly things and values into the spiritual realm. It's like pulling heaven down to earth. I have a bad habit of crying for the wrong reason, in the wrong place, at the wrong time."

"You've got it," said the pastor. "Well, you stopped crying and God has wiped away your tears. Here, let me read something to you. 'The Spirit and the bride say, "Come." And let him who hears say, "Come." Whoever is thirsty let him come. And whoever wishes, let him take the free gift of the water of life.' That's from Revelation 22:17 and is now available for all believers."

And here we may very well see an important key to why bad things happen to good prophecies— rightly dividing the Word of Truth doesn't mean cutting the Bible up in thousands of verses. Rightly dividing or correctly handling the Word of Truth cannot mean any more than making a clear distinction between the Old and New Testaments, between fulfilled and unfulfilled revelatory periods, and between literal and spiritual interpretation of divine inspiration. Take the words of the Son of God as final authority, over everything that has been said by prophets in the fulfilled past (Hebrews 1:1).

The Tree of Life

After the rebellion of Adam and Eve: The Lord God made garments of skin for Adam and his wife and clothed them. And the Lord God said, "The man has now become like one of us, knowing good and evil. He must not be allowed to reach out his hand and take also from the tree of life and eat, and live forever." So the Lord God banished him from the Garden of Eden to work the ground from which he had been taken. After He drove the man out, He placed on the east side of the Garden of Eden cherubim and a flaming sword flashing back and forth to guard the way to the tree of life.

It was a great thing for man that he could thus read so clearly his original destination to immortality. He knew that if he had remained steadfast in his allegiance to God, abiding in the order appointed for him, he should have continued to possess life in incorrupt purity and blessedness, possibly also might have been conscious of a growing enlargement and elevation of its powers and functions. But choosing the perilous course of transgression, he forfeited his inheritance of life, and became subject to the threatened penalty of death. The tree of life, however, did not lose its life-sustaining virtue because the condition on which man's right to partake of it had been violated. It remained what God originally made it. And though effectual precautions must now be taken to guard the center of the garden, the object of fond aspirations as well as hallowed recollections— though enshrined in a sacredness which rendered it for the present inaccessible to fallen man. *Why should its place have been so carefully preserved? And the symbols of worship, the emblems of fear and hope, planted in the very way that led to it? Why, but to intimate that the privilege of partaking of its immortal fruit was only for a season withheld—not finally withdrawn—waiting till a righteousness should be brought in, which might again open the way to its blessed provisions.* For as the loss of righteousness had shut up the way, it was manifest that only by the *possession of righteousness* could a fresh access to the *forfeited boon be regained*" (Patrick Fairbairn, *Typology of Scripture*, page 210).

Fairbairn points out that the preference of consumption of the Tree of Life is only withheld for a season. It turns out that the other or second Tree of Life is Jesus, who said, "I am the way, the truth, the life" (John 14:6), and also "and this is my body" (Matthew 26:26).

How Holy Is the Holy Land?

Over the last two thousand years, there's been unmitigated confusion caused by anti-biblical behavior and an attachment to divinely discarded Jewish things. Human and ecclesiastic entanglement with fleshly, emotionally useless Jewish paraphernalia, claimed to still have divine sanction and importance, has stifled the gospel in many nations.

In modern days, this false, stubborn opinion of dispensationalism has communicated, particularly to Arab and Islamic nations, that the Creator God of the universe still loves Jacob only and still hates Esau. This unchristian, perpetual, false and "other gospel" generated the Crusades and continues today, inflaming Islamic hatred for Jesus Christ.

Is it true that Jerusalem of today (called Sodom and Egypt, in Revelation 11:8), is more holy than Cairo, Mecca, Paris, Amsterdam, New Orleans, Moscow, and Rome? Certainly, all the big cities in the world are strongholds of Satan, and many millions of lost people wallow up to their eyeballs in sin. However, in those same cities are millions of holy people, regenerated, sanctified, and declared holy by God. No nation in the world is today void of holy people.

Consequently, since the resurrection of Christ, the only holy things that remain are holy people, engaged in true spiritual worship.

Jesus, speaking to a Samaritan woman, declared: "Believe me, woman, a time is coming when you will worship the Father neither on this mountain nor in Jerusalem. You Samaritans worship what you do not know; we worship what we do know, for salvation is from the Jews. Yet a time is coming and has now come when the true worshippers will worship the Father in spirit and truth, for they are the kind of worshippers the Father seeks. God is spirit, and his worshippers must worship in spirit and in truth" (John 4:21-24).

It's truly remarkable that the most profound and godly instruction about true worship of God was given by Christ, not to a high priest, but to an immoral non-Jewish woman. The value of true worship has to be consistent with the nature of God. God is Spirit.

Let's close this chapter with Paul's testimony:

> But whatever was to my profit I now consider loss for the sake of Christ. What is more, I consider everything a loss compared to the surpassing greatness of knowing Christ Jesus my Lord, for whose sake I have lost all things. I consider them rubbish, that I may gain Christ and be found in him, not having righteousness of my own that comes from the law, but that which is though faith in Christ—the righteousness that comes from God and is by faith (Philippians 3:7-9).

CHAPTER 16

Out of Context

⊷⇌⇋⊶

"The time is coming," declares the Lord, "when I
will make a new covenant with
the house of Israel and with the house of Judah.
It will not be like the covenant I made with their forefathers
when I took them by the hand to lead them out of Egypt,
because they broke my covenant, though I was a husband to
them," declares the Lord.
"This is the covenant I will make with the house of Israel after
that time," declares the Lord.
"I will put my law in their minds and write it on their hearts.
I will be their God, and they will be my people.
No longer will a man teach his neighbor, or a man his brother,
saying, 'Know the Lord,'
because they will all know me, from the least of them to the
greatest," declares the Lord.
"For I will forgive their wickedness and will remember
their sins no more."
(Jeremiah 31:31-34)

Israel's Door is Still Open

D o you believe the Bible is the infallibly inspired true word of
God?" said a man to a preacher after the worship service.

"Of course I do," said the preacher.

"So if I read something from the Bible, do you believe it?" said
the man.

"Yes!" answered the preacher.

Opening his Bible to Romans 11:26, he read, "And so all Israel
will be saved." Looking at the pastor he said, "End of argument,"

slammed his Bible shut and walked off without another word.

The flabbergasted preacher thought, "How on earth, Lord, am I going to help that man?"

This, however, isn't simply an isolated, unpublished, wrong use of Scripture. Steve Schlissel and David Brown's book, "Hal Lindsey and the Restoration of the Jews," begins, in the preface, exactly the same way: "And so all Israel shall be saved..."

However, to lift one brief statement completely out of its context and declare it to be fact is erroneous and misleading.

Chapters 9, 10, and 11 of Romans comprise one unit, dealing with one issue. Nothing can be interpreted apart from the whole. Because, just prior to Paul's deep emotional doxology (Romans 11:33-36) are the dispensationalist's and premillennialist's favorite verses: Romans 11:25-26. Much is made of these two verses and they're always interpreted in a certain way, and interpreted in isolation from Romans 9:1.

> I do not want you to be ignorant of this mystery, brothers, so that you may not be conceited: Israel has experienced a hardening in part until the full number of the Gentiles has come in. And so all Israel will be saved... (Romans 11:25-26a).

> Oh, the depth of the riches of the wisdom and knowledge of God! How unsearchable his judgments, and his paths beyond tracing out! "Who has known the mind of the Lord? Or who has been his Counselor? Who has ever given to God, that God should repay him?" For from him and through him and to him are all things. To him be the glory forever! Amen. (Romans 11:33-36).

The translators of the NIV have headed this section (verses 25-32) with the words, *All Israel Will Be Saved*. This is a dispensational heading, and will cause a wrong interpretation.

The *New Scofield Reference Bible* (King James Version) has the heading, *Israel Is Yet To Be Saved Nationally*. This is, of course, a worse dispensational heading, and will result in the same misunderstandings that many have about national Israel of today.

The New King James (1983) has entitled it, *Israel's Rejection Not Final*. This is a better heading, which allows the Bible to say what it wants to say.

It's important to recognize that these headings are *not* part of the Greek manuscripts, but are the arbitrary opinions of translators. No wonder the average Bible-believing Christian is confused. Ezekiel 39:23 says all Israel died by the sword. Why isn't there a heading by the NIV translators: *All Israel Is Dead*, or *All Israel Died*?

The Key Is in the Context

Questions from Romans 9 to be carefully considered in light of chapters 10 and 11:

> I speak the truth in Christ—I am not lying, my conscience confirms it in the Holy Spirit—I have great sorrow and unceasing anguish in my heart. For I could wish that *I myself were cursed and cut off from Christ for the sake of my brothers,* those of my own race, the people of Israel. Theirs is the adoption as sons; theirs the divine glory, the covenants, the receiving of the law, the temple worship and the promises. Theirs are the patriarchs, and from them is traced the human ancestry of Christ, who is God over all, forever praised! Amen. (Romans 9:1-5)

> *Observe! Why would Paul have great sorrow and unceasing anguish and be willing to be cursed for them if, in his heart, he believed that "all Israel," that is, the Jewish nation, would be saved?*

Then, the *all* of Romans 11:2 must mean *remnant* only. Remember, God used the 7,000 remnant Jews to encourage Elijah and release him from his sorrow. If Paul believed all Israel was going to be saved, would he not rejoice with exceeding joy at the prospect of seeing his kinfolk acknowledging Christ as their Messiah?

175

However, Romans 9:6 states clearly: "It is not as though God's word had failed. *For not all who are descended from Israel are Israel.*"

It's not the natural children of Abraham who are God's children. Abraham's spiritual children and God's children are one and the same. Compare Romans 9:6-8 with John 1:10-13 again:

> He was in the world, and though the world was made through him, the world did not recognize him. He came to that which was his own, but his own did not receive him. Yet to all who received him, to those who believed on his name, he gave the right to become children of God—children born not of *natural descent, nor of human decision or a husband's will, but born of God* (John 1:10-13).

Then, we read in Romans 9:17-24:

> For the Scripture says to Pharaoh: "I raised you up for this very purpose, that I might display my power in you and that my name might be proclaimed in all the earth." Therefore God has mercy on whom he wants to have mercy, and he hardens whom he wants to harden.
>
> One of you will say to me: "Then why does God still blame us? For who resists his will?" But who are you, O man, to talk back to God? Shall what is formed say to him who formed it, "Why did you make me like this?" Does not the potter have the right to make out of the same lump of clay some pottery for noble purposes and some for common use?
>
> What if God, choosing to show his wrath and make his power known, bore with great patience the objects of his wrath—prepared for destruction? What if he did this to make the riches of his glory known to the objects of his mercy, whom he prepared in advance for glory—even us, whom he also called, not only

from the Jews but also from the Gentiles?

If God raised up Pharaoh to proclaim His name and destroyed him to save Israel, can He not also destroy Israel and save Egypt? God does say "...Egypt my people..." (Isaiah 19:25). Is this not what is meant by Romans 9:25, "You who were not my people are my people"?

> As he says in Hosea: "I will call them 'my people' who are not my people; and I will call her, 'my loved one', who is not my loved one,"
>
> and, "It will happen that in the very place where it was said to them, 'You are not my people,' they will be called 'sons of the living God.'"
>
> Isaiah cries out concerning Israel: "Though the number of the Israelites be like the sand by the sea, only the remnant will be saved. For the Lord will carry out his sentence on earth with speed and finality."
>
> It is just as Isaiah said previously: "Unless the Lord Almighty had left us descendants, we would have become like Sodom, we would have been like Gomorrah" (Romans 9:25-29).

Both Jew and Gentile are objects of God's mercy. They are both one nation under God with liberty, grace, and mercy for all. Does this not negate ethnic privilege?

> What then shall we say? That the Gentiles, who did not pursue righteousness, have obtained it, a righteousness that is by faith; but Israel, who pursued a law of righteousness, has not attained it. Why not? Because they pursued it not by faith but as if it were by works. They stumbled over the "stumbling stone." As it is written: "See, I lay in Zion a stone that causes

177

men to stumble and a rock that makes them fall, and the one who trusts in him will never be put to shame" (Romans 9:30-33)

The stumbling stone is the Rock, Jesus Christ (see 1 Corinthians 1:23). If Christ is not the stumbling stone, then who or what is?

> The LORD spoke to me with his strong hand upon me, warning me not to follow the way of this people. He said: "Do not call conspiracy everything that these people call conspiracy; do not fear what they fear, and do not dread it. The LORD Almighty is the one you are to regard as holy, he is the one you are to fear, he is the one you are to dread, and he will be a sanctuary; but for both houses of Israel he will be a stone that causes men to stumble and a rock that makes them fall. And for the people of Jerusalem he will be a trap and a snare. Many of them will stumble; they will fall and be broken, they will be snared and captured." Bind up the testimony and seal up the law among my disciples. I will wait for the LORD, who is hiding his face from the house of Jacob. I will put my trust in him (Isaiah 8:11-17).

Questions from Romans 10 that need to be considered in the light of chapters 9 and 11:

Romans 10:1-2: "Brothers, my heart's desire and prayer to God for the Israelites is that they may be saved. For I can testify about them that they are zealous for God, but their zeal is not based on knowledge."

Paul prays for Israel's salvation because of their misplaced zeal. Paul is speaking from experience—remember that he, too, was a Jew with misplaced zeal when on his way to Damascus to kill Christians (Acts 9).

Meanwhile, Saul was still breathing out murderous

threats against the Lord's disciples. He went to the high priest and asked him for letters to the synagogues in Damascus, so that if he found any there who belonged to the Way, whether men or women, he might take them as prisoners to Jerusalem. As he neared Damascus on his journey, suddenly a light from heaven flashed around him. He fell to the ground and heard a voice say to him, "Saul, Saul, why do you persecute me?"

"Who are you, Lord?" Saul asked. "I am Jesus, whom you are persecuting," he replied. "Now get up and go into the city, and you will be told what you must do." (Acts 9:1-6)

Moses describes in this way the righteousness that is by the law: "The man who does these things will live by them." But the righteousness that is by faith says: "Do not say in your heart, 'Who will ascend into heaven?'" (that is, to bring Christ down) "or 'Who will descend into the deep?'" (that is, to bring Christ up from the dead). But what does it say? "The word is near you; it is in your mouth and in your heart," that is, the word of faith we are proclaiming: That if you confess with your mouth, "Jesus is Lord," and believe in your heart that God raised him from the dead, you will be saved. For it is with your heart that you believe and are justified, and it is with your mouth that you confess and are saved. As the Scripture says, "Anyone who trusts in him will never be put to shame" (Romans 10:5-11).

Salvation comes to the heart and is acknowledged by the mouth, and anyone can put their faith in Christ. "For there is no difference between Jew and Gentile—the same Lord is Lord of all and richly blesses all who call on him, for, 'Everyone who calls on the name of the Lord will be saved'" (Romans 10:12-13).

There is no difference between Jew and Gentile. Why would Paul contradict himself by emphasizing an artificial, unbiblical distinction again in the future?

> For I do not desire, brethren, that you should be ignorant of this mystery, lest you should be wise in your own opinion, that blindness in part has happened to Israel until the fullness of the Gentiles has come in. And so all Israel will be saved, as it is written: "The deliverer will come from Zion; he will turn ungodliness from Jacob (Romans 11:25-26, New King James Version).

> How, then, can they call on the one they have not believed in? And how can they believe in the one of whom they have not heard? And how can they hear without someone preaching to them? And how can they preach unless they are sent? As it is written, "How beautiful are the feet of those who bring good news!" (Romans 10:14-15)

> But not all the Israelites accepted the good news. For Isaiah says, "Lord, who has believed our message?" Consequently, faith comes from hearing the message, and the message is heard through the word of Christ. But I ask: Did they not hear? Of course they did: "Their voice has gone out into all the earth, their words to the ends of the world.

> Again I ask: Did Israel not understand? First, Moses says, "I will make you envious by those who are not a nation; I will make you angry by a nation that has no understanding."

> And Isaiah boldly says, "I was found by those who did not seek me; I revealed myself to those who did not ask for me."

> But concerning Israel he says, "All day long I have held out my hands to a disobedient and obstinate people" (Romans 10:16-21).

The non-Jews have always been more responsive to the gospel. (Approximately eight percent of Egypt is Christian; there are only a few thousand Christians in Israel).

Thoughts from Romans 11 for our careful consideration of chapters 9 and 10:

Israel is not totally rejected by God. Paul stresses the point that *just because you are a Jew does not mean you cannot be saved.* "I am an Israelite; I have not been rejected [Paul says]. I repented, I believed, and claimed God's promise and gift to His people." Isaiah 59:20: "...the Redeemer will come to Zion, to those in Jacob who repent of their sins," declares the Lord.

BUT: Paul *believed* in Christ. He *obeyed* Him; he *acknowledged Him as the Messiah;* he was grafted back into the *one* true olive tree.

> Again I ask: Did they stumble so as to fall beyond recovery? Not at all! Rather, because of their transgression, salvation has come to the Gentiles to make Israel envious. But if their transgression means riches for the world, and their loss means riches for the Gentiles, how much greater riches will their fullness bring! I am talking to you Gentiles. Inasmuch as I am the apostle to the Gentiles, I make much of my ministry..." (Romans 11:11-13)

All of Israel did not fall beyond recovery (verse 11a).

To make the Israelites envious was something Paul had experienced, and he argues here from that experience. This is not something that will only happen thousands of years from the time of writing—in Acts 13:44-48, we see the event played out. The Israelites were envious during Paul's time.

Romans 11:14: "...in the hope that I may somehow arouse my own people to envy and *save some of them.*"

Paul is happy and trying hard to save *some of them. Why talk of saving some if all Israel will be saved?*

> For if their rejection is the reconciliation of the world, what will their acceptance be but life from the dead? If the part of the dough offered as first-fruits is holy, then the whole batch is holy; if the root is holy, so are the branches.
>
> If some of the branches have been broken off, and you, though a wild olive shoot, have been grafted in among the others and now share in the nourishing sap from the olive root, do not boast over those branches. If you do, consider this: You do not support the root, but the root supports you. You will say then, "Branches were broken off so that I could be grafted in." Granted. But they were broken off because of unbelief, and you stand by faith. Do not be arrogant, but be afraid. For if God did not spare the natural branches, he will not spare you either.
>
> Consider therefore the kindness and sternness of God: sternness to those who fell, but kindness to you, provided that you continue in his kindness. Otherwise, you also will be cut off (Romans 11:15-22).

Now you see why Paul was crying so desperately in Chapter 9, verse 1. Again, there is only *one* olive tree, with cut-off branches in *fulfillment of Jeremiah 11-16.*

> *And if they do not persist in unbelief,* they will be grafted back in, for God is able to graft them in again. After all, if you were cut out of an olive tree that is wild by nature, and contrary to nature were

grafted into a cultivated olive tree, how much more readily will these, the natural branches, be grafted into their own olive tree!

I do not want you to be ignorant of this mystery, brothers, so that you may not be conceited: Israel has experienced a hardening in part until the full number of the Gentiles has come in. And so all Israel will be saved, as it is written: "The deliverer will come from Zion; he will turn godlessness away from Jacob. And this is my covenant with them when I take away their sins."

As far as the gospel is concerned, they are enemies on your account; but as far as election is concerned, they are loved on account of the patriarchs, for God's gifts and his call are irrevocable. Just as you who were at one time disobedient to God have now received mercy as a result of their disobedience... (Romans 11:23-30).

The key to the whole argument is in verse 23; "*And if they do not persist in unbelief, they will be grafted in, for God is able to graft them in again.*" Paul is simply saying that, like himself, Peter, James, etc., the salvation of the Jews will consist of *one branch at a time of believing repentant Jews* being part of the fullness of all the nations and realizing the fulfillment of God's promise to Abraham. So the one condition to be fulfilled by all alike, Jew and Gentile, is *individual, obedient repentance, and faith* in the Lord Jesus Christ.

In verse 26, the phrase *and so*, which in Greek (*kai houtos*), means *in like manner*, that is—not persistent in unbelief, in the manner of Paul's, Peter's, etc. conversions. This is the manner or way for them to be converted, *like messianic Jews only.*

Romans 11:31-32: "...so they too have *now* become disobedient in order that they too may *now* receive mercy as a result of God's mercy to you. For God has bound all men over to disobedience so that he may have mercy on them all."

Verse 31 is often overlooked. The disobedience was evidenced in the *present*. The mercy was also available in the *present once again:* "...so they too have *now* become disobedient in order that they too may *now* receive mercy as a result of God's mercy to you" (Romans 11:31).

In other words, the disobedience *is now* and the mercy *is now*, not thousands of years later during an imaginary tribulation, or a thousand-year reign.

All of this is beyond Paul's understanding and so he breaks out into a wonderfully inspired doxology.

> Oh, the depths of the riches of the wisdom and knowledge of God! How unsearchable his judgments, and his paths beyond tracing out! Who has known the mind of the Lord? Or who has been his counselor? Who has ever given to God, that God should repay him? For from him and through him and to him are all things. To him be the glory forever! Amen. (Romans 11:33-36)

Israel's last and only opportunity is now to be converted to Christ and become a Christian nation. If all the Jews living in the world today would be converted, that would still only be a remnant. Millions upon millions have died without hope and without God. Look at the diary of Anne Frank and observe the total absence of hope in God.

In summary, Paul, the sorrowful, tearful evangelist and apostle, is inspired to say in Romans 9: No, to the salvation of *all* the Jews, or the whole physical nation of Israel.

Romans 10: No, to the salvation of *all* the Jews, or the whole physical nation of Israel.

Romans 11: No, to the salvation of *all* the Jews, or the whole physical nation of Israel.

He does not change his mind in Romans 11:26 and contradict the prophets and himself.

CHAPTER 17

A New Age of Accountability

⤙⟹⟸⤚

Seek the Lord while he may be found;
call on him while he is near.

Let the wicked forsake his way
and the evil man his thoughts.
Let him turn to the Lord,
and he will have mercy on him,
and to our God, for he will freely pardon.

"For my thoughts are not your thoughts,
neither are you ways my ways,"
declares the Lord.
(Isaiah 55:6-8)

Let's Make the Connection

The reestablishment of the state of Israel and the Rapture of the church are interconnected by dispensationalists. But it's unbiblical, and that's why so many Christians are led astray when it comes to the teaching of the end times. It also explains why none of their predictions come to pass. There is absolutely no correlation between the miraculous Exodus of Scripture and the 1948 exodus of Jews from other nations to the Holy Land. The complaint of Gideon is veiled: "If the Lord is among us, where are the miracles"? (Judges 6:13)

Let's look at this at length. You may not, at this point, see the significance of Romans 11:25-26. However, it's extremely important to recognize that a major foundation of the whole system of futurism, dispensationalism, and the reign of Christ for a thousand years with Israel as the main nation, rests, to a great extent, on the interpretation of these two verses, in isolation from Romans 9:1. To link the very limited support in the New Testament with the Old Testament prophecies of Israel's literal restoration simply has no consistent support from Scripture.

Looking at the End Times Through Dispensational Glasses

The way it's understood and authoritatively propagated as the absolute true teaching of Scripture is:

1. A great immeasurable number of Gentiles, non-Jewish people, from all nations are going to be saved during the time of the church, or the church age.
2. Then, when the full number of all the Gentile elect has been reached, they will go to heaven at the Rapture. These Christians are of the spiritual seed of Abraham.
3. The unconverted Jews and unconverted Gentiles will stay behind to go through the Great Tribulation. But Israel as a nation always has its own place, and is yet to have its greatest exaltation as the "earthly people of God."
4. During the Tribulation, there will be "144,000 Jewish Billy Grahams turned loose on this earth... the earth will never know a period of evangelism like this period," and all Israel is going to be saved.
5. This precedes the second coming of Christ. After that, Christ will sit on His earthly throne in Jerusalem for a thousand years.
6. Gog and Magog, according to a television broadcast by Pastor John Hagee, will march 200 million Chinese soldiers around the world at the end of the thousand years to overthrow Jesus, who now has disappeared from Jerusalem, because God the Father had to snatch Him up to save Him. Fire will come from heaven and destroy them. Then eternity will begin and never end.
7. Remember: prior to all of this, the church has been secretly snatched away from all the Great Tribulation.

So then you understand that, in order for this scheme to work, Romans 11:25-26 needs to be understood as follows:

1. First, the Gentiles need to be saved.
2. The church mysteriously needs to disappear (called the Rapture).
3. And then, after that, in sequence, all Israel will be saved.
4. Then Christ and His church will come back from heaven for a thousand years, glorified and non-glorified living together.
5. Then Gog and Magog will declare war, at the end of the thousand years.
6. God the Father will snatch Jesus away to rescue Him from Gog and Magog.
7. Then eternity begins.

The Bible Does Not Tell Me So!

First, we need to do a study without getting too technical.

1. The word *Gentile* or *nation*.

In Hebrew, the words are *ummah* and *goi*, and are translated *nation*. In Greek, the word *ethnos*, most of the time, is translated *Gentile*. Translators have the liberty to translate the word into English to read either *nations* or *Gentiles* as they see it according to its context, or out of unintentional prejudice.

The NIV translates *ethnos* as *Gentiles* in Romans 1:5: "Through him and for his name's sake, we received grace and apostleship to call people from among all the *Gentiles* to the obedience that comes from faith."

The King James and the New King James versions use the word correctly; it is translated as *nations*. In this verse, I challenge the translators of the NIV to change it. For the way this reads, Paul was called to the Gentiles exclusively. But we know that, in his missionary journeys, he always started with the Jews (Acts 14:1). Jews are never called Gentiles. It's an insult to them. Even in Romans 1:16, the translators have translated the word *elleni* (meaning *Greek*) as *Gentile*. Why? The New King James has *Greek*.

Who Says Israel Is Not a Nation?

2. Sometimes the Jews, or Israel, are part of, or addressed as, *nation* or *nations*. For instance, I will make you into a great *nation* (Genesis 12:2); and, "Two *nations* are in your womb" (Genesis 25:23).

All the nations of the earth are blessed by those who openly or covertly worship Christ. Surely Israel was the first among the *nations* to be blessed. In John 11:48-52, Caiaphas was concerned that the Romans would take away the Jewish *nation*, and scatter all the children of God to make them one nation. That, of course, is exactly the purpose of the gospel and the burning passionate preaching of the former Pharisee, Paul.

The disciples were told to baptize all nations (Matthew 28:19): "Therefore go and make disciples of all nations, baptizing them in the name of the Father and of the Son and of the Holy Spirit."

After Pentecost they were, for the first few years, preoccupied with the Jewish *nation* and Jews from all nations.

It is impossible to be consistent biblically, if the term nation *is exclusively used for Gentiles and can never be used when appropriate for Israel as well!* It's true that sometimes *ethnos* is used to differentiate between Jew and Gentile. But remember the strongest condemnation in Paul's writings to the Galatians—"Consider Abraham: 'He believed God, and it was credited to him as righteousness.'" Understand, then, that those who believe are children of Abraham. The Scripture foresaw that God would justify the Gentiles by faith, and announced the gospel in advance to Abraham: "All nations will be blessed through you" (Galatians 3:6-8).

God has one people, one Shepherd, one fold, one holy nation.

I suggest that Romans 11:25 could read: "...Israel has experienced a hardening in part until the *fullness of the nations* has come in." If the word *Gentiles* is used as in most translations, then this verse is used to try to prove that God has a different plan for the Israelis. This doesn't fit in with Romans 9:1-3, Galatians, and the Great Commission.

The fullness of the nations fits perfectly, for the gospel has been completed in all the world and the last sheep has been found, and all the sheep are in the fold. Why is Israel not a part of the fullness of the nations? Where do all our Hebrew brothers, the Christian Jews, fit in who, for the last two thousand years have believed and followed Jesus Christ as their Messiah? Are these Jews part of the Gentile fullness of nations? Of course they are!

Furthermore, the hardening of Israel is only in part. No one can tell how small or how great that part is. But we know that there were many Jews who were experiencing God's redeeming fullness, just like Paul, and tens of thousands of other Jews in New Testament times. And it continues right up to now.

The next most important word is *pleroma*, which means *fullness*. The NIV translates this word as *full number* in Romans 11:25, and so has made two words out of one Greek word. The King James, the New King James and New American Standard use the word *fullness*.

Below are all the translations of *pleroma*. It should never be used as *full number* anywhere.

1. John 11:6	Of his *fullness* we have all received…
2. Romans 11:12	If their *fall*, how much their *fullness*…
3. Romans 11:25	(KJV, NKJV, ASV) Until the *fullness*…
4. Romans 15:29	I shall come in the *fullness* of blessing…
5. 1 Corinthians 10:26	(Quote from Psalm 24) The earth is the Lord's and the *fullness* thereof…
6. Galatians 4:4	But in the *fullness* of time…
7. Ephesians 1:10	That in the dispensation of the *fullness*…
8. Ephesians 1:23	Which is his body the *fullness* of him…
9. Ephesians 3:19	Filled to the measure of the *fullness* of God…
10. Colossians 1:19	All his *fullness* dwells in him…
11. Colossians 2:9	For in Christ all the *fullness*…
12. Colossians 2:10	And you have been given the *fullness*…

Go back and try to substitute *full number* for *fullness* in the corresponding verses: 1, 2, 4, 5, 8, 9, 10, 11, 12. It makes no sense. So, *full number* doesn't fit (at least) nine out of twelve times. *Fullness*, however, fits in each of these verses.

Second, and more importantly, Paul tells the Gentiles in Colossians 2:10 that they have already received fullness. Is there fullness that will follow the *full number* or does full *number* follow fullness? Consider Colossians 2:10: "...and you have been given fullness in Christ, who is the head over every power and authority."

Third, if according to the NIV, the full number of Gentiles is going to be saved and afterward, that is, if their full number has been reached, and all Israel is going to be saved, does that mean that, at that point, no other Gentile is ever going to be saved?

Does not dispensationalism teach that during the so-called Tribulation and Millennium, non-Jews are going to be born and saved? So there is going to be another full number after the first full number. This, of course, is absurd. Are the imaginary 144,000 Jewish Billy Grahams only going to save Jews, Mr. Lindsey? This is as much another gospel as the Koran and the Book of Mormon.

If there is no salvation possible for any or even *one* more Gentile during the Great Tribulation, why should God be concerned with them any longer? Why not just send them to hell? Let me quote C. I. Scofield, the high priest of dispensationalism: "The great tribulation will be, however, a period of salvation. An election out of Israel is seen as sealed for God (Revelation 7:4-8) and with an innumerable multitude of Gentiles (Revelation 7:9) are said to have come 'out of the great tribulation.'"

So even to dispensationalists, the full number can't be the full number, or the complete number. *Pleroma* in this verse (Romans 11:25) means the *fullness of the blessing of the gospel*. That is the fullness which Jew and Gentile enjoyed in the church at the time of Paul's writing and ever since.

A bad thing happens to a good prophecy when it is insisted that the word *ethnos* is translated as *Gentiles* only and *pleroma* (fullness) has to be translated as *full number* in this particular verse.

Are All Israelis Going to Be Saved?

The next verse (Romans 11:26) and its correct understanding is of vital importance. Let the verse say what it says. "And so all Israel will be saved." True Israelites are the only spiritual children of Abraham. Abraham is the seed of Christ and so the seed of Abraham are all believers.

And So What?

Once again, these two very simple words, *kai houtos* means *and so* or *in the same manner*. Look up any Greek lexicon and you will see that the meaning of *kai houtos* is *and so*, that is, "in the way described or in the same manner." It *never* means *afterward*.

Dispensationalists misuse the words and want you to believe that it means *afterward* as in, first, all the Gentiles are going to be saved and then *afterward*, all of the ethnic origin and traditions are going to be saved.

Beloved, that is wrong! It is false! It is deceptive! The very rich vocabulary of the Greek language has very different words for *afterward* (see 1 Corinthians 15:6).

This is how Romans 11:25-26 should be understood in *context* of what Paul has said in chapters 9, 10 and 11: "I do not want you to be ignorant of this mystery, brothers, so that *you may not be* conceited: Israel has experienced a hardening in part until the fullness of the nations has come in (been completed). And so (alongside and in the same manner) all Israel will be saved."

And so, alongside, and in the same manner as the Gentiles, all Israelites that are going to be saved are going to be saved in the same manner as Paul, the Jewish church, and all the Gentiles were, and are doing; that is, by faith in Christ. This is the manner in which people are going to be saved.

The Williams New Testament (a translation in the language of the people) has translated it, "And so in that way all Israel will be saved." That is, all true Israel is going to be saved. Of course! That's why Christ came in the first place—to fill heaven with the great multitude of Abraham's numberless children, made up of all nations from Arabia to Zambia. The spiritual seed within Abraham is the spiritual seed within Christ.

These are the ones Christ referred to when He said, "those you have given me" (John 17:24). This seed within Christ went to the cross with Him, and was infallibly atoned for.

The deliverer did come to Zion, the virgin did give birth, godlessness was turned away from Jacob, the covenant was fulfilled, and is being fulfilled. The sins of all people in all nations are being taken away from all those who believe. Those who have wrestled with God and man, and have surrendered to Christ, and consequently, have overcome, have received a new name, from Adam to the end. (See Genesis 32:28 and remember—the new name Jacob received was *Israel*.)

And so it is! It is totally impossible for all fleshly, ethnic Jews who have existed on this earth to be saved, who still, even now, don't want Christ to reign over them. See Luke 19:14.

> **Violence is done to the inspired writing of the converted Pharisee when it's insisted that Paul was excited about his kinsmen's conversion. NO! NO! NO! Paul knew that few would believe the report (Isaiah 53:1).** *That's why he cried, that's why he pleaded, that's why he was willing to be cursed instead of them, in order to save some.* **He did find some comfort, however, from Elijah and knew that not all were lost, but that God had preserved some to be elect.**

Any other interpretations of these three chapters don't make any sense. The interpretation that all physical Israel will be saved is forced, to try to prove a dispensational argument.

If dispensational teaching is correct, Paul would have said in Romans 9:1-2: "I speak the truth in Christ. I am not lying, my conscience confirms it in the Holy Spirit. *I have great joy and unceasing excitement,* for all Jews, my countrymen, are going to be saved. Hallelujah!" But that is not how Romans 9:1-2 reads.

No! Like Christ, Paul is a man of sorrows and acquainted with grief. He cried over Israel of the flesh like Christ cried over Jerusalem. He cried over today's Israelis, not Israelites. Can you imagine Christ doing that and foreseeing the city on the brink of disaster?

> O Jerusalem, Jerusalem, you who kill the prophets and stone those sent to you, how often I have longed to gather your children together, as a hen gathers her chicks under her wings, but you were not willing. Look, your house is left to you desolate. For I tell you, you will not see me again until you say, "Blessed is he who comes in the name of the Lord" (Matthew 23:37-39).

But who then, is numbered among all Israel that is going to be saved? Here are just a few: Adam, Eve, Noah and family, Melchizedek, Job and family, Abraham, Isaac, Jacob and family, all faithful prophets, seven thousand men who had not bowed to Baal, faithful believers in captivity, God's special jewels like Zechariah and others (see Zechariah 9:16), Jews and Gentiles throughout the Old Testament, John the Baptist, all believers in Christ, the centurion at the Crucifixion, and possibly some of whom Christ prayed for on the cross for their forgiveness. The whole Israel of God.

144,000 Christians

What does the Bible tell us in Revelation? "Then I heard the number of those who were sealed: 144,000 from all the tribes of Israel." Revelation 7:4

> Then I looked, and there before me was the Lamb, standing on Mount Zion, and with him 144,000 who had his name and his Father's name written on their foreheads. And I heard a sound from heaven like the roar of rushing waters and like a loud peal of thunder. The sound I heard was like that of harpists playing their harps. And they sang a new song before the throne and before the four living creatures and the elders. No one could learn the song except the 144,000 who had been redeemed from the earth.

These are those who did not defile themselves with
women, for they kept themselves pure. They follow
the Lamb wherever he goes. They were purchased
from among men and offered as first fruits to God
and the Lamb. No lie was found in their mouths;
they are blameless (Revelation 14:1-5).

There are various opinions in dispensational circles about who
and what are these 144,000? Here are just a few description and job
descriptions of the 144,000 that dispensational teachers want you to
believe.

1. An army of Jewish soldiers fighting for Christ during the
   Great Tribulation.
2. 144,000 Billy Grahams who will evangelize the world
   before the thousand-year reign of Christ in Jerusalem
   begins.
3. They will do in three-and-a-half or seven years what the
   church with billions of Christians has failed to do over two
   thousand years.
4. They are virgins.
5. Dispensationalism is forced to make up these fairy tales
   about them for evangelization is necessary, but the problem
   is the real Christian, the church, is raptured. Hence the need
   for extra-biblical creativity.

First of all, please recognize the significance of 144,000. It is:
12 tribes x 12 disciples x infinity = 144,000.

Second, notice that the above dispensational job descriptions
are not in the Bible.

Third, let's make a Biblical comparison between the 144,000
and an average, down-to-earth, born again Christian as described in
Scripture.

144,000 Israelites	144,000 Christians
1. Israelites	1. Children of Abraham Galatians 3:29
2. Chosen by God	2. Chosen by God Ephesians 1:4
3. Bearing Christ's name and Father's name	3. The Christian has Christ's name and prays "Our Father"
4. Sealed by God	4. Sealed by the Holy Spirit Ephesians 1:13
5. Servants of God	5. Servants of God Romans 6:22
6. Name written on forehead	6. Name of God and city of God written on them Revelation 3:12
7. Sing a new song	7. Sing new songs Revelation 5:9
8. Redeemed from the earth	8. Redeemed from the earth. Titus 2:14
9. Not defiled. (Female goddesses)	9. Not defiled but cleansed 1 Corinthians 6:9
10. Follow the Lamb	10. Follow Christ, the Lamb of God. John 10
11. Purchased from among men	11. Purchased from among men. 1 Peter 19-25
12. First Fruits	12. First Fruits James 1:18
13. No lie in their mouth	13. No Lie, Proclaimers of the Gospel of Truth. Romans 9:1
14. Blameless, not sinless	14. Blameless, not sinless 1 Corinthians 1:8

There is no difference between the 144,000 and Christians. These 144,000 have been in the world from day one to the end. God showed his absolute sovereignty by not announcing the whole number of the elect. Consequently, John saw a

great innumerable multitude from every tribe and nation in fulfillment of God's promise to Abraham. (Genesis 22:17-18)

After this I looked and there before me was a great multitude that no one could count, *from every nation*, tribe, people and language, standing before the throne and in front of the Lamb. They were wearing white robes and were holding palm branches in their hands. And they cried out in a loud voice: "Salvation belongs to our God, who sits on the throne, and to the Lamb." (Revelation 7:9-10)

CHAPTER 18

The Elusive Rapture

❖═◎═❖

"Do not let your hearts be troubled.
Trust in God; trust also in me.
In my Father's house are many rooms;
if it were not so I would have told you.
I am going there to prepare
a place for you.
And if I go and prepare a place for you,
I will come back
and take you to be with me
that you also may be where I am."
(John 14:1-3)

From Panic to Peace

Jack woke up suddenly from a very disturbed sleep. The noisy, cheap apartment complex in which he lived had been the scene of an unbelievable racket all night, with loud fireworks, and non-stop rock music blaring from boom boxes everywhere.

Jack had decided to go to bed early and had plugged his ears; he knew the Lord would silently take him away as a worthy participant of the Rapture. The things of the world had lost all their attraction, as far as he was concerned; "The Lord is coming," he thought. "Now I can go to sleep."

But early the next morning, he awoke suddenly and panic struck him. "Oh, dear Lord, it's January 1, 2000, the Rapture has come, and I've been left behind. Why am I still here?" Without putting on his shoes, he ran out of his apartment building, leaving his door wide open behind him. He ran the three blocks, without looking back, to his Independent Bible Church, of which he was a more or less faithful member.

The pastor had warned all the members about the soon return of Christ. Signs of the times were everywhere, and these times were pointing to Y2K as the appointed time for the secret, silent snatching away into heaven of all true believers in Jesus Christ, the so-called Rapture.

While running, he kept on praying and asking God, "Why am I still here? Lord, it's me, Jack! You know me! I made my decision at the Billy Graham Crusade eleven years ago."

Then suddenly, as if God had perhaps answered him, a comforting thought entered his troubled mind. "Maybe the church is full of people, it's about time for the early service; if so, the pastor will have a perfectly biblical reason and give a careful explanation of why Y2K wasn't the correct occasion for Christ's return. My faithful pastor isn't one of those liberal ministers who don't take the whole Bible literally."

Turning the corner and seeing the church parking lot almost empty, panic gripped his fast-beating heart. "The cars! Where are all the cars? There's nobody here. They're gone, all gone, and I've been left behind! Why didn't I witness more to my neighbors?"

Running up the front steps of the church, he found the door locked. "God has shut the door, and no one's going to open it," he thought. He banged and banged on the door—to no avail. Sinking to his knees, he clenched his sore fist and, trembling with fear, said: "Dear God, I don't want to go through the Great Tribulation.

"I've been judged by God," he thought for, all of a sudden, he realized the sound logical and biblical fact that it's impossible to have a Rapture of the whole Christian world without a universal judgment of sheep and goats. At the same moment, God has divided the righteous and the unrighteous, the wheat and the chaff. "I am chaff. Lord, have mercy!

"I'm no good. I've read the novels about being left behind." He wished he'd never read any of those silly books. "I'm it," he thought. "I've been left behind.

"Lord, have mercy," he prayed again. "I thought I was a Christian. It's no use."

"What in the world is the matter with you, Jack?" said Tim, the part-time janitor and theological student at a well-known reformed seminary. He had heard the banging and eventually found his way to the door, only to find a hunched-over Jack on the front steps.

Surprised, Jack looked at the inquisitive but relaxed face of Tim and cried, "You too? You too, Tim! That makes two of us who missed out on being raptured. Your reformed education didn't save you either. Oh! We're in so much trouble!" Jack cried, "so much trouble. What are we going to do, Tim? The church is empty. They've all gone into heaven and we're left behind. No one's here but us. Your old car is the only one in the parking lot."

"Jack, it's Saturday. Sunday's coming!"

Relieved, and red with embarrassment, Jack slowly limped home on sore feet to his lonely apartment, with the door still wide open, and his TV stolen.

Tim continued to vacuum the sanctuary, but he couldn't stop thinking about poor Jack. He called his wife, Sue, and told her he'd see if he could find Jack, and maybe help him. "So," he told her, "I'll be home a little later than usual."

He got Jack's address from the church directory, and went to his apartment. Jack opened the door slowly, still looking very sad.

"Jack, can I come in? My heart went out to you this morning. If you'll listen to me, maybe I can help you."

"My TV was stolen," said Jack.

"I'm sorry. I can't help you with that, but maybe I can help you feel better about your terrifying experience this morning. Jack, last night, the Lord *did* return."

"What?"

"Yes! Yes, He did return. Listen, I picked up the paper this morning, and the obituaries listed eighteen people who died. There'll be funeral services for thirteen of them in various churches in town. Jack, in our town alone, Jesus has been busy. If any of those who died had repented of their sins and had acknowledged Jesus Christ as their own personal Savior, He came last night to take them home with Him. Do you believe that, Jack? The first time Christ came to them was at conversion, the second time was for promotion to glory. Do you also get that, Jack?"

"Yes. Of course."

"Every day, for thousands of years, there have been many people who died and were waiting for him—and He came! Let me show you. Paul says here in 1 Corinthians 1:7, 'Therefore you do not lack any spiritual gift as you eagerly wait for our Lord Jesus Christ to be revealed.' Are they still waiting, Jack?"

"Of course not."

"You got it, Jack. Christ came to them exactly the same way He came to His apostles in John 14:3, 'And if I go and prepare a place for you, I will come back and take you to be with me that you also may be where I am.' Are those disciples still here? Of course, you know the answer.

"For thousands of years, Christ has been coming for those who have fallen asleep in Him, and the Lord will bring those people with Him at His *final* coming (1 Thessalonians 4:14).

"Jack, that's why the term, *the second coming*, isn't in the Bible. If you want to be very specific, the literal second coming really happened at the resurrection of Christ. Jesus went to hell first, to grab the keys from Satan (Revelation 1:18) and then went to heaven to drop off the thief on His right on the cross, and then came to minister to the frightened women and the rest. Jack, things as we know them will come to an end. Jesus said heaven and earth will pass away.

"Jack, you haven't missed out. Christ knows you; He saw you, head bowed and crying, as you walked forward to receive Him at the Billy Graham Crusade. He knows where to find you."

"Thank you, Tim," said Jack. "I wish I could study the Bible like you and go to a seminary and learn these things."

"Jack, you don't need to go to seminary to read the Bible. Just read the whole thing consistently, and don't jump from one verse to another, and you'll know the truth, and the truth will set you free to follow Jesus daily.

"You'll discover that earthquakes mean more than just the trembling of the soil under your feet. You'll learn that stars falling on earth means more than what it literally says (Revelation 6:12-17). And Jack, very importantly, you'll discover that coming in the clouds doesn't mean Jesus needs to use a cloud to travel through space.

"It means He's hidden from view and can only be seen, or perceived, by those waiting for Him. This is what happened when

Jerusalem was destroyed in 70 A.D. His people, the church in Jerusalem, in obedience to Christ's warning in Matthew 24, fled to the mountains. They knew it was Jesus coming back in judgment upon Jerusalem."

"Let me tell you this, Tim," Jack answered. "I did think this morning that if there is such a thing as the secret Rapture, how can it be secret if, in fact, it's a worldwide judgment by God, separating believers and unbelievers; the sheep and goats? At this Rapture, God has judged between believers and unbelievers. You can't have a secret, silent Rapture without the general judgment of God on all people."

"That's a brilliant insight, Jack. You're absolutely right. The blessed hope is that you've been made alive by Christ. You've been born again; resurrected from death to life. 'Blessed and holy are those who have part in the first resurrection' (Revelation 20:6). That's you and me. 'The second death has no power over them.' *Nothing more significant and wonderful can happen to you this side of eternity.* So, Jack, things can't get any better. So hang on to that. No, I should have said, 'Stand firm' I have to go now. God bless you!"

"Thanks, Tim," said Jack. "*My peace has been restored for good.*"

O Rapture, Where Art Thou?

While some type of pre-millennial teaching occurs in only a few writings of early church Fathers, the doctrine of a pre-tribulation Rapture of the church doesn't appear in theological books until the latter part of the nineteenth century.

The basic theology of dispensationalism is this: the church and Israel are two distinct groups with whom God has a divine purpose. The church is a mystery, unrevealed in the Old Testament, and she must disappear before the Great Tribulation, so that the 144,000 Jews can take over and finish the job. If this is so, then isn't the evangelical ministry of the 144,000 Jews the same as that of the church? There's no distinction. It's artificial and without biblical warrant.

Such opinions all arise from the literal method of interpretation and are preached consistently in churches, and by a number of international TV preachers. But even dispensational teachers are not consistent in literal interpretation of the work of Christ.

A very clear literal example has been given by Christ regarding the washing of feet: "I have set you an example that you should do as I have done for you" (John 13:15).

Shouldn't we expect to see this in churches where dispensationalism is preached? Foot washing should be a very prominent ceremony. It can very easily be done literally. Is it interpreted spiritually by these churches? Has foot washing been spiritualized away by them?

When it's insisted that the church is a "mystery unrevealed in the Old Testament," one must ask the question: "Under whose control or sovereignty were these people who were created in the image of God during those many centuries from Adam to Christ?" Didn't Moses say that God has been our dwelling place throughout all generations? (Psalm 90:1-2). Was not the Lamb slain from the foundation of the world? (Revelation 13:8).

Whose blood but Christ's blood was represented on the doorposts of Israel in Egypt? Did not Christ dwell with Israel in the wilderness? They drank of that spiritual rock. That rock was Christ (1 Corinthians 10:4). They tempted Christ and were destroyed by the serpent (1 Corinthians 10:9).

Furthermore, Christians are chosen in Him before the foundation of the world (Ephesians 1:4). That is the great multitude. So then, it's clear that the first, second, and third revelation periods are all the generation under the Father, Son and Holy Spirit.

I met a very faithful and effective evangelist in Australia in 1965. This particular man of God, after his conversion to Christ, in early 1900, refused to go to college to prepare himself for ministry because, as for as he was concerned, it would mean a total waste of three years, for the church would be raptured before his graduation.

He gave me a little book titled, "The Blessed Hope." In it, the Rapture is based on Titus 2:13: "While we wait for the blessed hope—the glorious appearing of our great God and Savior, Jesus Christ..."

> The blessed hope, for which we wait, is the appearing of Jesus Christ in glory. The saving grace of God has already appeared to us; the work of salvation, which it has begun, is perfected by the appearing of the Saviour in glory, who, in His state of humiliation

here, wrought out our redemption. The appearing of the kingdom of God in Christ gives us the earnest of its appearance hereafter in glory, quickens our desires after it, and draws us away from worldly lusts (Lange's Commentary; Vol. 11, P.18).

CHAPTER 19

Mistaken Signs

❖➤◗❖

...Then a great and powerful wind tore the mountains apart
and shattered the rocks before the LORD,
but the LORD was not in the wind.
After the wind there was an earthquake,
But the Lord was not in the earthquake.

After the earthquake came a fire,
But the LORD was not in the fire.
And after the fire came a gentle whisper.

When Elijah heard it, he pulled his cloak over his face
And went out and stood at the mouth of the cave.
Then a voice said to him,
"What are you doing here, Elijah?"
(1 Kings 19:11-13)

2,000-Year-Old Signs of the Times

Waiting for the Rapture with feverish anticipation has millions of Christians confused, disappointed, and embarrassed. What's the holdup? These so-called infallible signs of the times have been with us now for almost 2,000 years and, when the elusive Rapture fails to happen, more "infallible" signs are sighted. Here are some serious mistaken signs:

1. Many Jews are back in the land.
2. The world is morally worse.
3. Earthquakes are on the increase, causing tsunamis (tidal waves) and killing thousands.

4. The gospel is preached to every nation.

5. Knowledge has increased.

6. A unified Europe is in the making. (The ten toes of the great statue in Daniel 2:41 used to be seen as a sign of ten European nations. It's not mentioned anymore because there are more nations involved now in the European Union, so the statue of Daniel is embarrassing.)

7. There are wars and rumors of wars.

8. Anything else you were made to believe related to the imminent Rapture of the church is now in progress.

9. The twin towers of the World Trade Center have been destroyed by a criminal act of warfare. Still no Rapture.

10. The year 2000 has come, but still no Rapture.

The Rapture is reluctant because it's a phantom. It's because none of the above signs has been interpreted biblically, and therefore, they're totally unrelated to the final coming of Christ. None of the above has anything to do with the last days, the final coming, the end of the earth, or eternity. Unbiblical literal interpretation will continue to prove dispensationalism wrong. People are no longer quoting Samuel: "Speak, Lord, for thy servant heareth." Instead, it's: "Hear, Lord, for thy servant speaketh. It's time for the Rapture."

The Unblessed Hope

In order to prove that the Rapture (or translation), that is, the secret, quiet taking of the church out of the earth, isn't to be confused with the second coming, dispensationalists want you to know the great difference between them.

Dispensationalists are full of *artificial, careful distinctions*. There is, however, not one verse in the whole New Testament that clearly teaches that there's a distinction between spiritual Israel and the church, or that there's an additional divine plan in sequence after the church is secretly removed. This makes Christ, who said, "I will build my church," into a complete and embarrassing failure.

"We believe that Jesus died and rose again and so, we believe that God will bring with Jesus those who have fallen asleep in him" (1 Thessalonians 4:14). Not those who were part of a so-called Rapture, *but for the billions "who have fallen asleep in him."* Please note that God the Father will bring with Jesus those who have fallen asleep. Is this the first coming of the Father and the second coming of the Son?

The dispensational program is this: you've been with God in heaven, and now you have to leave that unimaginable glory and go back to earth for a thousand years, at which time you'll again be subject to a rebellion.

The final coming may or may not be imminent, and sign seekers are part of an adulterous generation. Jesus said so! What signs are we talking about? Scripture, please!

Futurologists maintain that the Rapture will be an event that will bring great comfort, but the second coming is a time of judgment. This is a very troublesome statement, particularly for Christian parents whose children are still lost.

There cannot be a translation, or Rapture, *without a general universal judgment*, even at the so-called secret snatching away of the church. At the moment of the Rapture, God has to make a divine judgment between believers and unbelievers.

a. God has to judge between those who are in Christ, and those who are not.

b. As argued before, God has to judge those who are not in Christ and are supposed to go through the Great Tribulation. *Those taken are judged; those left behind are judged!* It's impossible to have a secret snatching away of the Christians out of the world without a general, universal judgment of God. God has to judge or discriminate between the Christians and non-Christians.

c. Dispensationalism demands a secret Rapture, without a general judgment by Christ, but even Christ can't ascertain the righteous from the wicked without judging them. Consequently, the general judgment of the wicked must take place at the so-called Rapture. And then there are no more judgments. *"Just as man is destined to die once, and after that, to face judgment..."* (Hebrews 9:27). At each deathbed, the triune God is the supreme judge of the universe, right down to every individual.

Here then, in generic form, is the teaching of dispensationalism, with regard to the secret, silent coming of Christ to take the church (all true believers) bodily out of the world. It's not a summary built on Scripture, but on sentiment.

When Creativity is Boundless, but Bibleless

Two illustrations from futuristic dispensational books should be enough to amaze and alarm the reader at the unbelievable fairy tales, conclusions, and unfettered imaginations of the producers of these unbiblical fantasies. The reason for this amazing creativity is because the writers believe and thus are forced to comply with literal interpretation of all of Scripture.

Robert Van Kampen provides an imaginary description of the New Jerusalem in his book, *The Sign*: Jerusalem will be rebuilt in forty-five days sometime between Armageddon and the beginning of the thousand-year reign. The temple will be in the middle of Jerusalem, but will not touch the ground. It will be hovering above it and at the same time it will be situated on Mount Zion.

Hebrews chapter 1 tells us clearly that the Son of God, who is the exact representation of God's glory, made the universe. Think about the following divinely inspired truth of the Word of God:

> He is the image of the invisible God, the firstborn
> over all creation. For by him all things were created;
> things in heaven and on earth, visible and invisible,
> whether thrones or powers or rulers or authorities;
> all things were created by him and for him. He is
> before all things, and in him all things hold together.
> And he is the head of the body, the church; he is the
> beginning and the firstborn from among the dead, so
> that in everything he might have the supremacy
> (Colossians 1:15-18).

We know the opening miracle of creation took place in six days. The psalmist tells us that God spoke and it came to pass. *What has happened to the glorified Christ who now takes forty-five days to restore the imaginary temple or city? Talk about faded glory!*

My only comment: nowhere have I read in the Bible that Jesus said, "I will come again and again and again and again" —except to gather individual believers unto Himself.

In that same book, Van Kampen says the highway of holiness (Isaiah 35:8) is a real highway from Assyria to Egypt to be used by some Jews. This, of course, is absurd literalism.

More serious still is his opinion that, at the final judgment, people who have helped Jews in their time of trouble will inherit salvation. This, of course, is bordering on heresy.

Have you noticed how complicated dispensationalism is? There are so many artificial distinctions between the past and future. Compare this with the method of Jesus' teaching as the great storyteller. He had common folk following Him.

Dispensationalism is the history of salvation backward. It's a gospel in reverse. At least, Van Kampen could have added that those people who helped Christians in the former Soviet Union, who were persecuted for seventy years, will also go to heaven. This sort of thing is light years removed from two thousand years of orthodox Christianity. But the futuristic teachings are so interesting, so extremely fascinating, and can be embellished with great creativity and endless excitement and sensationalism. *And it makes the doctrines of personal holiness so boring.*

There are millions upon millions of people in churches all over the world, where the emphasis is not on God, but on man. Many people come together who ignorantly worship an unknown god. People come together so often because:

1. They've always gone to church.
2. It makes them feel good.
3. It's a meeting place of like-minded people and friends.
4. They love the helpful, encouraging messages.
5. It helps them to get on with life.
6. They love the uplifting music.
7. It sets a good example for the kids.

8. The week isn't the same if they skip going to church.
9. They love to hear sermons on the end times and Armegeddon.
10. They don't want to go through the Tribulation.
11. They don't want to be left behind.
12. It makes them feel safe.

Two Different Bible Conferences in the Same City

Is it not an insult to our great God and Father that the focus on Him is secondary? For example, imagine two Christian conferences in the same city at the same time, equally advertised. One conference is about future events, the Second Coming, the Great Tribulation, the Rapture, and what happens to those left behind in the thousand-year kingdom. The main speakers are Hal Lindsey and Jack Van Impe.

The other conference is on holiness, featuring a well-known Bible teacher. The first conference will be held in the largest auditorium available, with a long platform to spread out a big End Times chart. There's standing room only. The other conference will half fill a Sunday school room.

Now go to your Bible, and see how much emphasis is given in Scripture on what will happen in the future. And then search Scripture to see how much emphasis is given to knowing God, holiness of life, Christlikeness, evangelism, and growing in grace.

The Bible says to remember Christ's death till He comes. But most Christians get excited and go overboard with the non-biblical requirement to remember *His birth*. It's so much more fun, and the Rapture is much more interesting than His lonely atonement.

The shameful, pernicious condition of today's Christianity is that there isn't much, if any, real interest in God Himself, His Word, or His glory.

A famous preacher said, *"It is very difficult to get Christians excited to come to a meeting when the only attraction is God."*

CHAPTER 20

New Wine in Old Skins

⊹⟫⊜⟪⊹

Formerly, when you did not know God,
you were slaves to those
who by nature are not gods.
But now that you know God –
or rather are known by God –
how is it that you
are turning back
to those weak and miserable principles?

Do you wish to be enslaved
by them all over again?

You are observing special days
and months and seasons and years!
I fear for you,
that somehow
I have wasted my efforts on you.
(Galatians 4:8-11)

Were the Old Testament Prophets Better Informed than Jesus?

Some time ago, I received a letter from a church in town, asking me to take up a special offering to collect money for rebuilding the temple in Jerusalem. What?

You're reading me correctly. Dispensationalism can be looked upon as a gospel in reverse. Consequently, the physical rebuilding of the temple in Jerusalem is a logical requirement of its theology. You can't be a consistent dispensationalist without believing in rebuilding the temple, the reestablishment of the literal priesthood, and temple sacrifices.

I discarded the letter, thinking it to be a small, unknown congregation in town headed by a pastor with similar theology to my friend at the gas station (I described him in the introduction to this book). Not correct! One day, in my office, there arrived a copy of *The Chosen People*, a Messianic (Christian) Jewish publication, at the back of which was an artistic impression of the proposed new temple in Jerusalem.

There is actually a Temple Institute, founded by Rabbi Israel Ariel. The institute has already completed over 100 vessels required to conduct temple worship. Now, of course, all the people who are excited about this must all be Jews; non-messianic Jews. Right? Wrong!

The rebuilding of a material, physical temple in Jerusalem is consistent and is the logical outcome of dispensational teaching. Now we have a clearer, concrete example that this teaching leads us all the way back into the Old Testament, and Jesus Christ is reduced to an earthly king with rebellious subjects at the end of His millennial reign.

It's astonishing how followers of the Lord Jesus Christ are so misreading the Bible, and are so hooked on an absolute, literal interpretation of God's Word, that they actually believe Christ is interested in a material, man-made temple again. According to *The Chosen People* magazine, plans for the new temple have been drawn and funds are being raised.

In order to understand my serious response to all of this, we need to go back about two thousand years. Consequently, the first question that arises is: Who repaired the veil?

Matthew, Mark, and Luke record that, at the moment Jesus died, the veil of the temple was torn in two, from top to bottom.

How significant is this? Nothing more is said about it in the gospels. Obviously, the Holy Spirit expects you to reach a sound biblical conclusion yourself. God is indicating by this that it's now safe to go and look into the Holy of Holies, because the temple has been reduced to a historical artifact. God no longer dwells in temples built with man's hands. (See John 4:21-24, and Hebrews 11:8-10.)

> Talking to a very immoral Samaritan woman, Jesus declared: "Believe me, woman, a time is coming when you will worship the Father neither on this mountain nor in Jerusalem. You Samaritans worship what you do not know; we worship what we do know, for salvation is from the Jews. *Yet a time is coming and has now come* when the true worshipers will worship the Father in spirit and truth, for they are the kind of worshipers the Father seeks. God is spirit, and his worshipers must worship in spirit and in truth" (John 4:21-24).

Hundreds of years before Christ said these things to the Samaritan woman, Abraham understood that the temple and the city of God were not structures built by men's hands, but by God Himself.

> By faith Abraham, when called to go to a place he would later receive as his inheritance, obeyed and went, even though he did not know where he was going. By faith he made his home in the Promised Land like a stranger in a foreign country; he lived in tents, as did Isaac and Jacob, who were heirs with him of the same promise. *For he was looking forward to the city with foundations, whose architect and builder is God* (Hebrews 11:8-10; see also Revelation 22:2).

I'm suggesting to you that the moment Jesus died, the veil was rent. The temple in Jerusalem lost its spiritual significance, and was reduced to nothing more than a beautiful building for people to gather for worship; a meeting house; a church building. That's why Paul and other Christian Jews had no problem going back into the temple during his last visit in Jerusalem (Acts 21:26).

Previously, the temple had been a special place where God was present by His Spirit (Luke 1:5-25). This is illustrated by the appearance of the angel Gabriel to Zechariah, the father of John the Baptist:

Once when Zechariah's division was on duty and he was serving as priest before God, he was chosen by lot, according to the custom of the priesthood, to go into the temple of the Lord and burn incense. And when the time for the burning of incense came, all the assembled worshipers were praying outside.

Then an angel of the Lord appeared to him, standing at the right side of the altar of incense. When Zechariah saw him, he was startled and was gripped with fear. But the angel said to him: "Do not be afraid, Zechariah; your prayer has been heard. Your wife Elizabeth will bear you a son, and you are to give him the name John. He will be a joy and delight to you, and many will rejoice because of his birth, for he will be great in the sight of the Lord. He is never to take wine or other fermented drink, and he will be filled with the Holy Spirit even from birth. *Many of the people of Israel will he bring back to the Lord their God.* And he will go on before the Lord, in the spirit and power of Elijah, to turn the hearts of the fathers to their children and the disobedient to the wisdom of the righteous—to make ready a people prepared for the Lord." (Luke 1:8-17)

Zechariah asked the angel, "How can I be sure of this? I am an old man and my wife is well along in years." The angel answered, "I am Gabriel. I stand in the presence of God, and I have been sent to speak to you and to tell you this good news. And now you will be silent and not able to speak until the day this happens, because you did not believe my words, which will come true at their proper time" (Luke 1:18-20).

Very specifically, the Holy of Holies was the room where the Ark of the Covenant and other sacred paraphernalia stood, and was the place in which the yearly offering on the Day of Atonement was made. The curtain, or veil, separated the Holy Place from the Most Holy Place. Let the Holy Spirit tell us about it in the following Scripture:

Now the first covenant had regulations for worship and also an earthly sanctuary. A tabernacle was set up. In its first room were the lampstand, the table and the consecrated bread; this was called the Holy Place. Behind the second curtain was a room called the Most Holy Place, which had the golden altar of incense and the gold-covered Ark of the Covenant. This ark contained the gold jar of manna, Aaron's rod that had budded, and the stone tablets of the covenant. Above the ark were the cherubim of the Glory, overshadowing the atonement cover. But we cannot discuss these things in detail right now.

When everything had been arranged like this, the priests entered regularly into the outer room to carry on their ministry. But only the high priest entered the inner room, and that only once a year, and never without blood, which he offered for himself and for the sins the people had committed in ignorance. The Holy Spirit was showing by this that the way into the Most Holy Place had not yet been disclosed as long as the first tabernacle was still standing. This is an illustration for the present time, indicating that the gifts and sacrifices being offered were not able to clear the conscience of the worshiper. They are only a matter of food and drink and various ceremonial washings—external regulations applying until the time of the new order. (Hebrews 9:1-10)

Who Repaired the Veil?

No one could enter or even look into the Most Holy Place. Why was the veil rent? Who repaired the veil? What happened to the priest who first discovered that the curtain had been torn from top to bottom? As far as we know, it didn't matter—no one died. The special, unique Most Holy Place had become desolate. The glory of Israel had departed. The temple, as far as being God's dwelling place, was destroyed when the veil was rent. However, in three days, the real temple was rebuilt (John 2:19-22).

> Jesus answered them, "Destroy this temple, and I
> will raise it again in three days." The Jews replied,
> "It has taken forty-six years to build this temple, and
> you are going to raise it in three days?" But the
> temple he had spoken of was his body. After he was
> raised from the dead, his disciples recalled what he
> had said. Then they believed the Scripture and the
> words that Jesus had spoken (John 2:19-22).

Hallelujah!

Once again, it's clear that, almost always, prophecy has a double
purpose. First, there's the physical reality, followed by a spiritual
fulfillment. First, there's the shadow, and then the substance.

For example, the writer to the Hebrews explains that the tabernacle or sanctuary is a copy or shadow of what's in heaven.

> The point of what we are saying is this: We do have
> such a high priest, who sat down at the right hand of
> the throne of the Majesty in heaven, and who serves
> in the sanctuary, the true tabernacle set up by the
> Lord, not by man.
>
> Every high priest is appointed to offer both gifts and
> sacrifices, and so it was necessary for this one also
> to have something to offer. If he were on earth, he
> would not be a priest, for there are already men who
> offer the gifts prescribed by the law. They serve at a
> sanctuary that is a copy and shadow of what is in
> heaven. This is why Moses was warned when he was
> about to build the tabernacle: "See to it that you
> make everything according to the pattern shown you
> on the mountain." But the ministry Jesus has
> received is as superior to theirs as the covenant of
> which he is mediator is superior to the old one, and

is founded on better promises.

For if there had been nothing wrong with that first covenant, no place would have been sought for another. But God found fault with the people and said:

"The time is coming," declares the Lord, "when I will make a new covenant with the house of Israel and with the house of Judah. It will not be like the covenant I made with their forefathers when I took them by the hand to lead them out of Egypt, *because they did not remain faithful to my covenant*, and I turned away from them," declares the Lord. "This is the covenant I will make with the house of Israel after that time," declares the Lord. "I will put my laws in their minds and write them on their hearts. I will be their God, and they will be my people. No longer will a man teach his neighbor, or a man his brother, saying, 'Know the Lord,' because they will all know me, from the least of them to the greatest. For I will forgive their wickedness and will remember their sins no more."

By calling this covenant "new," he has made the first one obsolete; and what is obsolete and aging will soon disappear. (Hebrews 8)

The writer to the Hebrews was quoting from the prophecy of the New Covenant that the Holy Spirit had given to Jeremiah, and which is recorded in Jeremiah 31:31-34. This prophecy found its fulfillment in the pages of the New Testament and is being fulfilled within Christ's church today.

Temples Built with Many Hands

It had been the desire of King David's heart to do something significant for God before he died, so he tried for a long time to

217

build a permanent place for God to dwell, and to replace the old, worn-out tabernacle that housed the Ark of the Covenant. But God did not allow him to do so because, as a warrior, he had shed too much blood. Then David, as directed by God, addressed his son Solomon, and said:

> "And you, my son Solomon, acknowledge the God of your father, and serve him with wholehearted devotion and with a willing mind, for the Lord searches every heart and understands every motive behind the thoughts. *If you seek him, he will be found by you; but if you forsake him, he will reject you forever.* Consider now, for the LORD has chosen you to build a temple as a sanctuary. Be strong and do the work."

> David also said to Solomon his son, "Be strong and courageous, and do the work. Do not be afraid or discouraged, for the LORD God, my God, is with you. He will not fail you or forsake you until all the work for the service of the temple of the LORD is finished. The divisions of the priests and Levites are ready for all the work on the temple of God, and every willing man skilled in any craft will help you in all the work. The officials and all the people will obey your every command" (1 Chronicles 28:9-10, 20-21).

David had related to the Israelite officials God's word to him: "Solomon your son is the one who will build my house and my courts, for I have chosen him to be my son, and I will be his father. I will establish his kingdom forever *if he is unswerving in carrying out my commands and laws, as is being done at this time*" (1 Chronicles 8:6-7).

Please note the emphasized conditional clauses and read what's recorded in 1 Kings 11:9-11:

> The LORD became angry with Solomon because his heart had turned away from the LORD, the God of Israel who had appeared to him twice. Although he had forbidden Solomon to follow other gods, Solomon did not keep the LORD's command. So the LORD said to Solomon, "Since this is your attitude and you have not kept my covenant and my decrees, which I commanded you, I will most certainly tear the kingdom away from you and give it to one of your subordinates."

What do you make of this? If you feel like reading on in your Bible, then consider what Paul had warned: "Do not be deceived; God cannot be mocked. A man reaps what he sows. The one who sows to please his sinful nature, from that nature will reap destruction..." (Galatians 6:7-8a).

Moses reaped what he sowed; David reaped what he sowed; Solomon reaped what he sowed; and so did all the others mentioned in the Old Testament. *God is faithful to both sides of His covenant.*

> Know therefore that the LORD your God is God; he is the faithful God, keeping his covenant of love to a thousand generations of those who love him and keep his commands. But those who hate him he will repay to their face by destruction; he will not be slow to repay to their face those who hate him.
>
> Therefore, take care to follow the commands, decrees and laws I give you today.
>
> Do not bring a detestable thing into your house or you will be set apart for destruction, even as it is. Utterly abhor and detest it, for it is set apart for destruction. (Deuteronomy 7:9-11, 26)

The earthly kingdom of David and his descendants was subject to obedience. They disobeyed and followed after other gods; the result was that, eventually, the house was left to them desolate. However, dispensationalists teach that this desolation was caused by heathens. The truth is, the temple had been destroyed on three different occasions because of the disobedience of the people.

There is no incident in Scripture where the people of God are punished and forsaken by God for whatever evil heathens did to them.

In the Old Testament (2 Samuel 6), we read that Uzzah, a descendant of Abraham, out of love for God and respect for the Ark of the Covenant, dropped dead for trying to save the ark from falling when an ox stumbled. In Uzzah's time, God was present in the Ark of the Covenant. But after the veil was rent, the temple, as a former dwelling place of God, became a structure like any other place of worship, a house of prayer, as Jesus referred to it.

In our time, it would be like a church building sold by a congregation and replaced by a supermarket. The congregation could then buy a bigger and newer church building on more acreage in the suburbs.

CHAPTER 21

The Branch

⊹⇌◎⇋⊹

"Give thanks to the LORD, call on his name;
make known among the nations
what he has done.

Sing to him, sing praise to him;
tell of all his wonderful acts.

Glory in his holy name;
let the hearts of those
who seek the LORD rejoice."
(1 Chronicles 16:8-10)

The Branch is Too Late.

Is the branch too late? Plans have been laid without Him.
The prophet Zechariah, under the inspiration of Christ (1 Peter 1:11), prophesied that the man named Branch would build the temple (Zechariah 6:12).

In the notes of his study Bible, C. I. Scofield comments that the Branch is Christ. It is a name of Christ, used in a fourfold way: (1) The Branch of Jehovah, Isaiah 4:2; (2) The Branch of David, Isaiah 11:1; Jeremiah 23:5, 33:15; (3) Jehovah's Servant, the Branch, Zechariah 3:8; (4) The man whose name is the Branch, Zechariah 6:12.

"In that day the Branch of the LORD will be beautiful and glorious, and the fruit of the land will be the pride and glory of the survivors in Israel" (Isaiah 4:2).

"A shoot will come up from the stump of Jesse; from his roots a Branch will bear fruit" (Isaiah 11:1).

"The days are coming," declares the LORD, "when I will raise up to David a righteous Branch, a king who will reign wisely and do what is just and right in the land" (Jeremiah 23:5).

"In those days and at that time I will make a righteous Branch sprout from David's line; he will do what is just and right in the land" (Jeremiah 33:15).

"Listen, O high priest Joshua, and your associates seated before you, who are men symbolic of things to come: I am going to bring my servant, the Branch" (Zechariah 3:8).

What Scofield doesn't make clear in his uninspired footnotes on the inspired pages of the Bible is how the Branch will build the temple of the Lord (Zechariah 6:12-15).

> Tell him this is what the LORD Almighty says, "Here is the man whose name is the Branch, and he will branch out from his place and build the temple of the LORD. It is he who will build the temple of the LORD, and he will be clothed with majesty and will sit and rule on his throne. And he will be a priest in his throne. And there will be harmony between the two. The crown will be given to Heldai, Tobijah, Jedaiah, and Hen son of Zephaniah as a memorial in the temple of the LORD. Those who are far away will come and help to build the temple of the LORD, and you will know that the LORD Almighty has sent me to you. This will happen if you diligently obey the LORD your God" (Zechariah 6:12-15).

Now take note of how Jesus interpreted the Old Testament when He said, *"I will build my church"* (Matthew 16:18). But Jesus never picked up one stone to begin building His church. Jesus never once picked up a brick or stone to put together a foundation to build something earthly. "And I tell you that you are Peter, and on this rock I will build my church, and the gates of Hades will not prevail against it" (Matthew 16:18).

Obviously, the building of the temple and the building of the church is the same thing. The unbiblical insistence of a literal interpretation wrongly divides and misinterprets the inspired Word of

God. The Branch builds the temple by means of branching out.

"I tell you that one greater than the temple is here" (Matthew 12:6).

"But the temple he had spoken of was his body" (John 2:21).

"Don't you know that you yourselves are God's temple and that God's Spirit lives in you?" (1 Corinthians 3:16).

"Do you not know that your body is a temple of the Holy Spirit, who is in you, whom you have received from God? You are not your own" (1 Corinthians 6:19).

"What agreement is there between the temple of God and idols? For we are the temple of the living God. As God has said: 'I will live with them and walk among them, and I will be their God, and they will be my people'" (2 Corinthians 6:16).

The book of Revelation speaks of a temple coming down from heaven. It's foolish to think of that building in terms of brick and mortar, or gold and crystal.

The New Temple

The book of Malachi prepared the way for a new and universal means of worship without any need for a physical temple. As has been stated before, there's no mention in the last book of the Old Testament of a return to the land. It had been fulfilled at the time of the writing of Malachi; they were there, and there's no further promise in the Bible relating to 1948.

> "Oh, that one of you would shut the temple doors, so that you would not light useless fires on my altar! I am not pleased with you," says the LORD Almighty, "and I will be great among the nations, from the rising to the setting of the sun. In every place incense and pure offerings will be brought to my name, because my name will be great among the nations," says the LORD Almighty (Malachi 1:10-11).

The Numbers 14:4 Mindset

Hindus need temples, Muslims need mosques, Mormons need temples, Buddhists need temples. A Christian is a living temple of

God. The church is made up of living stones, of which Christ is the chief cornerstone. If the so-called millennium needs a physical temple, it's nothing short of millennial madness, and an inferior condition to what a Christian experiences now.

To go back to the need of a brick and mortar temple is to:

- contradict the Word of Christ
- confuse Christianity with cults
- build on an obsolete foundation
- misrepresent the Messiah
- fill old skins with new wine

It's the way back into Egypt; it's a gospel in reverse. "And they said to each other, 'We should choose a leader and go back to Egypt'" (Numbers 14:4).

All of this is looking for the old country, an earthly one, and God will be ashamed to be called their God, and so will Abraham.

"Instead, they were longing for a better country—a heavenly one. Therefore God is not ashamed to be called their God, for he has prepared a city for them" (Hebrews 11:16).

Moses would be embarrassed with the Numbers 14:4 mindset:

> "But do not think I will accuse you before the Father. Your accuser is Moses, on whom your hopes are set. If you believed Moses, you would believe me, for he wrote about me. But since you do not believe what he wrote, how are you going to believe what I say?" (John 5:45-47).

As a believer in Jesus Christ, you will permanently be joined to Christ. He is a living temple, a living holy tabernacle. How this relationship continues in heaven, no one knows. God has not revealed this.

You are in Christ, and Christ is in you! That's all you need for now. The law of Christ and the gospel of God go with the Christian wherever he moves or has his being (Colossians 1:27).

Dispensationalism Before a Watching World

A very troublesome thing happened in August 2003 in Montgomery, Alabama. A godly state Supreme Court judge managed to have a two-and-a-half ton granite block with an abbreviated Ten Commandments chiseled on top in the foyer of his courthouse. The ACLU, of course, got busy and managed to persuade courts to have it removed.

I've never witnessed anything like this before. More and more Christians were personally motivated to stop it. They were kneeling in prayer, crying, pleading, being arrested. Someone called out, "Don't remove my God!"

Where are these people when a baby is aborted? If Christians all over the nation had objected to the teaching of evolution in the public schools, the only problem today might be chewing gum in class.

Well-meaning Christians were wrong to break the law. It was a very bad testimony. Here's why:

1. The purpose of the law of God is not to chisel it on a dead rock to irritate unbelievers and the ACLU, but to have the law of God written on the heart of the Christian (Jeremiah 31:32).

2. In the New Testament there are no Christian relics, no shrines, no temples, or holy places. Any close-ended typology—stone commandments, brass serpent, temple, etc.—can very easily become a malignant idol.

3. Christians are living stones, living the Commandments, being temples of God, with the law of God written on their hearts (Jeremiah 31:33).

4. Consequently, *there's no such thing as separation between church and state. Wherever the Christian goes, the law of Christ and prayer goes with him.* In courts or in schools, godly children pray before exams. Every government agency is permeated with implanted living Ten Commandments. For seventy years, the former Soviet Union tried to wipe out Christianity, but Christ was everywhere. It collapsed without a shot fired. Hallelujah!

5. The real disaster is that a serious Christian state Supreme Court judge was removed from his vital position, missing a unique opportunity to be a godly subordinate Christian leader in Alabama. With all due respect, a better Christian witness would have been for him to obey 1 Peter 2:13-18:

    > Submit yourselves for the Lord's sake to every authority instituted among men: whether to the king, as the supreme authority, or to governors, who are sent by him to punish those who do wrong and to commend those who do right. For it is God's will that by doing good you should silence the ignorant talk of foolish men. Live as free men, but do not use your freedom as a cover-up for evil; live as servants of God. Show proper respect to everyone: Love the brotherhood of believers, fear God, honor the king. Slaves, submit yourselves to your asters with all respect, not only to those who are good and considerate, but also to those who are harsh.

    That would have pleased God.

6. One more troublesome incident:

    That incredibly refreshing and safe *World Magazine* (www.worldmag.com) featured an article in the May 2004 issue, called *Wages of Sin*.

    > A pastor of a Pentecostal church in Jonesville, VA, celebrated Christ's victory over the serpent this Easter by handling one—and it killed him. No one at the Easter service sought help after the rattlesnake bit the pastor because the church teaches that God commands the handling of snakes and the refusal of medical help for snakebites. "We don't anticipate any charges," said Sheriff Gary Parsons. "That's their belief."

The sheriff is right when he said, "That's their belief." I maintain that it's another very disturbing result of literal interpretation of God's Word. Mark 16:15-18 clearly expects us to understand this symbolically.

> He said to them, "Go into all the world and preach the good news to all creation. Whoever believes and is baptized will be saved, but whoever does not believe will be condemned. And these signs will accompany those who believe: In my name they will drive out demons; they will speak in new tongues; they will pick up snakes with their hands; and when they drink deadly poison, it will not hurt them at all; they will place their hands on sick people, and they will get well."

Why is it that pastors shouldn't handle snakes? Because these words of Christ, from a problematic passage, *are not supposed to be interpreted literally*. It's a lonely paragraph, with no support anywhere else.

Every serious Christian handles all kinds of demonic snakes from day to day. Healings of minds and souls continue wherever the true gospel is preached and experienced. If one interprets this literally and dies, then Christ has made a false promise; His words can kill you. This sort of thing is such a bad testimony to the unbelieving world. It's once again a bad thing happening to a good prophecy.

What is Replacement Theology?

In dispensational circles, the negative term "replacement theologians" has become popular. A preacher who teaches that the church replaces the true Israel is identified by that unkind distinction, as if replacement is man-made and not in Scripture.

But who are the bad replacement theologians?

1. Being in contempt of Scripture and history by declaring fulfilled prophecy unfulfilled and replacing it somewhere in the future.

2. Replacing the faithful body of Christ, His church, with 144,000 Jewish male virgins to finish the job during the Great Tribulation.
3. Replacing the ruined temples of the Old and New Testaments (by the way, God didn't lift a finger to prevent their destruction) and building a greater and more elaborate one for worship in the Millennium.
4. Replacing the once and for all sacrifice of Christ on the cross by reinstituted temple sacrifices during the thousand years.

This is replacement theology of the worst kind. The church doesn't replace the Jews. True followers of God in any other revelatory period are redeemed because of Christ, and in good standing as members of the body of Christ. No replacement has taken place or is necessary.

There are, of course many, replacements in the Bible, not done by man but executed by God himself.

1. God moved Adam and Eve from the inside to the outside of the Garden.
2. God replaces former things for better things (Hebrews 7:28-19).
3. God replaces stony hearts with hearts of flesh.
4. God replaces the old ways of entering the sanctuary with a new and living way (Hebrews 10:19).
5. God replaces shadows of the law with the coming of good things (Hebrews 10:1).
6. God replaces the prophets by His gift of His Son (Hebrews 11).
7. God replaces the old Jerusalem with a spiritual new Jerusalem.
8. God replaces circumcision of the flesh with spiritual circumcision of the heart.
9. God replaces the Holy Land with holy living.
10. God replaces the broken down physical temples with living temples.

11. God replaced the Old Covenant with the New Covenant

That new term used by dispensationalists to identify non-dispensationalist *replacement theology* turns out to be a badge of honor.

CHAPTER 22

Go Down, Jesus!

The Passion of Christ

Who, being in very nature God,
did not consider equality with God
something to be grasped,
but made himself nothing,
taking the very nature of a servant,
being made in human likeness.

And being found in appearance as a man,
he humbled himself
and became obedient to death – even death on a cross!

Therefore God exalted him
to the highest place
and gave him the name that is above every name,
that at the name of Jesus
every knee should bow,
in heaven and on earth
and under the earth,
and every tongue confess
that Jesus Christ is Lord,
to the glory of God the Father.
(Philippians 2:6-11)

The Thousand Years—Delight or Disaster?

First and foremost, this book is about the glorious and only Son of God, the Lamb slain before the foundation of the world, the sin bearer, the one who bore within Himself all those whom God had chosen. He was the one who could have called more than twelve legions of angels to protect Him. But He went willingly to the cross.

He was the only one who overcame Satan and all the host of hell. We're talking about Jesus, the one of whom the church has been singing:

> Jesus the name high over all,
> In heaven, earth, and sky
> Angels and men before Him fall
> And devils fear and fly.

What is Jesus Doing Right Now?

Consider just a tiny fraction of what Scripture tells us Jesus is doing right now. It's overwhelming:

- The exalted Christ is at God's right hand, permanently.
- He is interceding for all His sheep; He is in contact with each one.
- He keeps each sheep before Him day and night.
- His promise stands: "I will never leave you or forsake you."
- He knows each Christian by name.
- He knows where we live.
- He plans our paths; each one is mapped out by Him.
- He listens to each prayer.
- He disciplines each believer.
- He never slumbers or sleeps.
- He opens and closes doors.
- He comes constantly to take dying saints to be with Him, the real Rapture.
- He carries on a truceless war on behalf of us with Satan.
- He is defeating Satan, and all evil with him.

He is the one the book of Hebrews talks about: "...but in these last days he has spoken to us by his Son, whom he appointed heir of all things, and through whom he made the universe. The Son is the radiance of God's glory and the exact representation of his being, sustaining all things by his powerful word. After he had provided purification for our sins, he sat down at the right hand of the Majesty in heaven" (Hebrews 1:2-3).

We're talking about the second person of the Godhead. He is in heaven with millions of souls saved from this earth. Christ has gathered them from the four corners of the world to be with Him in heaven eternally. It's an environment that's totally different from anything we're capable of imagining.

The place is sinless, joyful, glorious, timeless, spaceless, and painless. It's God's gift to believers, a place of unencumbered grace. Nothing is soilable or spoilable. There is sinless worship with unspeakable joy. It's the place where God's plan for history has come together perfectly with great celebration. There is purpose, and sinless worship.

The best songs have been kept for heaven; the greatest music has been reserved. The greatest voices on earth will sound like crows with laryngitis, compared with the sounds never heard on earth, but in heaven only.

There are no limitations. The seed form of the flesh (1 Corinthians 15:36) has been planted in heaven and has sprung up to a glorious other spiritual form, called glorified saint. We'll be as different in heaven from what we are now, as a small acorn is from a mighty oak tree.

There is togetherness, harmony, and love. In heaven are many rooms. Jesus said, "I am going to prepare a place for you" (John 14:2); we will be together with Him forever.

I remember a horrible time when I was a youngster at home. I was about twelve years old when I must have done something wrong, for which I was taken to the proverbial woodshed. My Christian father loved me and made sure that when I did wrong, pain followed.

After the thunder and lightning had passed, I was sent to my room. An hour or so later, my dad came into the bedroom.

"Son," he said, "you claim to be a Christian. You claim that you accepted Christ as your Savior at age six in Sunday school, but I doubt it. You have absolutely nothing in your life to show that you're a Christian. And listen to me—I fear for you, that if you should die tonight, you'll go straight to hell!"

"Not so fast, Dad," I said, wiping salty tears from my red eyes. "You and Mother are good Christians, and both of you will go to heaven, and I know you won't be happy if you know your boy didn't make it."

"Son, listen to me carefully, for once. When Mother and I are in heaven in the presence of God the Father, Jesus, His Son and our Savior, and the Holy Spirit permeating all there is, when we gaze upon the beauty of God and enjoy sinless worship, if you're not there, in all eternity my memory of you won't enter my glorified mind for one split second. Your soul will just be a dead seed, which was incapable of germinating into a glorified body. There's no evidence that your dead soul was resurrected." What a great and wonderful dad I had.

A Point of No Return

You can't put a one-day-old chicken back into its eggshell. The mosquito can't go back into the pond to visit his unglorified, left-behind larva. The butterfly can't go back into the old limitations of his now-damaged cocoon. Neither can a glorified saint live in this fallen world again. Why would he want to?

Does Scripture support the above illustration from creation (Romans 1:19-20)? Yes! It's called natural revelation. But what about supernatural revelation?

> Brothers, we do not want you to be ignorant about those who fall asleep, or to grieve like the rest of men, who have no hope. We believe that Jesus died and rose again and so we believe that God will bring with Jesus those who have fallen asleep in him. According to the Lord's own word, we tell you that we who are still alive, who are left till the coming of the Lord, will certainly not precede those who have fallen asleep. For the Lord himself will come down from heaven, with a loud command, with the voice of the archangel and with the trumpet call of God,

and the dead in Christ will rise first. After that, we who are still alive and are left will be caught up together with them in the clouds to meet the Lord in the air. And so we will be with the Lord forever. Therefore encourage each other with these words (1 Thessalonians 4:13-18).

Jesus said, "It is finished," not, "So far, so good"

In praying to His Father shortly before His arrest, Jesus said: "I have brought you glory on earth by *completing* the work you gave me to do" (John 17:4). Yet, according to dispensationalist interpretation, His work was *not* completed. In order to validate that position, God the Father has to say to Jesus, "Son, I know you said it was finished at the cross, but guess what—it's not finished! Before, you went willingly to the earth for thirty-three years. Now I want you to go for a thousand years! So, *Go Down, Jesus!*

"You still have to prove to the world that you are the king and the ruler of the world. You still have to prove that you are able to take the throne of David and sit in your palace in Jerusalem. Satan won't bother you, for he will be bound with a great chain for the thousand years."

Dear reader, do you think I'm kidding? No, I'm not kidding! Those of you who have turned to this book for encouragement because you've been disappointed by the elusive Rapture know this is the teaching of dispensationalism, or pre-millennialism, as recorded in Dwight Pentecost's major work, and popularized by the *Left Behind* series.

This, as we've said before, is the problem with insisting that things that can be interpreted literally must be interpreted literally. Oh, what a disaster and humiliation for the exalted Christ, and for what purpose? God has to violate, and call null and void, all His warnings and curses in Scripture, and say, "I didn't really mean it."

I repeat: if God still looks upon Israel as the apple of His eye, His warnings and curses are empty and void. The Old Covenant has not disappeared and is superior to the New Covenant.

No! Christ proved He was supreme victor of the whole universe and all sin when He had His moment in the darkness. "He became obedient unto death—even death on a cross! Therefore God *exalted Him* to the highest place" (Philippians 2:8-9).

Nothing else needs to be said, apart from the fact that pre-millennialists take away the *emphasis of the cross.* Paul didn't say that "in the kingdom of Christ, I glory." No, it was only in the cross of Christ (Galatians 6:14).

To prove that the pre-millennialists de-emphasize the cross of Christ, consider that during the supposed thousand-year reign of Christ—we've already talked about this—they believe a temple will be built and sacrifices will again be burned on the altar as a memorial. As if Christ's death wasn't enough. Jesus said, "Remember my death till I come."

CHAPTER 23

How Can One Day Be a Thousand Years?

⋆⇒◦⇐⋆

...faith comes from hearing the message,
and the message is heard
through the word of Christ.
(Romans 10:17)

An Unbeliever Criticizes the Bible

The Bible is full of contradictions," said an agnostic to a church deacon.

"What do you mean?" the deacon retorted.

"Well, this Jesus of yours is supposed to have said to His disciples, 'Go out into all the world and make disciples.' And also, He said something like, 'Go out into the highways and byways and compel sinners to come to Me.' Right?"

"Right!"

"But in the Old Testament, it says in Psalm 1, 'Blessed is the man who does not walk in the counsel of the ungodly (wicked) or stand in the way of sinners, or sit in the seat of mockers.'"

"So?"

"Well, it's obvious you're obedient to Jesus, but disobedient to the Old Testament. You're sinning by just talking to me. How can you make someone a Christian like yourself if, in the Old Testament, you're not even allowed to walk, stand, or sit with him or her at the table and go through your silly little *Four Spiritual Laws*?"

"Well," answered the deacon, "walk doesn't always mean walk. Stand doesn't always mean stand. And sit doesn't always mean sit."

"You're crazy, and so is your Bible."

"Listen to me. It means simply this. Walk means to go the same direction, so don't go the same direction as ungodly people, and don't take your stand with them. And don't sit at the table that would identify you as one of them."

The deacon went on and explained that the Bible isn't a book you read once and you've read it. It's a *study* book. Children can be blessed by it, and the world's greatest minds cannot fathom all its wisdom. They stand in awe of it as an unfathomable well.

The same thing applies to the number 1000, or the thousand-year earthly reign of Christ. This is particularly so when you read books that primarily use apocalyptic language, like Daniel, Ezekiel, and Revelation. There are very few things in Revelation that are unique to that book. Most of it is borrowed from the Old Testament. So, let's study the number 1000.

For Example, When Is 1000 Not 999 + 1?

Is 1000 in the Bible equal to 999 plus one? Or does 1000 not always really mean a literal 1000? Here are some examples in the Bible where the word *thousand* is used. Let's consider whether each should be translated literally:

> Deuteronomy 7:9—Know therefore, that the LORD your
>   God is God; he is the faithful God, keeping his covenant
>   of love to a *thousand* generations...
> Joshua 23:10—One of you routs a *thousand*...
> Judges 15:16—...I have killed a *thousand* men.
> 1 Chronicles 16:15—He remembers his covenant *forever*,
>   the word he commanded for a *thousand* generations...

Literally 40,000 years? Does *forever* equal 40,000 years? Perhaps the last verse of *Amazing Grace* should be:

> When we've been there 10,000 years,
> Bright shining as the sun,
> There's only 30,000 left,
> And then we'll all be done.

This is silly, of course. One thousand generations equals eternity.

Psalm 50:10—The cattle on a *thousand* hills [are mine].

Psalm 68:17—The chariots of God are tens of *thousands* and *thousands* of *thousands*.

Psalm 84:10—Better is one day in your courts than a *thousand* elsewhere.

Psalm 90:4—For a *thousand* years in your sight are like a day.

Psalm 105:8—He remembers his covenant *forever*, the word he commanded for a *thousand* generations.

Isaiah 7:23—In that day in every place where there were a *thousand* vines worth a *thousand* shekels.

Isaiah 30:17—A *thousand* will flee at the threat of one.

Isaiah 60:22—The least of you will become a *thousand*, the smallest a mighty nation. In its time, I will do this swiftly.

Micah 5:2—But you, Bethlehem, ... you are little among the *thousands* of Judah.

(There weren't thousands of towns in Judah!)

2 Peter 3:8—A day is like a *thousand* years and a *thousand* years are like a day.

Often—almost always—the word, or number 1000 in the Bible is *not* taken literally—A thousand generations...one routs a thousand...I have killed a thousand men...He remembers his covenant *forever*, but his commands for (only) a thousand generations. See also how many times in the Psalms we have the term, all *generations*—so *all* and *a thousand years* are equal. *Forever* and *a thousand generations* are equal. "The cattle on a thousand hills are mine"—New Zealand alone has over a thousand hills. To be immovable about a literal 1000 is just plain silly.

Why This Book?

My *major objection* to this whole misinterpretation of future events has to do with the *person, honor, and glory of Christ.* For argument's sake, let's compare King Hezekiah with King Jesus. King Hezekiah, an earthly man with no supernatural powers, took an evil kingdom and more or less restored it. The devil was loose with evil people everywhere, and Hezekiah (through the power of the Holy Spirit) turned people's hearts to the Lord in twenty-nine years.

According to the futurists, Jesus receives a kingdom with only righteous people—glorified and non-glorified saints. What a wonderful, unprecedented start. The devil is bound, tied up, inactive; yet, after a thousand years, things are fouled up under Christ's rule. Who did a better job? Who's a greater king? Who ruled better? What a disaster! This is further humiliation for Christ!

Getting back to reality, Christ is now exalted and seated at the right hand of God. Stephen saw it. We know that Christ is reigning in inexpressible glory over the measureless universe; this whole concept is incomprehensible to anyone on earth—billions of times more wonderful than anything we can imagine! We can now see again that the last verse in John's gospel is *not* an exaggeration, but fact.

"Jesus did many other things as well. If every one of them were written down, I suppose that even the whole world would not have room for the books that would be written" (John 21:25).

The Natural and Supernatural World

The late Dr. Francis A. Schaeffer, in his most excellent book, *True Spirituality*, points out in his fifth chapter, *The Supernatural World*, the reason for failing spiritual development in the life of the Christian: the Christian of this generation has lost sight of his access to the spiritual world, because of his overwhelmingly naturalistic world view and behavior.

Dr. Schaeffer points out very clearly that most Christians are totally ignorant of the fact that here and now, in time and space, the converted believer lives in a natural and supernatural universe.

Suddenly, it hit me! How could I have missed it?

Let's go back to the first chapter of this book—you'll remember that the murderous Cain feared greatly that he was cut off from the supernatural world, where others walked with God. It seems to me that during those early years after creation, people were acutely aware of the two worlds in which they naturally lived, illustrated by an angel with a flaming sword for everyone to see and get away from (Genesis 3:20-24).

Clearly, Enoch walked in both worlds with God. Later on,

Abraham walked in both worlds; Moses walked in both worlds; Elisha walked in both worlds, as is so magnificently illustrated in 2 Kings 6:17. Elisha and his servant were completely surrounded by a large band of murderous Arameans. His servant was about to fall apart, but Elisha asked God to give this young man a vision of God's supernatural world.

And Elisha prayed, "O LORD, open his eyes so he may see." Then the LORD opened the servant's eyes, and he looked and saw the hills full of horses and *chariots of fire* all around Elisha" (2 Kings 6:17).

In other words, God gave him a vision of the other universe, the supernatural one, in which he lived, but was not aware of.

Eric Liddell, the Olympic athlete who refused to compete on The Lord's Day, as portrayed in the film *Chariots of Fire*, was clearly operating in both the natural and supernatural worlds, while others around him were not. They were amazed at what to them was his strange behavior.

Our Lord Jesus operated in both worlds and, after conversion, so did Paul, Peter, and John. And every other truly converted person at the moment of rebirth is invited to walk in the supernatural kingdom, or universe (Hebrews 8:8-13).

I believe that the well-meaning yet relentless proponents of the physical thousand-year kingdom of Christ have no idea of, or have lost sight of, the fact that, here and now, the believer lives in the natural and supernatural worlds *already.* We struggle on earth, and are enthroned with Christ in heaven.

Consequently, having yet another thousand-year kingdom is totally unnecessary, redundant, embarrassing to Christ, and unbiblical. Study the realities of Ephesians 1:18, 2:1-10, 5:8, and rejoice!

This is our present position in Christ for all people of all nations who have committed their lives to Him. Millennialism has been weighed in the balance and found wanting.

Herein lies the problem:

1. It implies that the Gospel of Christ is not the total power of God unto salvation. It will need millennial aids.
2. The power of the Holy Spirit leading to repentance and

faith has failed during the pre-rapture of the church.

3. Jesus should have been more specific and should have said "I and the 144,000 male virgins will build our church, for the gates of hell have overcome the pre-rapture church."

4. The dividing wall of hostility (Ephesians 2:14) was really never broken down.

5. It contradicts the New Testament teaching as to the oneness of God's people.

6. It reverses God's order: First that which is natural or material, afterward that which is spiritual and eternal. Earth, heaven, earth again.

7. It makes the thousand years a time of less blessing for those who have already been in heaven.

8. It means a number of second comings of Christ: first second coming, second second coming, third second coming, etc.

9. It arbitrarily means a number of final judgments.

10. It means three resurrections: the church dead; the millennial, sainted dead; the totally wicked dead.

11. It's a time of learning war again to protect the camp of the saints.

12. It means an impossible binding of immortals and spiritual beings with the unspiritual and mortals. That's why Christ has to use the "iron scepter" to bring law and order.

13. It divorces the church from the Old Testament and major portions from the New Testament.

14. The thousand years is founded on two isolated, "symbolic," not-literal, lonely verses.

15. It's a reestablishing of earthly worship, temples, and sacrifices.

16. Finally, it all comes to a deteriorating end of disorder, disaster, and disgrace. Christ disappears to heaven and fire from heaven saves the remnant.

"The reason the Son of God appeared was to destroy the devil's work" (1 John 3:8b).

Christ certainly does not need another humiliation or another thousand years to accomplish His mission. He is highly exalted right now, and Satan is on the way out, systematically under the feet of His people in the past, present, and in a final future (Romans 16:20).

CHAPTER 24

The Purpose of History

⊹⇒◉⇐⊹

"Oh, that my words were recorded,
that they were written on a scroll,
that they were inscribed
with an iron tool on lead,
or engraved in rock forever!

I know that my Redeemer lives,
and that in the end
he will stand upon the earth.

And after my skin has been destroyed,
yet in my flesh I will see God;
I myself will see him
with my own eyes – I, and not another.
How my heart yearns within me!"
(Job 19:23-27)

Candidates for Heaven

It's obvious that in futuristic dispensationalism, Christ has been pushed into the background, and the focus is now on the Jews. No wonder the Arabs don't want anything to do with Christ. They think Christ only lifts up Israel and puts down Arabs. This needs correction.

What is the gospel really? Why did Jesus come? What is the church? What is the responsibility of an individual Christian?

In reading the New Testament, don't flip from one page to another, or from the Old Testament to the New, and vice versa. You may want to at least read one book of the New Testament at a time.

The great discovery will be God's only means to fulfill His original ultimate purpose, and that is to recreate man in His own image.

The purpose of history is to gather people from all nations for Himself, to be with Him forever in eternity. Jesus is the means by which this infallible plan is executed. Every converted person is a *positively approved candidate for heaven*. The following insights, from the pen of 17th century British minister John Flavel, will fill you with awe:

> Our glorious Mediator executes the design of our redemption. *Had he not, as our Prophet, opened the way of life and salvation to the children of men, they could never have known it; and if they had clearly known it, yet except as their Priest, he had offered up himself to obtain redemption for them, they could not have been redeemed virtually by his blood; and if they had been so redeemed, yet had he not lived in the capacity of a King, to apply this purchase of his blood to them, they could have had no actual, personal benefit by his death*; for what he revealed as a *Prophet*, he purchased as a *Priest*; and what he so revealed and purchased as a *Prophet* and *Priest*, he applies as a *King*; first *subduing the souls* of his people to his spiritual government, then *ruling them* as his subjects, and ordering all things in the kingdom of providence for their good. So that Christ has a twofold kingdom, the one *spiritual and internal*, by which he subdues and rules the hearts of his people; the other *providential* and external, whereby he guides, rules, and orders all things in the world, in a blessed subordination to their eternal salvation.

All there's left for us to do is summarize:

1. Jesus is the eternal Word of God.
2. Jesus is the only Son of God.
3. Jesus is the exact image of God.

4. Jesus is the only way back to God.
5. Jesus is the only lamb and sacrifice of God.
6. Jesus is the fulfillment of the Word of God
7. Jesus is the only glory of God.
8. Jesus is the only answer to man from God.
9. Jesus is the only glory of the Israel of God.

As has already been discussed in chapter 1, every book in the Old Testament has hidden in its content the mystery of God—Jesus Christ our Lord. So then, Jesus, and Him crucified, is to occupy our thoughts and actions. It is He who saves people from their sins. It is He who is the light and life of all who believe.

Someone has said that since His resurrection, all of history has been a *cleaning up* operation, wherein the implications of His work are gradually being implemented throughout the world.

It is the salvation of all the world, in which we personally live out the time allotted to us, that ought to demand our attention, by using all the means available to be holy persons, suitable to be used by God, in prayer and serious worship, together with His people.

At the same time, it's God who saves people. It's God who makes believers out of unbelievers. It's God who, by His sovereign electing grace, regenerates a dead soul. It's God who opens the heart of a sinner (Acts 16:14).

It's God, whom everybody has to face one day at the judgment, and then it's no longer an issue of Jew or Gentile, pre-millennial or a-millennial, but what you have done with Jesus. Are you in Christ or not?

If you're not sure, ask God to make Jesus known to you as your Savior.

You don't need to see Him or feel Him, but you must have faith to believe in Him. Ask God for it, for even God's grace and faith to believe in Christ are gifts from God.

"For it is by grace you have been saved, through faith—and this not from yourselves, it is the gift of God—not by works, so that no one can boast" (Ephesians 2:8-9).

It's Sunday, but Friday's Coming

Be blessed by the following story of the nearly unbelievable, yet greatest conversion in the Bible, which could only have taken place by God's sovereign work of redeeming grace.

Humanly speaking, the most unlikely person to be a king and savior was Jesus Christ, as He hung, slowly dying in indescribable agony on that horrible Roman cross.

The public ministry of Christ can be looked upon as one long beautiful Sunday. It was an extended Sunday of teaching, preaching, praying, healing, helping, and worshipping His Father. He was busy. It was a long, wonderful Sunday of carrying out the ministry His Father told Him to do.

Yet, hanging over His head, was a constant awareness that a Friday was coming. He knew right at the beginning of His ministry that He had come to die.

It's thrilling for us to know that, yet I wonder what went on in the mind of Christ as He knew that, down the road, not too far in the future, there was a Friday where He would have to meet the judgment of God and drink the cup of His wrath on behalf of all His sheep.

Many people left in tears after seeing the movie, *The Passion of the Christ.* I've listened to great sermons on the suffering of Christ, how agonizing His death was. But I have news for you. Millions of faithful Christians have suffered physically far longer than our Lord Jesus Christ. Many have died in prison over the last two thousand years.

However, Jesus died alone, separated from God. No Christian ever dies like that. We have the testimonies of martyrs that when the suffering is worst, His presence is unbelievably wonderful. Not so for Christ. He was cut off from God. But knowing all this, knowing He had come to die, He was determined to be the Savior.

So then, the most unlikely person to be recognized as the Son of God and Savior was Jesus, when He was dying on the cursed tree. This was the one who had promised freedom to the people when He said, "You will know the truth and the truth shall make you free." Yet now He was on that cross.

This was the one who said, "If God can clothe the lilies of the field, will He not clothe you, O you of little faith?" Yet He was stripped of His clothes and hung embarrassingly naked. Here was the one who healed the sick and cleansed lepers, yet He was dirty and dying. Hands that had healed the sick were being torn to pieces. The one who promised living water to those who were thirsty was now crying out for a drink.

The one who had claimed to be a king was without subjects, without a throne. The one who had so wonderfully defeated the devil was now crushed in a satanic grip. The one who was sinless had now become the bearer of sin. He who knew no sin had become sin for us.

The Most Unlikely Person to Be Saved

Let's leave Him for a moment and look at the most unlikely person to be saved—the thief hanging on the cross on the right of Jesus. His whole life had been one long Sunday, doing his own thing; a godless Sunday, a godless life, indulging his own sinful pleasure whenever he wanted to, with no thought or fear of God.

This man also had a Friday coming, but, unlike Christ, he didn't know it. He'd lived one long, godless Sunday of a life, but now Friday had come his way, the day of judgment, the day of reckoning. This was the day when he had to face God.

Consider this man: no one would think he'd be invited to paradise. His criminal, godless life was about to come to a brutal end. "Sin, when it is finished, brings forth death." He had made no preparation for eternity. He was in the most unholy, horrible surroundings possible, far from the beauty of the architecture of a church, the sweetness and the music of a congregation singing *Just as I Am*.

No, he was in a most unholy, godless place. There was cursing, blaspheming, screaming and hatred, the stench of previous crucifixions, millions of blowflies, indifferent people laughing, calloused and cruel soldiers carrying out inhumane orders. His Friday had come and he wasn't ready. He hadn't prepared or thought about it. He may never have been warned about it. Maybe no one ever prayed for his conversion. He may never have heard a preacher say, "Prepare to meet your God."

What happened next? I believe this is the most incredible opportunity for us to witness God's redeeming grace. I believe this is the Bible's most incredible conversion. As we read this passage of Scripture, we discover the first thing that happens when God, by His sovereign grace, touches someone.

I wonder if there was some person somewhere in the crowd looking at this criminal who began to pray for him. I don't know. All we know is that Jesus was praying and the grace of God came upon and within this man. Consequently, we see the most incredible conversion in the Bible. And what happens when God opens someone's heart to receive the truth of the gospel? Let's look at it in sequence.

First of all, it stops a man from mocking and insulting God. In Matthew 27, we read that both criminals were insulting Christ: "In the same way the robbers who were crucified with him also heaped insults on him" (Matthew 27:44).

Both thieves cursed, both blasphemed God, but in Luke's gospel, only one thief mocks Christ. At one stage, both mocked. Then the grace of God came into this man's life and all of a sudden, *he stopped mocking.*

The second thing that happens is that the saving grace of God *implants the fear of God.* When the grace of God takes hold of an individual, there comes a realization that God is holy and that we are to fear Him and face Him. Turning to the other thief, he said, "Don't you fear God?"

You know the answer: "Of course I don't fear God." The Bible says the unconverted don't fear God. "There is no fear of God before their eyes." They fear everything else, but they don't fear God.

He had never been taught to fear God. He had never heard sermons on the holiness of God, or on the wrath of God, or about hell.

You know what was happening to the thief on the right? He was slowly becoming aware of his Friday. His Sunday was over. Judgment was upon him and, whether he wanted to or not, he had to face his holy Creator.

The third thing that happens in this incredible conversion is that *God's grace convicts of sin.* He says, "We deserve our punishment. We're punished justly; it's nobody else's fault."

What an unbelievable breakthrough! He didn't blame his father;

he didn't blame his family, his circumstances, or his environment. He said, "We deserve our punishment right now." So when the Spirit of God enters a person, he's convicted of sin—his own sin, his rebellion—and his contempt for God's law.

The next thing that happens is that *he recognizes the Savior.* The supernatural world opened up to him. Consequently, God's saving grace will always lead a repentant sinner to the Savior. This is the very reason why I think it's the most incredible and the most outstanding conversion in the Bible.

Nicodemus believed in Jesus because he had a personal interview with Him and said, "You must have been a teacher come from God for no one can do these miracles that you do." So he believed something about Jesus because he saw the miracles.

Nathaniel believed because Jesus told him, "I saw you under a tree. You didn't even know it, but I knew you." "Is this not the Messiah?" Nathaniel said to his friends. He believed, for Jesus showed him His omniscience.

The woman at the well believed in Jesus because He was a prophet and He asked her for water and she received the living water. Then she told everyone, "Is this not the Christ? He told me everything that I have ever done wrong."

A whole lot of people believed in Him when He was feeding the five thousand. It's easy to believe in someone who can do miracles. People must have said to each other, "He must have come from heaven. He's able to do some mighty miracles. Here He is, breaking bread for five thousand people; let's follow Him, for the prophet Isaiah has foretold that 'He will feed His flock', and that's what He did."

It must have been a terrible moment when those men stood around the sepulcher where the body of Lazarus lay. He'd been in there for some time now, when Jesus told them to roll away the stone. "Lord, don't do that, don't do that—he stinks!" They rolled away the stone and the stench of death hit everybody – mothers with little children hanging on to their skirts; fathers trembling. Even the birds in the trees stopped singing.

Then, with the same divine voice that brought the whole universe together, Jesus said, "Lazarus, come forth." He who had been dead was dead no longer. People everywhere were saying,

"It's the Son of God, it's the Messiah!" No one else can do that. It was easy to believe in Him.

Sleeping in the boat was, for Jesus, a break from people. When the disciples thought the boat was about to capsize, Jesus stood up. "Oh, there is a storm on, isn't there? I was sound asleep. Sorry about this, guys. Peace, be still." "Wow, You are the Son of God" (paraphrase mine).

We talk about the incredible conversion of Paul the apostle. Paul would have to be insane if he wasn't going to be converted after what happened to him. The lightning hit and he fell to the ground, blind as a bat. "Saul, Saul, why are you persecuting me?" "Who are you, Lord?" "I am Jesus of Nazareth." Of course, Paul believed! He was made an apostle by the will of God.

Beloved, think of this. *The thief believed in Jesus when there was nothing physical to make a believer out of him. There was nothing left.* God's saving grace, that taught his heart to fear, now led to the sinner's prayer, *"Lord, remember me."*

Oh, what a wonderful Savior we have. As the Lord Jesus is hanging in intense pain between two criminal sinners, he doesn't say to this wretched soul, "Why should I remember you? I'm suffering here. I have enough pain to worry about, without having to worry over you!" I think we'd have understood if He hadn't said anything to this guilty man. Instead, our Savior, who refused to answer the king, who wouldn't talk to him in the palace, turned His head in agony to answer the prayer of a repentant sinner.

God's redeeming grace finally opened paradise. "Today," He said, *"you will be with me in paradise." What a conversion!* It was a wonderful conversion because, without repentance, no one will enter paradise.

Christ is always the Savior. Today is the day of salvation. Today is the day when the gospel can go out. There are people who are being led astray in this world, who don't realize there's a judgment coming, who don't realize they may be enjoying a long Sunday, but that there's a Friday coming in their lives, at God's appointed time.

Heaven and Hell

Now what happened? What's the end of all this? The thief was regenerated; his soul silently, quickly, invisibly, mysteriously, unmistakably ascended to heaven. The other thief was left behind. Christ descended into hell. He obediently drank the cup of God's wrath. The converted thief drank the cup of salvation, as the psalmist, in a divinely inspired moment of revelation, said:

"How can I repay the LORD for all his goodness to me? I will lift up *the cup of salvation* and call on the name of the LORD" (Psalm 116:12-13).

We know that wasn't the end. We know something else happened. Christ rose again, the eternal temple was rebuilt in three days, and Christ is seated at the right hand of God in heaven, ruling forever over the immeasurable universe! He will not return from there until all enemies are made a footstool for His feet.

"The LORD says to my Lord: 'Sit at my right hand until I make your enemies a footstool for your feet.'" (Psalm 110:1).

"The Lord said to my Lord: 'Sit at my right hand until I put your enemies under your feet'" (Matthew 22:44).

"...until I make your enemies a footstool for your feet" (Luke 20:43).

"...until I make your enemies a footstool for your feet" (Acts 2:35).

"To which of the angels did God ever say, 'Sit at my right hand until I make your enemies a footstool for your feet'?" (Hebrews 1:13).

So we see the thief, unworthy, but ascending into heaven, and Jesus going obediently to hell. We rejoice that He came out of hell and took the keys of death and hell with Him (Revelation 1:18), and is at the right hand of God the Father.

In the first chapter of Revelation, we have an incredible description of someone who went to hell and back. John writes about his vision:

> I turned around to see the voice that was speaking to me. And when I turned, I saw seven golden lamp-stands, and among the lampstands was someone

"like a son of man," dressed in a robe reaching down to his feet and with a golden sash around his chest. His head and hair were white like wool, as white as snow, and his eyes were like blazing fire. His feet were like bronze glowing in a furnace, and his voice was like the sound of rushing waters. In his right hand he held seven stars, and out of his mouth came a sharp double-edged sword. His face was like the sun shining in all its brilliance.

When I saw him, I fell at his feet as though dead. Then he placed his right hand on me and said: "Do not be afraid. I am the First and the Last. I am the Living One; I was dead, and behold I am alive forever and ever! And I hold the keys of death and Hades.

"Write, therefore, what you have seen, what is now and what will take place later. The mystery of the seven stars that you saw in my right hand and of the seven golden lampstands is this: The seven stars are the angels of the seven churches, and the seven lamp-stands are the seven churches." (Revelation 1:12-18)

In the meantime, we have a great responsibility to warn everyone that it's Sunday, but that Friday's coming. Are you ready? We don't know when Christ will come for the last time, but you know your life is but a few decades. Ask Jesus to be your Savior, if you're not already sure He is.

Jesus has come, is coming constantly, and will come.

We believe the whole purpose of history, beginning with Adam and going to the end of the world, is for God, the triune God, to call people, in the time and space allotted to each individual, unto Himself to populate eternity, which is an unbelievable, timeless, spaceless, unimaginable

existence. Consequently, history is not fulfilled by the activities and decisions of man, but by God.

Let me put it this way. God-ordained, true history is made when a little child, kneeling before his father, says, "I would like to receive Jesus as my Savior and ask Him to come into my heart." Then the whole host of heaven shouts for joy. Christ is building His universal church. All the redeemed and angels fall down and worship God.

CHAPTER 25

Love in the City

-◆⟹⟸◆-

But you have come to Mount Zion,
to the heavenly Jerusalem,
the city of the living God.

You have come to thousands
upon thousands of angels
in joyful assembly,
to the church of the firstborn,
whose names are written in heaven.

You have come to God,
the judge of all men,
to the spirits of righteous men
made perfect, to Jesus the mediator
of a new covenant,
and to the sprinkled blood
that speaks a better word
than the blood of Abel.
(Hebrews 12:22-24)

From Here to Eternity

First think about the Scriptures above. Here and now on earth, we are loved by God in the city, the heavenly Jerusalem, the church, the Bride of Christ. The apostle Paul gives a description of that love in the city:

> And we know that in all things God works for the
> good of those who love him, who have been called

according to his purpose. For those God foreknew he also predestined to be conformed to the likeness of his Son, that he might be the firstborn among many brothers. And those he predestined, he also called; those he called, he also justified; those he justified, he also glorified.

What, then, shall we say in response to this? If God is for us, who can be against us? He who did not spare his own Son, but gave him up for us all—how will he not also, along with him, graciously give us all things? Who will bring any charge against those whom God has chosen? It is God who justifies. Who is he that condemns? Christ Jesus, who died—more than that, who was raised to life—is at the right hand of God and is also interceding for us. Who shall separate us from the love of Christ? Shall trouble or hardship or persecution or famine or nakedness or danger or sword? As it is written: "For your sake we face death all day long; we are considered as sheep to be slaughtered." No, in all these things we are more than conquerors through him who loved us. For I am convinced that neither death nor life, neither angels nor demons, neither the present nor the future, nor any powers, neither height nor depth, nor anything else in all creation, will be able to separate us from the love of God that is in Christ Jesus our Lord (Romans 8:28-39).

These above quotes from Scripture are reality. These verses, however, involve a unimaginably momentous task of spiritual, hidden administration by Christ on behalf of all God's people who have been and are rescued from the realm of darkness (Colossians 1:13). This is going on all the time in this very exciting history of redemption.

When Baffling Things Happen to God's People in the City

Fred, a new convert to the saving grace of the Lord Jesus Christ, was totally confused and devastated. "I've been lied to, I've been misled, and this is a total disaster. There's no way out of this eternal, sinful mess," he groaned. "We're in this war and sin struggle forever. There's no escape from this. All those promises in the Bible and from sermons about peace and joy, righteousness and holiness in heaven where God is, are wishful thinking."

Fred had disciplined himself to read the Bible through in one year, but because of this excitement about his new life as a Christian, he was way ahead of schedule.

"We're never going to be without strife," he thought, as he read over and over again this passage from Ephesians: "For our struggle is not against flesh and blood. But against the rulers, against the authorities, against the powers of this dark world, and against the spiritual forces of evil in the heavenly realms" (6:12).

"Lord, have mercy, what a disaster," he said to himself. "I've been fighting my whole life against flesh and blood, but now it seems I'll still get no relief when I get to heaven. The fight is still on, except it will be worse when we fight against spiritual forces. What's so good about going to heaven? If we have to be fighting more battles, I don't want to go there.

"I wonder if Eric, my first-ever pastor, is in his office this early. I'll bet he's never read this verse before." He phoned his church and asked to speak to the pastor.

"This is Pastor Eric. Who is this?"

"This is Fred. Do you remember me? You baptized me three months ago. I was saved in prison when Chuck Colson spoke at a special meeting. I joined your church as soon as I was released on probation."

"Oh, yes, Fred. How are you, my friend?"

"Not good, I'm very disappointed with the whole thing. Why haven't you told me about this passage in Ephesians 6, about the continual battle we face when we're in heaven?"

"Why?" Eric said. "What's up? Ephesians 6:12? Fred, I've read this verse a hundred times. I've preached a whole series of sermons on the armor of God. The whole chapter deals with that."

"Well, OK, I'm sorry, but why didn't you tell me that when we're in heaven, we still have to fight against sin and all sorts of evil spiritual forces? I've suffered enough in this world. Why bother going to heaven if it's no different than the hell I've been through on earth?"

"Fred, my dear friend," Eric said. "The heavenly realms you've been reading about are not heaven where God sits with Jesus on His right hand forever, but it's another term used for an evil spiritual realm. It's here that Satan and his hordes operate and influence and insidiously manipulate the physical world or realm.

"But don't be afraid, Fred. You're in the process of growing in the knowledge of God, and learning to put on the whole armor of God, so you'll be able to stand up against the schemes the devil has for you in the present age. By doing this, the devil will be defeated. He has no absolute power anymore.

"Before Christ defeated him on the cross, Satan ruled, with a few exceptions, over all the nations in the world. But since Christ's resurrection, every nation has a multitude of believers who bow the knee to Jesus Christ. Satan is handicapped figuratively, bound by a chain, frustrated, limited, but not dead. His activities go on and on, just like the head of an organized crime syndicate being in prison, but his criminal organization goes on."

"Oh, I know what I did," Fred acknowledged, much relieved. "I took it literally as the heaven where God sits on His throne. It's not heaven where the saints reign with Christ. Thanks, I'm OK, now."

"Before you go, Fred, let me read three verses from Psalm 113 to you," said Eric.

"The LORD is exalted over all the nations, *his glory above the heavens.* Who is like the LORD our God, the One who sits enthroned on high, *who stoops down to look on the heavens and the earth?*" (Psalm 113:4-6).

"Fred, why don't you check out a book from the church library dealing with that subject?"

"Thank you, I will," Fred said and hung up. Eric phoned his assistant minister of Christian education to keep an eye on Fred and help him with good reading. Fred, on his way to work, stopped at McDonald's and bit into an Egg McMuffin. "The Lord is good," he mumbled to himself. "I'm loved by God himself. He knows me. I don't have to wait or focus on some mysterious future kingdom. I'm looking now to Jesus, the author and finisher of my faith, and enjoying myself with my brothers and sisters in the city of God."

When Burdensome Things Happen to God's People in the City

The difference between the four Gospels and Revelation is: the Gospels display Jesus on earth, as the Son of Man and Son of God, while Revelation shows us Jesus and the whole host of heaven working behind the scene, invisible fighting evil in a spiritual realm called the Heavenlies.

> For our struggle is not against flesh and blood, but against the rulers, against the authorities, against the powers of this dark world and against the spiritual forces of evil in the heavenly realms (Ephesians 6:12).

The book of Revelation was written during great tribulation, in fulfillment of Christ's warning to His beloved disciples in Matthew 24. Tens of thousands of Christians were slaughtered. It was a word of warning that would soon take place. The first and foremost principle of interpreting God's Word must always be this question: What was the message of the prophecy or letter to the first recipients? What did it mean to them first?

> I, John your brother and companion in the suffering and kingdom and patient endurance that are ours in Jesus, was on the island of Patmos because of the word of God and testimony of Jesus (Revelation 1:9).

Those who interpret the Bible literally, as do the dispensationalists, make an artificial distinction between tribulation and the Great Tribulation. The Great Tribulation, they say, will come later to the world just after the church is raptured up into heaven. By this standard, the Bible also speaks of two salvations in Hebrews 2:3, where we have a description of *such a great salvation.*

Does this mean there are two salvations? One ordinary salvation and one great salvation? It's absurd. What makes a tribulation great? The number of people murdered? The duration? Millions of people, maybe 40,000,000, suffered tribulation under communism in Eastern Europe and China for many years, not just seven years.

According to dispensationalists, the Great Tribulation will only last three-and-a-half or seven years. From very good internal and external, carefully researched evidence, more and more scholars believe that Revelation was written before the fall of Jerusalem.

Keep in mind the first principle of interpretation and that, according to Revelation 22:20, *soon* means soon. Israel and the united European countries and the 1980 oil crisis would be totally useless to the First Century churches.

But think clearly about this fact: John was given a vision that dealt with a warning to the churches of the destruction of Jerusalem by Roman armies. He needed to give the warning to Christians to get out of Jerusalem. Why? Because the time had come of which Christ had warned them:

> "When you see Jerusalem being surrounded by armies, you will know that its desolation is near. Then let those who are in Judea flee to the mountains, let those in the city get out, and let those in the country not enter the city. *For this is the time of punishment in fulfillment of all that has been written*" (Luke 21:20-22).

Please read the italicized part of the verse above a few times. Think of it in context, and let the Holy Spirit say what He clearly and truly says here. These are the words of Jesus.

The Language of God's People in the City.

It's worth repeating that the church obeyed, for they missed out on the sack of Jerusalem because they believed and obeyed Christ, who had warned them in non-figurative terms. But there would have been no way that John's literal written warning would have passed the guards on Patmos. By just quoting Christ's own words in his writings, it would not have been allowed to leave Patmos and warn everyone about the invasion of Rome, and the planned destruction of Jerusalem.

But now consider a Roman official, who's responsible for outgoing letters to relatives or friends from prisoners, looking at John's revelation. This official, of course, would have been completely ignorant about Old Testament terminology of apocalyptic descriptions of things to come. Would he have thought it anything but the senile ravings of a harmless old seer? No one's going to read this fairy tale. It's not hard to imagine the tremendous burden put on John to get the revelation out as the testimony to the churches.

And that's why the Holy Spirit used Old Testament apocalyptic terminology—He knew that only those who were followers of Christ would be able to interpret the figuratively described events, which took place some eighteen months after receiving Revelation.

When Breathtaking Things Happen to God's People in the City

Just like the story in the introduction to this book, of the man looking up into the sky, this next story is also true. A young woman named Alice, who was handicapped because of Down Syndrome, was a faithful member of the congregation I served as pastor. She had acknowledged that she knew the Lord Jesus Christ as her personal Savior by slowly nodding her head when asked that most important question.

She was severely limited in speech and particularly in any physical movement of her arms, legs, and her whole body. So she never made a quick movement with her hands or feet. Every Sunday morning after church, she'd come to me at the door for a weekly hug and then leave with her mother. When she was twenty, she became very sick and was in the hospital at the point of death. This is how the breathtaking scene was told to me by her mother and the relatives who testified unanimously to what had happened to Alice.

She was struggling for each slow breath: death rattles were gurgling deep within her chest; anytime now, she would breathe her last. With her eyes closed, she was unaware of anyone in the room. All of a sudden, she sat straight up with a very quick movement, as if jumping out of bed. Her head and arms straight, reaching for the ceiling for less than two seconds, and then she fell back with a smile on her face. Breathless!

According to Christ's apocalyptical description in Matthew 24:30-35, the mourning Christians around her bed saw the sign of His coming. Alice saw and met her Lord in the air. At that same hour, tens of thousands of Christians in the world had the same experience of being carried away from death to life.

It was the second coming of Christ for her, the first coming at conversion, and the second coming at her jubilant transformation. Alice had been resurrected. The second death had no power over her (Revelation 20:6). Alice had entered the eternal, true spiritual wonderland.

"No eye has seen, no ear has heard, nor mind has conceived what God has prepared for those who love him" (1 Corinthians 2:9; see also Isaiah 64:1-4).

When one carefully looks at the entire biblical plan of salvation throughout the whole of Scripture, and not miscellaneous Old Testament and New Testament fulfilled and unfulfilled prophetic announcements mixed together, then the history of redemption will become a harmonious revelation believers will take from here to eternity!

When Bad Things Happen to "Left Behind" People Outside the City

"Whoever believes in him is not condemned, but whoever does not believe stands condemned already because he has not believed in the name of God's one and only Son" (John 3:18).

My secretary informed me that a crying woman on the phone needed to talk to me urgently. "Who is it?" I inquired. "She didn't give her name; she just said she needed to talk to Dr. Kuiper."

Picking up the phone, I said, "I'm Pastor Kuiper. It sounds like you need someone to talk to. Please don't apologize for crying."

She said, "You don't know me, but I've attended your church a few times. I'm a Christian, but my dying father in intensive care is not. He hates religion, and has used bad language all his life. Could you please go and see him and tell him his daughter sent you, and please, oh please, pray with him and ask him if he wants to receive

Christ as his Savior.

"As far as I know, he's never been to church. But now that he knows he's dying, he may repent and get saved at the last moment, just like the thief on the cross."

"Where are you calling from? Are you with him now at the hospital?" I asked.

"Oh, no sir," she said. "He doesn't want to see me. He doesn't want me near him. But please go if you can."

I said, "This is very unusual, but I'll go immediately."

After she gave me his name and room number, she quickly hung up the phone.

The nurse in the ICU pointed to a lonely, cold cubicle. Walking in slowly, I turned back the faded curtain and stared at an old, worn out, shriveled up, bony little man, totally spent, like a withered brown leaf about to be released from a mighty oak. He looked discarded and worthless, like nature's reject.

I stood there for a moment—the silence was deafening. The eyes in his hairless head were closed; in his toothless mouth, he had a tube which went somewhere deep down inside him. I gently touched his exposed hand above the thin blanket.

Immediately, his bloodshot eyes opened. He looked angry and annoyed. I smiled at him and said, "I'm here at the request of your daughter. I'm a minister of the Lord Jesus Christ. She told me you're not a Christian, but if I would visit with you, and explain what's involved in being a Christian, she thought you might repent and ask Christ to save you. It's not too late."

Without giving him time to respond, I asked, "Would you like me to pray for you?"

He stiffened himself and, with what seemed to me to be a great effort to take a deep breath, he said with a loud, gurgling voice, "*Nooooooo!*"

This is what the Bible means being left behind. Banished and condemned, the power of the second death finished him off (Revelation 20:6), forever separated from the life-giving and sustaining God.

Being left behind isn't new—it began in Genesis and continues until the end. It must have been a terrible experience for Noah and his family to hear banging on the ark's closed door, the screaming and crying of drowning people judged by God. "God loves you and has a wonderful plan for your life" no longer applied, as in the case of that wasted old man. The invisible angel with a flaming sword protecting the tree of life came back and stood in that cold cubicle. He died, without hope, and without God, outside the city.

The Worship of God in the City

God is love. God shows his love in the City of God by the gift of his eternal son, Jesus Christ, to be the atoning sacrifice for the one and only possibility to open the way for cleansed, redeemed sinners to worship God in spirit and in truth.

The worship of God is the only activity in this passing world which will continue in heaven. God's ultimate purpose for history is to populate heaven with true worshippers. Unrepentant self-worshippers will violently rebel against the worshipping of God.

> "Yet they say to God, 'Leave us alone! We have no desire to know your ways. Who is the Almighty, that we should serve him? What would we gain by praying to him?'" (Job 21:14-15)

> "The Godless in heart harbor resentment; even when he fetters them, they do not cry for help. They die in their youth, among the male prostitutes of the shrines." (Job 36:13-14)

This is blatant contempt of God. They believe God is egotistical and self-centered, and show no fear of God by disgustingly quoting him. "Honor me, worship only me, don't worship anything else." Little do they know that they rebel against the greatest of all lovers in the whole universe. By that very behavior, having created a god in the lesser image of themselves, the result is a slow hemorrhage of the purpose, the potential of life sucked dry.

God's divine mandate to worship Him only saves us, and protects us from false affection and worship of satanic substitutes which lead to eternal destruction.

God's decree to worship him only will fill us with the blessing of God, the presence of God, the life of God in the soul of men, fulfilling the ultimate purpose of God, in the City of God.

CHAPTER 26

The One World Government Is Here

⋆⇒⟨⋆

Do you not know? Have you not heard?
Has it not been told you from the beginning?
Have you not understood
since the earth was founded?

He sits enthroned above the circle of the earth,
and its people are like grasshoppers.
He stretches out the heavens like a canopy,
and spreads them out like a tent to live in.

He brings princes to naught
and reduces the rulers of this world to nothing.

No sooner are thy planted,
no sooner are they sown,
no sooner do they take root in the ground,
than he blows on them and they wither,
and a whirlwind sweeps them away like chaff.
(Isaiah 40:21-24)

Our Great Comfort in Life and Death

Throughout history, those who feared God have been made alive, protected, provided for, rescued, resurrected by this *Supernatural One-World Government of three persons: the Father, the Son, and the Holy Spirit*. This absolute, unchangeable government has kept its eyes on the righteous, heard their cries, wiped away their tears, and treated them as precious members of the family. The whole Bible is full of those unchanging prophetic promises.

Let's look at one of the most brilliant questions ever printed, and its answer:

> Q: What is your only comfort, in life and in death?
> A: That I belong body and soul, in life and in death, not to myself but to my faithful savior, Jesus Christ, who at the cost of His own blood has fully paid for all my sins and has completely freed me from the dominion of the devil, that He protects me so well that without the will of my Father in heaven not a hair can fall from my head, indeed, that everything must fit His purpose for my salvation. Therefore, by His Holy Spirit, He also assures me of eternal life, and makes me wholeheartedly willing and ready from now on to live for Him. (*Heidelberg Catechism*)

From the time Enoch was taken from the earth, or raptured (Genesis 5), God has constantly, silently, and secretly, across the world, snatched believers away to be in glory with Him for eternity. The earthly shell was discarded and the indestructible seed (the soul) has sprung forth into an unimaginably glorious spiritual being, never to return to this speck of dust in God's great universe (1 Corinthians 15:42-49).

Most often, this doesn't happen during great world-shaking events, but in silent stillness. God whispers to His faithful child, "Come up here," or "Come ye blessed of the Father; inherit the kingdom prepared for you before the beginning of the world."

World-shaking events will happen. Jesus warned His disciples, "In the world you will have tribulation." As far as we know, experience has taught us that things will go wrong; we have a frustrated, powerful, and busy devil to deal with.

However, all those who are in Christ don't sorrow like those who have no hope. They're always safe, even in a hijacked airplane about to dive into the hard, unforgiving earth.

What good will the *one-world government* develop from the September 11, 2001 terrorist attacks? No one knows. We have no ability to imagine that. There's infinitely much more about God for us to discover, and it will take all of eternity to do it.

Here's a biblical example from God's words to King Solomon:

> "When I shut up the heavens so that there is no rain, or command locusts to devour the land or send a plague among my people, if my people, who are called by my name, will humble themselves and pray and seek my face and turn from their wicked ways, then will I hear from heaven and will forgive their sin and will heal their land" (2 Chronicles 7:13-14).

We know from Scripture that they did *not* humble themselves or pray, nor did they seek His face. Notice that verse 13 starts with the word "When," but verse 14 starts with the word "If." We all love verse 14, but no one likes verse 13. Take note: all one has to do is fly across the Negev and the Dead Sea, and instantly, becomes aware that God means what He says. It used to be, long ago, a *fertile crescent. Whatever happened to the land flowing with milk and honey?*

Think about this amazing bit of history for awhile. Caesar Augustus, the supreme ruler of Rome, that great world power of the past, was made aware that an enormous amount of wealth was slipping through his godless, thieving fingers. Because of the vastness of his conquered territory, he had no idea of the sum total of the populations of the nations he had subdued. Hence, he had no idea of how much revenue from taxes he was supposed to accumulate.

And so, as we know from Scripture (Luke 2:1), and world history, he ordered that a census be taken of the entire Roman world, which ultimately enabled Rome to keep tabs on all people and receive revenue to develop and maintain its war machinery. Having to travel, often for great distances, in order to enroll, must have been most difficult for many people, young and old, healthy and infirm. Caesar must have been so proud of himself for being so successful and powerful. But, unbeknownst to him, the only permanent purpose of all this feverish running about this world is in the next paragraph.

Whatever took place during that long-ago census has very little bearing on us today as we look at Ground Zero in New York, or any other earth-shattering disasters, *with one very important exception.*

During that census, a unique birth took place. "The Word became flesh." Joseph and Mary, who were expecting a child, were forced by a worldly government to move from Nazareth to Bethlehem, in order for God's infallible word to be fulfilled. Who says God doesn't have a sense of humor?

Originated and administered by the *One-World Government of Three Persons*, the sovereign God of the universe took hold of poor old Caesar Augustus, who had no idea that he was just a little pawn in the hands of that infallible power by which God fulfilled his prophesied eternal purpose, *to lead a young man and a pregnant teenager from Nazareth to Bethlehem, that's all.*

The effect of that birth, that life, that death, and that resurrection enabled millions of people to look at this *sinful world with horror, but without despair*; with sadness, but also with hope. It is the teaching of Scripture that God will work, and is at work, to fulfill His sovereign purpose. What incredible irony that this *one-world government* can covertly set the whole world in motion, just to plan infallibly for a baby boy to be born in a stable, and change history and lives, and the purpose of those lives for eternity.

Strange? No! Wonderful! Jesus was and is alive and on center stage. Augustus is dead. Someone has said, "We name our big dogs after Roman emperors, and our sons after the disciples of Jesus."

Throughout history, and particularly since the Great Commission (Matthew 28:18), the one-world government has had available and used hundreds of millions of Christian soldiers – an army of international warriors armed with double-edged swords, obedient to the Author of their salvation. All worldly armies together are totally outnumbered by this great multitude. No one can count the redeemed citizens of the one-world government who fight the good fight of faith.

On September 20, 2001 (just days after the World Trade Center disaster), the Ukrainian government recognized the Evangelical Presbyterian Church of Ukraine as an official Ukrainian church. Jesus said, "...I will build my church" (Matthew 16:18). God *is* at work. Who would have believed it possible just a few years ago?

The *man of lawfulness* sits on His throne at the right hand of His Father. By the power of His eternal sovereignty over the universe, He has the power to execute His promise that no matter how bad things get in this troubled world, "all things will work together for good to them that love God" (Romans 8:28).

The so-called seven-year Great Tribulation is unbiblical nonsense to millions of Russian brothers and sisters in Christ, who had to come through a seventy-year great tribulation. Countless millions lost their lives for Christ. Yet, without a shot being fired, the great, powerful, satanic Soviet Union disintegrated, when the one-world government of three persons said, *"It is enough."*

I know a faithful Christian man, who, for sixty years as a dispensational, futuristic Bible class teacher, finally died at the age of eighty-one. One of the last things he said to his tearful wife was, *"I have taught and believed that the Rapture would come during my lifetime. I am frustrated and disappointed that it has not."*

A major problem with futuristic excitement is that people who preoccupy themselves by waiting for something in the future, or for some supernatural event to prove or substantiate their faith in Christ, are actually dissatisfied with what is being done invisibly by God. They question God about their allotted usefulness in His appointed time (see Acts 13:36). Countless millions thought that, at the stroke of midnight on January 1, 2000, Christ would come back.

The excitement and preoccupation about a future participation in an extraordinary, supernatural event is a clear sign of day-by-day discontent with God.

There are millions of Christians who want to be part of an earth-shaking, visible coming of Christ in the clouds. If you feel this way, just remember that you may not be part of it; stop fretting about it. Get over it. *How sad it is to die as a believer with a complaint against God on one's lips.*

God is supernaturally at work, continually, every day, every time, everywhere for every believer, forever.

On the Brink of the Rapture?

With my early and only real cup of coffee in my hand, I turned on the TV to watch the typically one-sided liberal news. Flicking through the channels, my interest in the news took second place to yet another prophecy broadcast. The big letters, "ON THE BRINK OF THE RAPTURE," were displayed on a large banner behind a panel of male dispensational teachers. As I listened, I thought, "Here we go again, and again, and again!"

Having felt this, I need to communicate very clearly to my readers, however, that I don't think for a split second that this book will silence the relentless occupation of exciting dispensational fantasies, and the unmitigated longing of many Christians to be taken into the clouds with Jesus in front of all the terrible unbelievers.

I hope, however, that much greater minds than mine, hopefully serious theologians, will do more research, particularly in the period before Abraham, without isolating it from biblical or systematic theology, and help Christians everywhere in the world with a clearer understanding of the biblical origin and continuation of Christianity.

Whatever the case, we've been told to:

1. Make disciples of all nations.
2. Live holy lives.
3. Increase in the knowledge of God.
4. Think biblically. Think bravely. Think big.

Don't ask, "What would Jesus do?" The answer to that question is in the Bible. Just rejoice in *what Jesus has done*! He came, He conquered, He reigns. He finished His task on this little Planet Earth, and is in heaven, in the process of crushing the head of Satan (Genesis 3:15). Ask what would Jesus do through me today?

In Contempt of this Present Age

Those Bible-believing gifted preachers, who constantly energize great gatherings with loud sermons about the future, the imminent Rapture, the Great Tribulation and climaxed by Christ's thousand-year reign, seem to be in contempt or at least fed up with this present age. It's like overworked and underpaid slave laborers in a sweatshop, longing for an anticipated future vacation, but it slips further away into some distant dream.

These servants of Christ don't emphasize the incredible value and divine privilege of being engaged in greater works than Jesus in this present age.

> Jesus demanded that, "Anyone who has faith in me will do what I have been doing. He will do even greater things than these because I am going to the Father" (John 14:12).

This is not merely a suggestion. No! Jesus actually demands that by his help at his Father's right hand we outperform him. I can hear someone say, "Out-performing Christ? You're out of your mind!" Look at it historically. It's obvious that everyone Jesus healed eventually died. Lazarus died and went back into a smelly sepulcher.

A very serious misunderstanding of this mandate is evidenced by preachers who try to heal sick saints by interpreting this verse literally, and, of course, they fail miserably. They're not engaged in greater works than Christ, but alarmingly inferior works. They wait for people to come to them in a meeting. They don't go to funeral homes and raise the dead, and they don't visit hospitals and say, "Arise, leave your bed and walk."

I've watched TV shows where people come to the platform in front of a great lively crowd and, after being touched by the evangelist, fall backward. The only Biblical support of that strange exhibition is in John 18:5-6, when the murderous enemies of Christ come to arrest Him and were met by Christ who amazes them with divine majesty and said, "I AM" and they stepped back and fell to the ground. The greater works than Jesus obviously is spiritual work, inspired, empowered, directed and purpose-driven by Christ at God's right hand.

> Jesus said, "I tell you the truth, whoever hears my word and believes him who sent me has eternal life and will not be condemned; he has crossed over from death to life. I tell you the truth, a time is coming and has now come when the dead will hear

the voice of the Son of God and those who hear will live" (John 5:24, 25).

Christ demands that every true Christian outperform him and participate in the building of His church. Of course we'll never be a Jesus. Throughout eternity, the "creator-creature" distinction will never be compromised.

Stop looking for any other age this side of eternity. Don't be in contempt of God's place for you in this temporary "Phase One" of your eternal destiny. Here and now is where you have the divine privilege to do greater works than Jesus. Don't forget – God is full of surprises.

An Imaginary Conversation in Heaven

The above heading isn't so strange. In Scripture, there's a narrative of this actually happening between the Lord and Satan, with regard to Job and his family.

Now let's imagine a conversation between Jesus in Heaven and the Arab named Abraham.

Abraham: "Lord, you're sovereign and almighty. I'm not, but I am concerned about the overall inability of the gospel to reach the Arab world. We've tried many times."

Jesus: "Abraham, I have a plan."

Abraham: "What kind of plan, Lord?"

Jesus: "I'm developing a movie to penetrate the Islamic world and contradict the erroneous belief of Islam regarding my death."

Abraham: "Let it be a movie about you raising Lazarus, or feeding the five thousand. You could use an evangelical movie company to produce it."

Jesus: "It's not about Lazarus, or feeding the five thousand. You've already been involved in greater works than that, and no, I don't want some Christian organization to be involved with it."

Abraham: "Well, what non-Christian organization would be interested in producing a general audience movie?"

Jesus: "It's not going to be a general audience movie. It's going to be R-rated, and I want Hollywood to produce it."

Abraham: "Oh, I get it. It's going to be a movie on forgiveness, and I can guess it's going to be the occasion of the woman taken in adultery. Hollywood thrives on that; they can really make much of that sinful behavior with an R-rated film."

Jesus: "No, it's not going to be about that subject. It's going to be a movie about my crucifixion. You know, I went down into the world in order to die."

Abraham: "The Quran states that you didn't die on the cross. They'll never watch it. Lord, Hollywood won't touch a movie like that. Furthermore, no bank in the world will finance a movie on your crucifixion that only a handful of Christians are interested in. They love Christmas, much more than Good Friday. It's going to be a low budget production."

Jesus: "I'm going to inspire Mel Gibson, my servant, to produce it and pay for it with his own money."

Abraham: "What! Oh, I'm sorry, Lord, but Mel has been involved in some very bloody R-rated movies. Mel, your servant?"

Jesus: "Abraham, you know everyone in the world is my servant. Pharaoh, Nebuchadnezzar, Cyrus, Augustus, Gorbachev, Dobson, Colson, and Bush, believers and unbelievers, are all my willing or unwilling servants. And you, Abraham, don't know the heart of Mel Gibson, do you?"

Abraham: "I'm sorry, Lord."

Jesus: "It's going to be the historical event of the slow, agonizing murder of the Lamb of God. It will give insight into the extent God-haters have degenerated since Adam and Eve. It also will show the greatest display of love in the world."

Abraham: "You should entitle the movie, *The Greatest Crime in the World,* or *The Brutal Murder of the Son of God,* or *The God Killers.*

Jesus: "No, Abraham. It's to be called, *The Passion of the Christ.* Unbelieving Jews will cry, 'Anti-Semitism.' Islamic authorities will immediately see it as an opportunity to irritate the Jews. Consequently, they'll let it be shown in their countries, and will be the means by which many thousands of Muslims will walk out of darkness into the Light of Life by accepting me.

"Abraham, that's why my Apostle John introduces me correctly in Revelation 3:14 as, 'The Ruler of God's Creation.' I'm not finished with the world until my last sheep has been found. This takes place in the greater spiritual realm of 'wars and rumors of wars.' Worldwide earthly events have nothing to do with it. I will build my church. Surprise, surprise!"

With this fictitious scene, we come to the end of this book. Some will be blessed; others will be angry and discard it. I've shown that Christianity, according to Scripture, is a spiritual relationship with the triune God, lived out in this temporal physical world. That means, of course, that all futuristic battles, including Armageddon, are not physical but spiritual, which is the most insidious and dangerous warfare.

"We wrestle not against flesh and blood," not in the past, not now or in the future. The devil's onslaught, however, continues as a testimony to his knowledge that there is more to life than this temporary existence on this present little Planet Earth.

I recommend you read Dr. Peter Jones' book, *Spirit Wars* (Wine Press Publishing), where you'll discover that the Great Tribulation has always been. The onslaught of Satan and his host has been our violent, relentless, and only enemy since Eden.

> May the God of peace, who through the blood of the eternal covenant brought back from the dead our Lord Jesus, that great Shepherd of the sheep, equip you with everything good for doing his will, and may he work in us what is pleasing to him, through Jesus Christ, to whom be glory forever and ever. Amen (Hebrews 13:20-21).

Bibliography

Berkhof, L. *Principles of Biblical Interpretation.* Grand Rapids, MI: Baker Book House, 1950; 10th printing, 1969.

Boettner, Loraine. *The Millennium.* Philadelphia, PA: Presbyterian and Reformed Publishing Company, 1974.

Brakel, Wilhelmus A. *The Christian's Reasonable Service.* Grand Rapids: Reformation Heritage Books, First Publishing, 1700.

Carver, Everett I. *When Jesus Comes Again.* Phillipsburg, NJ: Presbyterian and Reformed Publishing Company, 1979.

Charnock, Stephen. *Discourses Upon the Existence and Attributes of God.* Grand Rapids, MI: Baker Book House, Reprint 1979 from 1853 edition.

Cox, William E. *An Examination of Dispensationalism.* Philadelphia, PA: Presbyterian and Reformed Publishing Company, 1974.

Cox, William E. *Biblical Studies in Final Things.* Philadelphia, PA: Presbyterian and Reformed Publishing Company, 1972.

Cox, William E. *Amillennialism Today.* Philadelphia, PA: Presbyterian and Reformed Publishing Company, 1966.

Fairbairn, Patrick. *The Typology of Scripture*. Grand Rapids, MI: Baker Book House, 1900.

Flavel, John. *The Fountain of Life*. Grand Rapids, MI: Baker Book House, 1671, reprint 1977.

Frydland, Rachmiel, *When Being Jewish Was a Crime*. Nashville, TN: Thomas Nelson, Publisher, 1978.

Gentry, Kenneth L. *Before Jerusalem Fell*. Tyler, TX: Institute for Christian Economics, 1989.

Gurnall, William. *The Christian in Complete Armour*. Edinburgh: The Banner of Truth 1961, (first printing 1696).

Hamada, Louis Bahjat. *God Loves the Arabs Too*. Jackson, TN: Hamad Evangelistic Outreach, Inc., 1986.

Hughes, Philip E. *Interpreting Prophecy*. Grand Rapids, MI: Eerdmans, 1976.

Jones, Peter. *Spirit Wars*. Mukilteo, WA: WinePress Publishing, 1977.

Kik, Marcellus J. *An Eschatology of Victory*. Philadelphia, PA: Presbyterian and Reformed Publishing Company, 1971.

Mauro, Philip. *How Long to the End*. Boston, MA: Hamilton Brothers Publishing, 1927.

Ridderbos, Herman. *The Coming of the Kingdom*. Philadelphia, PA: Presbyterian and Reformed Publishing Company.

Ryle, J. C. *Practical Religion*. Grand Rapids, MI: Baker Book House (reprint), 1927.

Robertson, O. Palmer. *The Christ of the Covenants*. Phillipsburg, NJ: Presbyterian and Reformed Publishing Company, 1980.

Schaeffer, Dr. Frances A. *True Spirituality*. Wheaton, IL: Tyndale House Publishers

Scott, Jack B. *God's Plan Unfolded*. Wheaton, IL: Tyndale House Publishing, Inc., 1976.

Thomas, Lawrence R. *A Symposium of Prophecy*. By the author: Australia.

Van Gemeren, William A. *Interpreting the Prophetic Word*. Grand Rapids, MI: Zondervan, Academie Books, 1990.

Witsius, Herman. *The Economy of the Covenant*. London: T. Tegg & Son, 1693.

Yerby, R. B. *The Once and Future Israel*. Swengel, PA: Reiner Publishing, 1977.

Printed in the United States
42116LVS00006BA/49

9 781597 814553